POSTCARD HISTORY SERIES

Biloxi

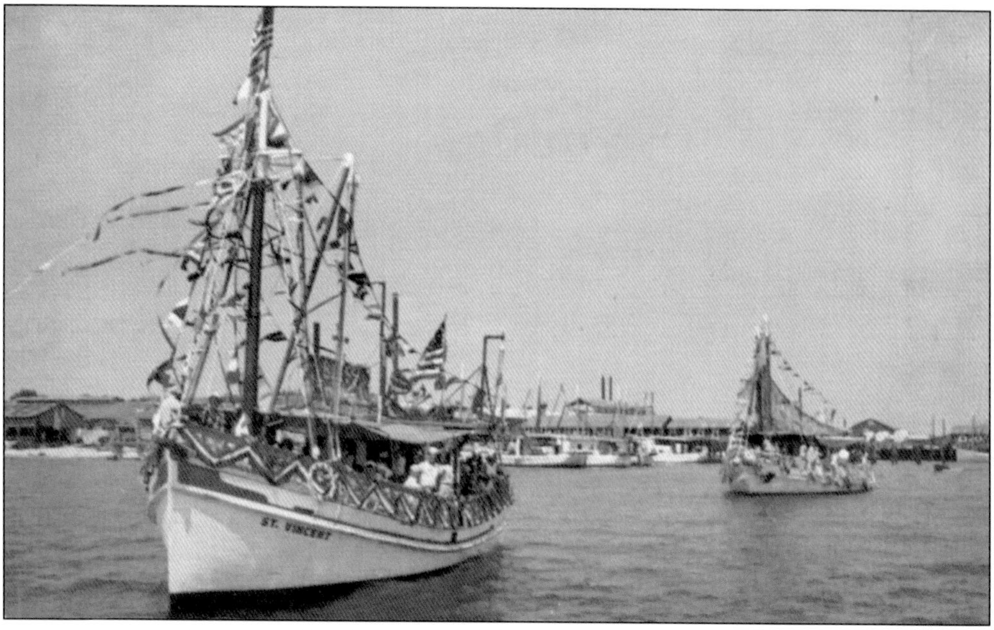

On the Front Cover: This 1960s postcard shows gaily decorated shrimp boats in the Biloxi channel during the annual Blessing of the Shrimp Fleet and Shrimp Festival. Picnics on the islands and a day on the boat made up the family activities of blessing day. The mixture of an old-world religious festival and a modern-day party highlighted the day. (Not Mailed; Santa Cruz collection.)

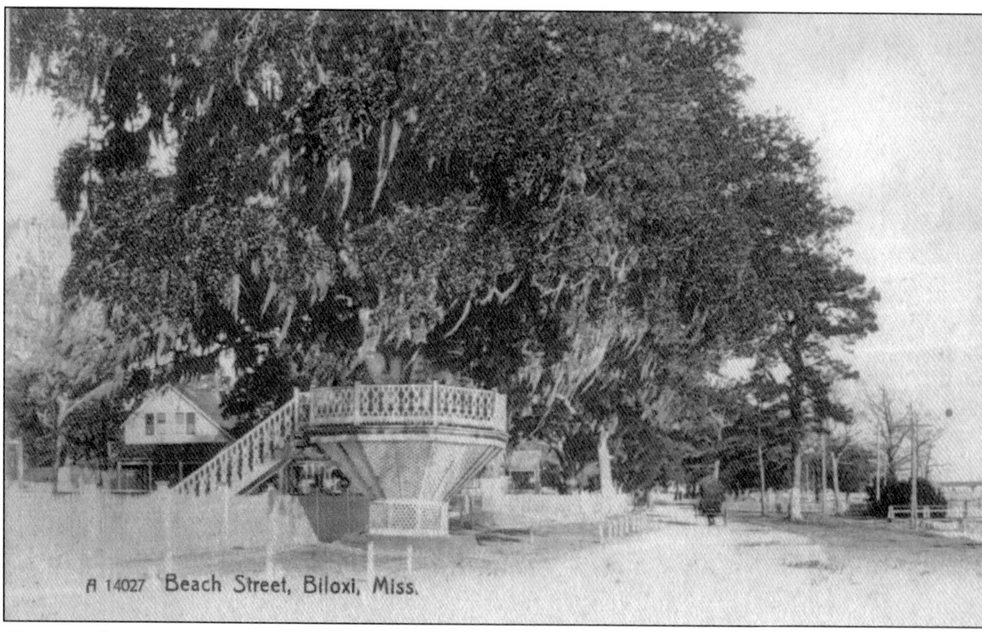

On the Back Cover: This wooden structure stood in East Biloxi, along Highway 90, until Hurricane Camille in 1969. Shooflies, carried over from the plantation era, were retreats from the summer heat, much like a gazebo shaded by the canopy of an oak tree. It was high enough off the ground to catch a breeze that whisked away biting flies, thus named Shoofly. (Not Mailed; Santa Cruz collection.)

POSTCARD HISTORY SERIES

Biloxi

Alan J. and Joan C. Santa Cruz and Jane B. Shambra

ARCADIA PUBLISHING

ISBN 978-0-7385-9150-6

Published by Arcadia Publishing
Charleston, South Carolina

Printed in the United States of America

Library of Congress Control Number: 2011940227

For all general information contact Arcadia Publishing at:
Telephone 843-853-2070
Fax 843-853-0044
E-mail sales@arcadiapublishing.com
For customer service and orders:
Toll-Free 1-888-313-2665

Visit us on the Internet at www.arcadiapublishing.com

Contents

ACKNOWLEDGMENTS

The combined postcards of the Biloxi Public Library and the Santa Cruz collection show many views of the city and surrounding area for the 80-year period covered in this publication. However, the text explaining the stories, legends, and history of each of the views would not have been possible without the research and publications of many individuals and groups who have researched the city and surrounding area for many years.

As we try to thank all of these people and organizations, we will surely fail to mention something or someone. Please rest assured that it is not intentional. We would like to thank the *Daily Herald* and its predecessors and successors, *Biloxi-D'Iberville Press*, the Harrison County Library System, Mississippi Department of Marine Resources, Mississippi Department of Archives and History, *Down South Magazine* and radio show, the maritime and seafood industry, and the writers, authors, artists, and photographers who contributed to the knowledge of the area. Joe and Colleen Scholtes, Julia Cook Guice, Murella Hebert Powell, Kat Bergeron, Edmond Boudreaux, Ray Bellande, Val Husley, Charles Sullivan, Ray Thompson, and Deanne Stephens Nuwer are just some of the researchers, compilers, and writers that contributed to the stories, legends, and facts referred to in this volume; thank you for your many hours of effort, intellectual abilities, and hard work.

Throughout this book, each caption includes the postmark year or indicates that it was never mailed. Only two collections of postcards were used in this publication. The letters BL indicate the postcards from Local History and Genealogy Department/Biloxi Public Library/ Harrison County Library System collection, and SC indicates the Alan J. and Joan C. Santa Cruz collection.

Introduction

The birthplace of Mississippi and the territory encompassed by the Louisiana Purchase was discovered by the French in 1699, under the command of Pierre Le Moyne d'Iberville. The abundance of timber and the many abundant variations of seafood provided the French explorers with a coastal location on the natural peninsula of what was to become Biloxi. Although the capital of the colony was moved to New Orleans in the 1720s, Biloxi remained a small fishing and trading village.

Worldwide economic and political decision brought changes in governance to Biloxi and the Gulf Coast. The flags of France, England, Spain, and what was known as the Republic of West Florida flew over the area. Results of the Louisiana Purchase solidified nationality of the inhabitants for a while, although they remained a very independent breed.

When Mississippi was granted statehood in 1817, the people of the area became Mississippians, at least in name. The religious and cultural differences between the people of North Mississippi (north of Wiggins) and the people of Biloxi and the Gulf Coast made for a very odd combination. The people of the area felt sure they were part of the United States, but they were not sure they were part of Mississippi, a feeling that is still present today.

Biloxi became a city, and by 1850, several hotels started to appear. But the Civil War of the 1860s brought its own group of challenges. Fort Massachusetts on Ship Island and the Union blockade of coastal shipping strengthened the ties to the people of the New Orleans area and the source of coastal independence. Ties to the West strengthened further with the popular use of the steamboat and the completion of the east-west rail line from Mobile to New Orleans.

The last three decades of the 19th century were a time of significant change for the people of the region. Biloxi would not be a sleepy fishing village any longer. The railroad and steamboat travel brought visitors and commerce. As people needed places to stay, hotels, rooming houses, and restaurants began to appear and flourish; a tourist industry was becoming a vital component of the economy. Biloxi has never forgotten the old adage, "Once a visitor has made his or her first trip here, and you treat them nice and feed them well, they will return every chance they get."

Another piece of the economic and growth puzzle of the area began during this time period. In 1881, the first seafood-canning factory opened in Biloxi. The harvesting and processing of seafood was very labor intensive, and many workers were needed. Along with the cannery owners and related suppliers, such as the boatbuilders, the seafood industry left its mark on Biloxi, which was called the "Seafood Capital of the World."

Biloxi and the Gulf Coast have a very unique place historically and geographically, in that during the time frame depicted in this volume (1900–1980), we have had the opportunity to totally replace and rebuild many times. In 1905, 1906, 1915, 1916, 1947, 1969, and 2005, the hurricanes of Hurricane Alley have given us the sadness of loss and the opportunity for growth.

In a volume of less than 230 pictures and captions of less than 70 words, we tried to show life in Biloxi from about 1900 to the 1970s; eight decades that showed the things that have made us who we are. Many of the stories and legends of our area have been handed down through our families, friends, and the newspapers we read. Although they are probably based on factual experiences, all writers have their own slant to the story. This volume is a combination of those facts, stories, and legends, along with the accompanying picture postcards.

The glorious accommodations of the signature hotels, which were for the most part built in the 1920s, our beach, motels, and some of our restaurants and lounges are featured early on in this volume. The seafood industry, boats, and waterways have added to our history and memories of our beloved hometown. The part played by our commerce and military have supplied both a livelihood and population to the area. The attractions and places of interest of the city and the surrounding area complete this volume.

Through picture postcards, we hope to show the history, legends, and stories of Biloxi through the eyes of business, government, promoters, and chambers of commerce. This volume is intended to bring back good memories, inviting conversations and discussions as we rebuild our lives in Biloxi and the Gulf Coast again.

One

The Grand Visit

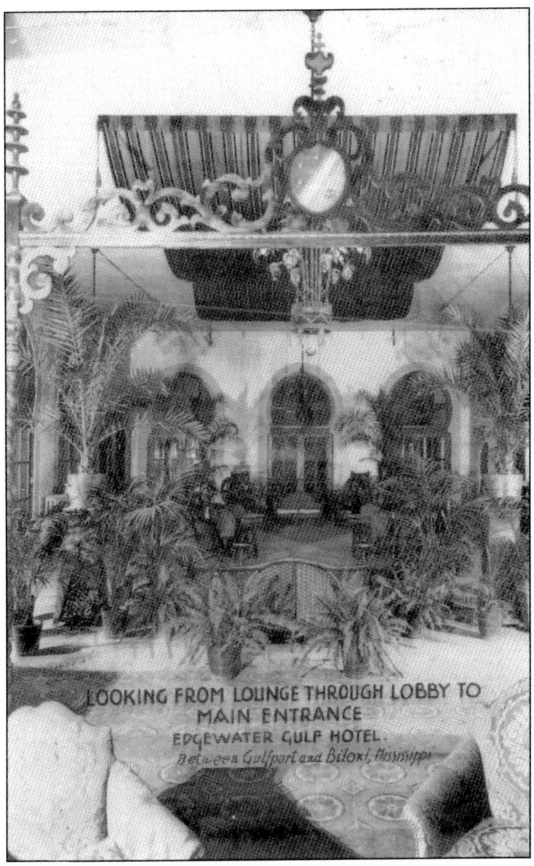

Main Entrance, Edgewater Gulf Hotel, 1927. This postcard features the view from the lounge through the lobby. The boom time of the 1920s again opened Biloxi to vacationing visitors, and signature resort hotels were built to appeal to visitors from the northern Midwest. These popular spots offered year-round options from quiet rest to active recreation. Beauty, climate, and attractions were highlighted in hotel and area advertising. (Postmarked 1927; SC.)

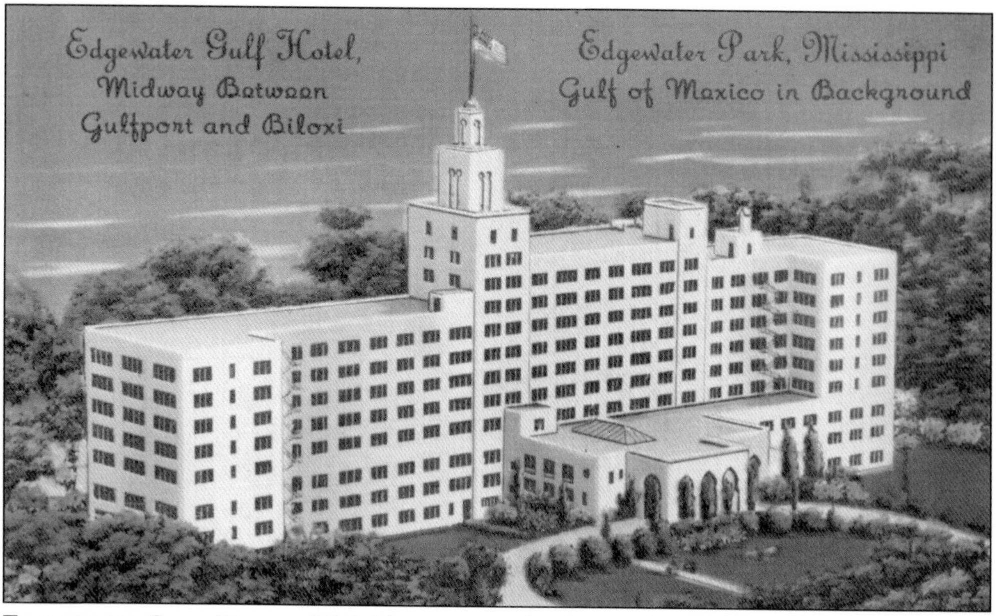

EDGEWATER GULF HOTEL, 1927. Elegance was the theme of the grande dame of coast hotels. This 400-room hotel featured every convenience. Located six miles from Biloxi and Gulfport, over 90 percent of the rooms directly overlooked the Gulf of Mexico. Fashioned after its parent hotel, the Edgewater Beach Hotel in Chicago, this hotel was built to appeal to wintering Midwesterners. (Postmarked 1948; SC.)

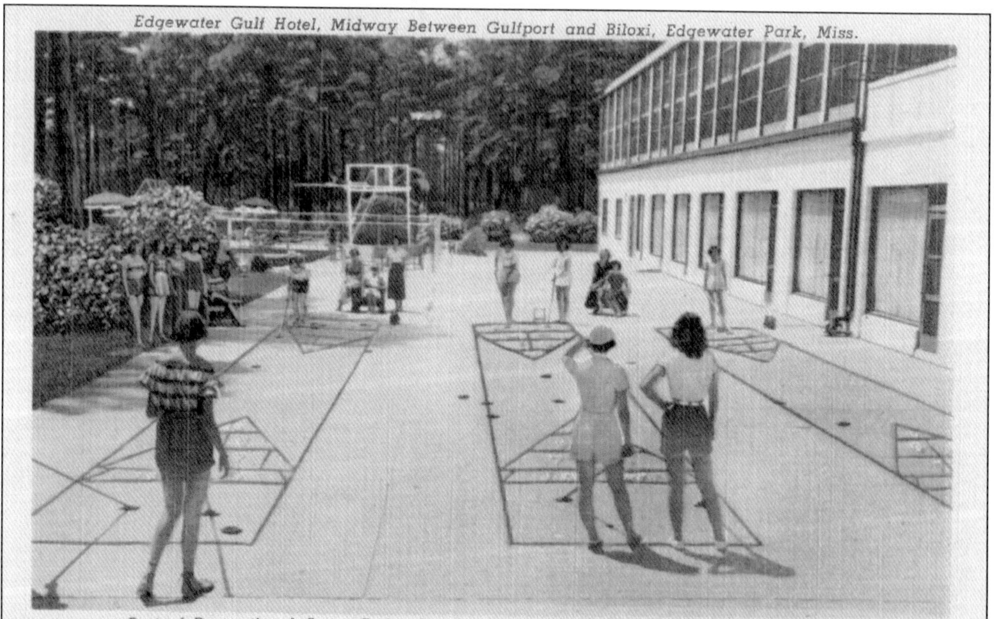

RECREATION AREA, EDGEWATER GULF HOTEL, 1949. The shuffleboard courts in the foreground of this postcard and the diving board of the swimming pool in the background were just two of the many recreational amenities featured on the 600-acre hotel property. An attempt was made to provide guests with everything their hearts desired, without leaving the hotel property. (Not Mailed; SC.)

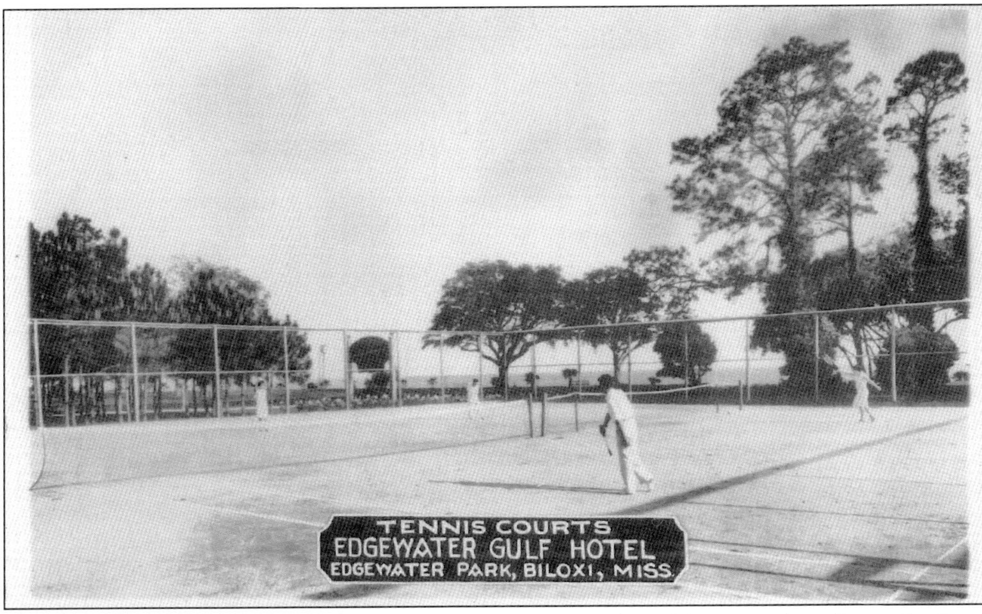

TENNIS COURTS, EDGEWATER GULF HOTEL, C. 1930. This 400-room, American-plan hotel (meals included) was a recreational haven for its many visitors. Tennis, an 18-hole golf course, horseback riding, boating, fishing, horseshoes, softball, swimming, and a children's playground were some of the activities offered. (Not Mailed; SC.)

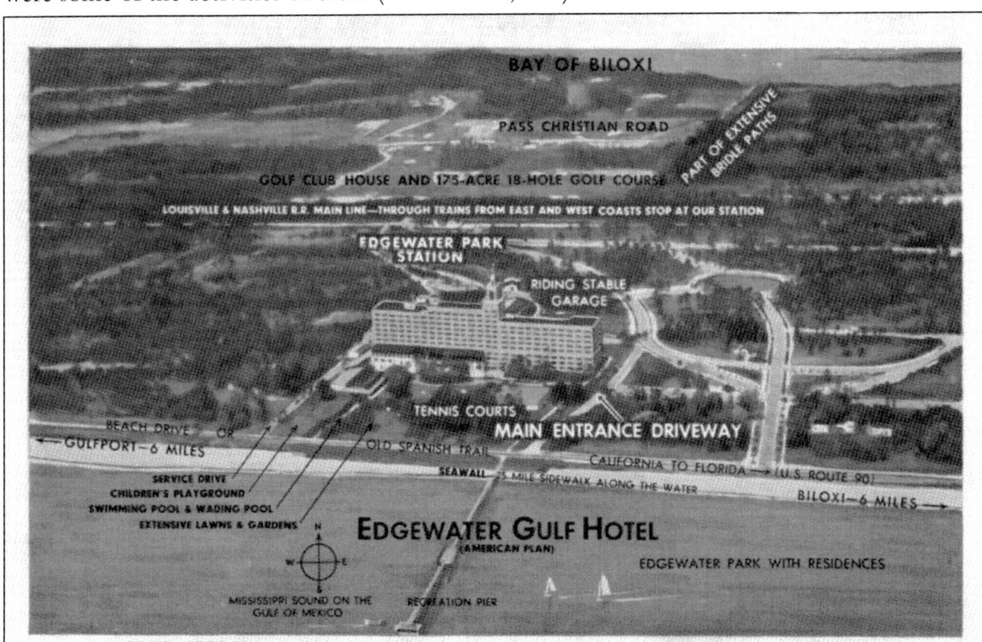

EDGEWATER GULF HOTEL, EDGEWATER PARK, 1938. This early postcard of the Edgewater Hotel and general area features several interesting items. Note that the property stretches from the Gulf to the Bay, the presence of Pass Christian Road (Pass Road), the L&N tracks and Edgewater Station, Edgewater Park subdivision located just east of the hotel, the Old Spanish Trail (Highway 90), and the presence of the seawall. (Postmarked 1938; SC.)

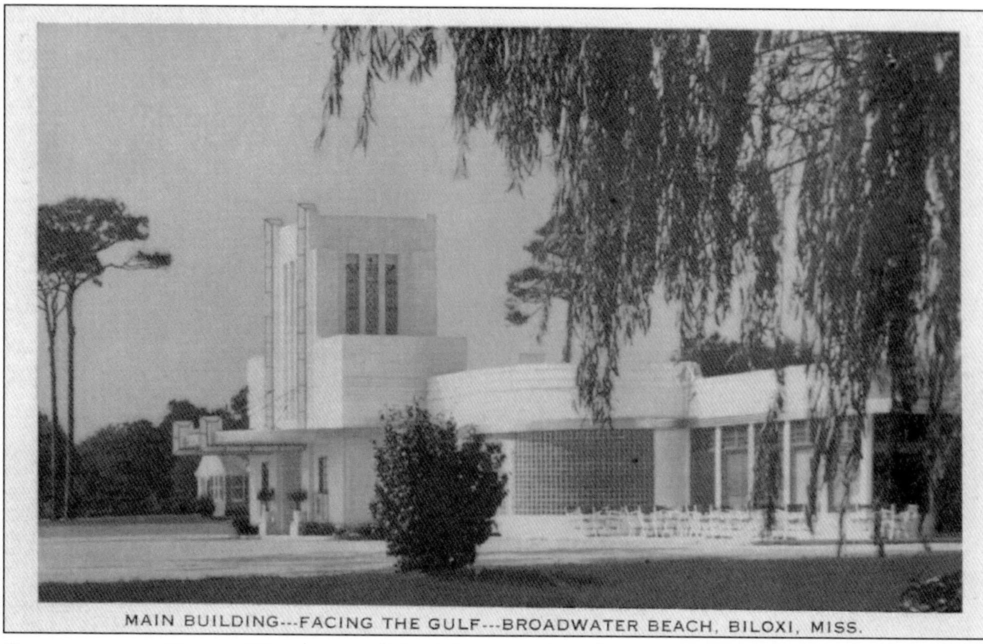

BROADWATER BEACH HOTEL, c. 1940. The main building, shown here, reflects an Art Deco theme for this 66-room hotel, which featured luxurious accommodations and hotel services. The hotel faced the Gulf of Mexico, providing its own private beach south of the seawall for guests' enjoyment, along with golf, fishing, hunting, and available sports. (Not Mailed; SC.)

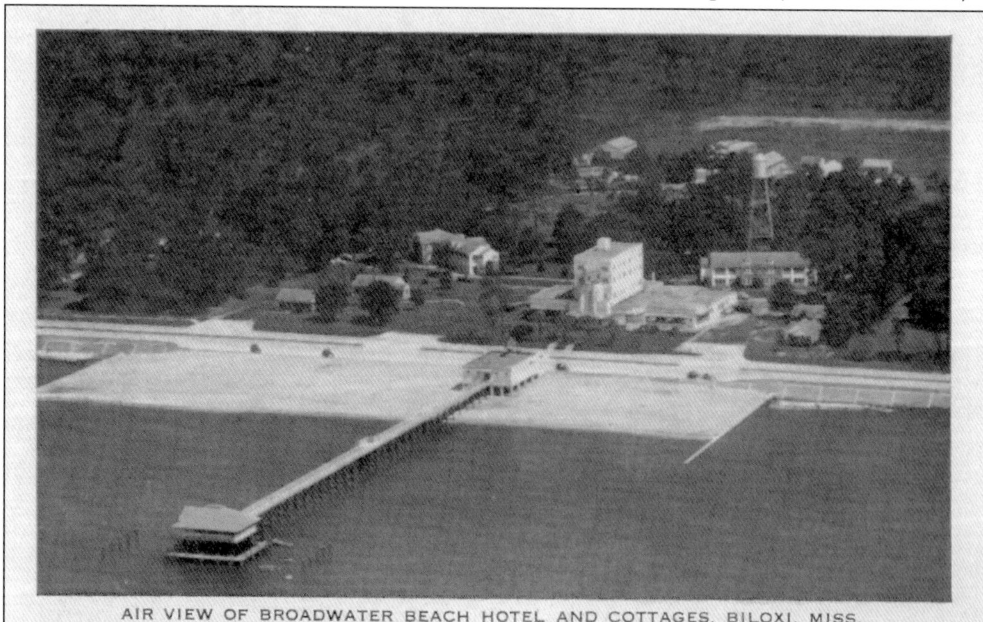

BROADWATER BEACH HOTEL AND COTTAGES, AERIAL VIEW, c. 1940. Constructed in 1938, the Broadwater Beach was built to accommodate out-of-state gamblers. Gambling was viewed during the Great Depression as a way to stimulate the local economy. Although today it is thought of as a time of illegal gambling by some people, this postcard states on the reverse side, "Dancing, Casino and Sports Results, Bathing, Fishing, etc. available." (Not Mailed; SC.)

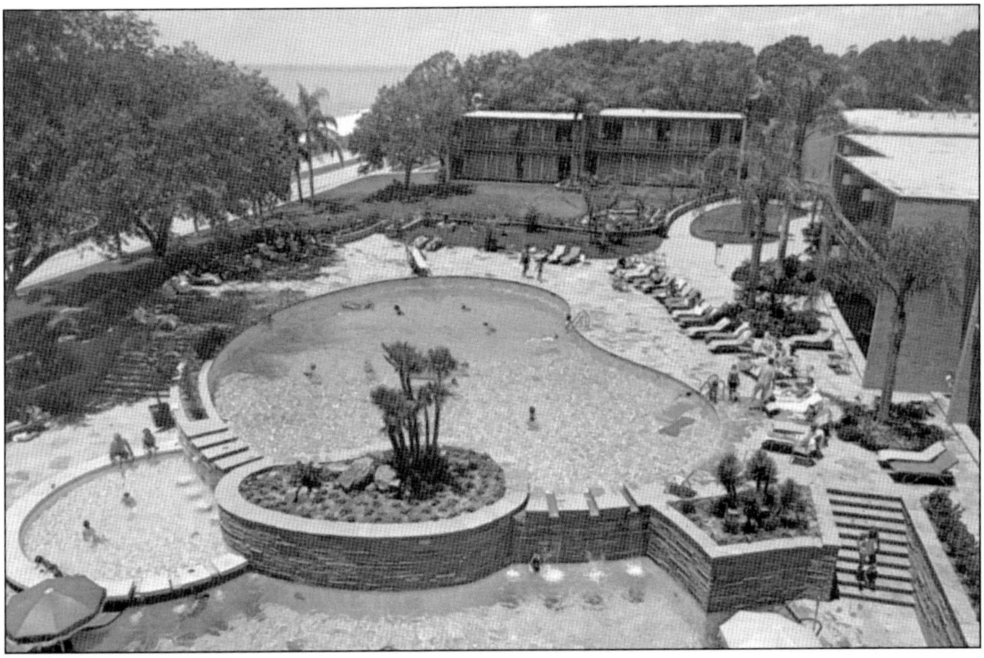

THE BROADWATER BEACH, 1960S. When owner Dorothy Brown focused on upgrading the hotel complex, its glory days began. She spent $3 million on the marina alone, and added rooms, pools (shown here), golf courses, men and ladies apparel shops, and featured entertainment nightly. Leigh MacConnell was given operational control of the hotel and resort. She was one of the few female CEOs of that era. (Postmarked 1965; SC.)

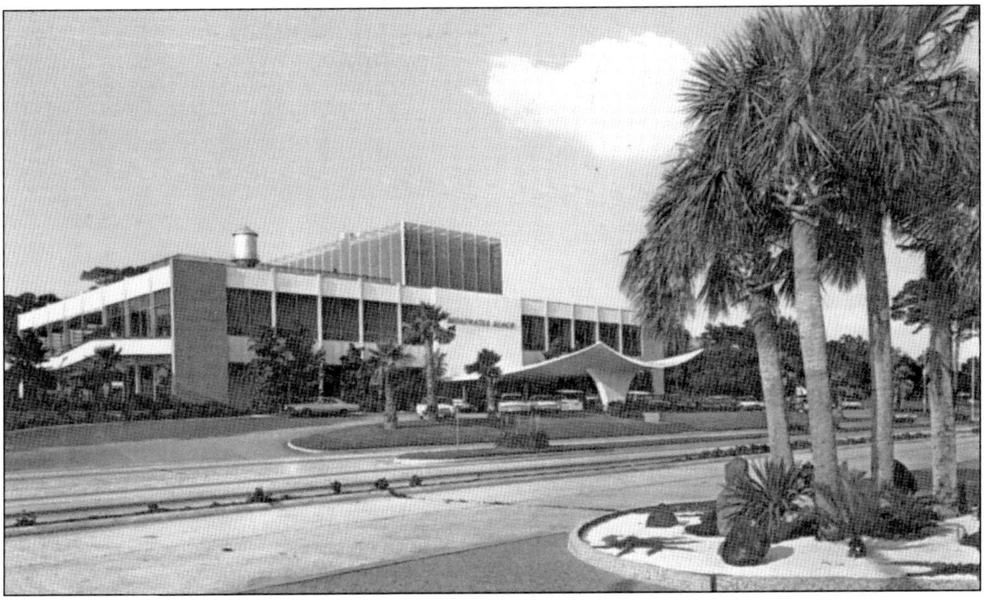

BROADWATER BEACH HOTEL, 1966. During the 1940s and early 1950s, the Broadwater flourished. In 1958, the property was purchased by Texas oilman Joe Brown, whose wife, Dorothy, renovated the hotel. Brown died shortly after the purchase, but his widow wanted to make the newly named Broadwater Beach the pacesetter hotel along the entire coast of the Gulf of Mexico. (Postmarked 1966; SC.)

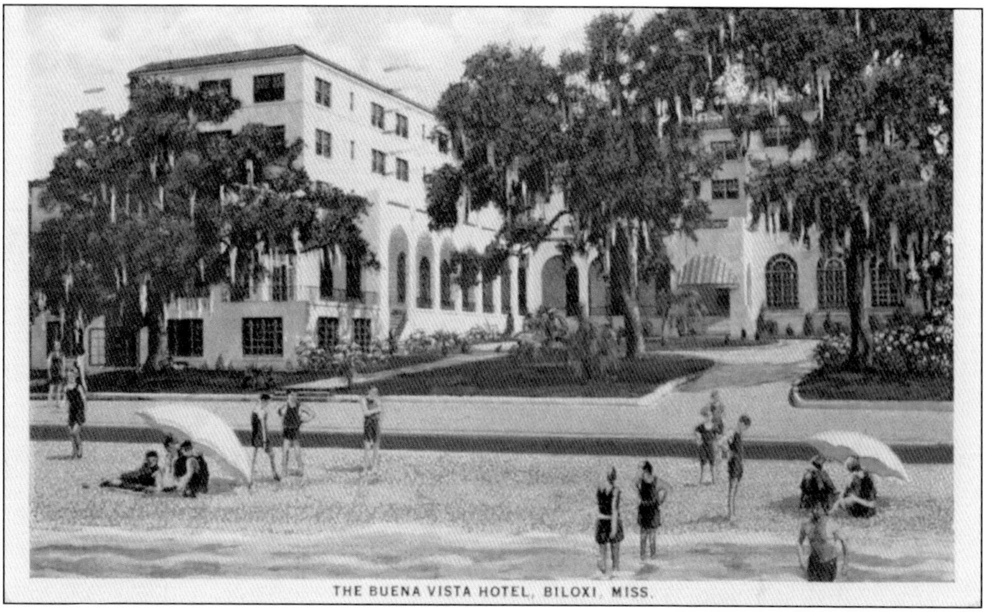

THE BUENA VISTA HOTEL, 1926. On July 4, 1924, there was a grand celebration in the city of Biloxi. Eager spectators marveled at the beige stucco walls, soaring arches, and tile roofs of the beautifully landscaped Buena Vista Hotel, located on Highway 90. The $400,000 hotel featured an expansive lobby and would become a landmark of central Biloxi for many years to come. (Postmarked 1926; SC.)

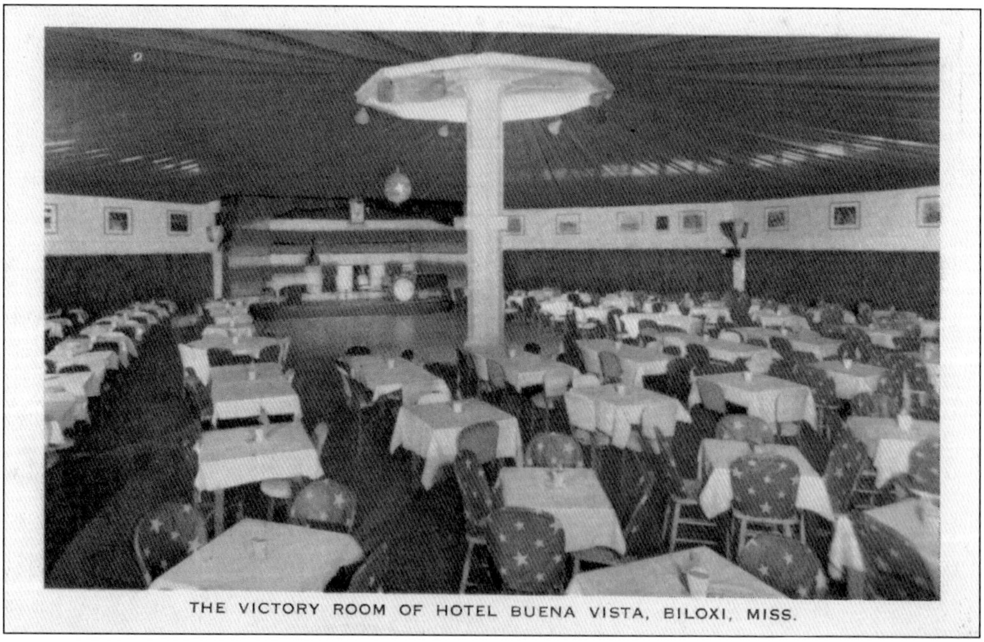

THE VICTORY ROOM OF THE BUENA VISTA, C. 1940. The Victory Room (dining), the Hurricane Room (ballroom), the Marine Room (downstairs lounge), and the Deck (rooftop bar) were some of the amenities of this grand hotel. Outstanding orchestras and live entertainment and fine dining, beverages, and casino games were featured nightly. Convention business was added to the hotel repertoire when it changed hands in 1938. (Not Mailed; SC.)

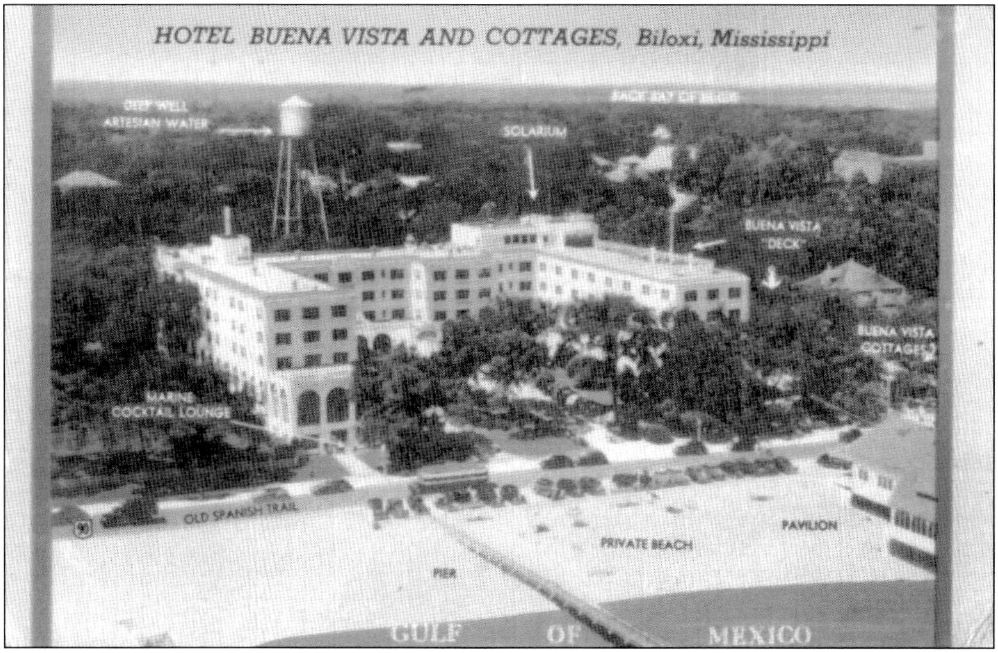

HOTEL BUENA VISTA AND COTTAGES, 1943. A closer look at this World War II–era postcard of the Buena Vista Hotel property reveals some unique amenities of the facility. Cottages were located at the southern terminus, where I-110 is now. On the eastern side was a private beach with a dancing and recreation pavilion, a solarium, and a water tank. (Postmarked 1943; SC.)

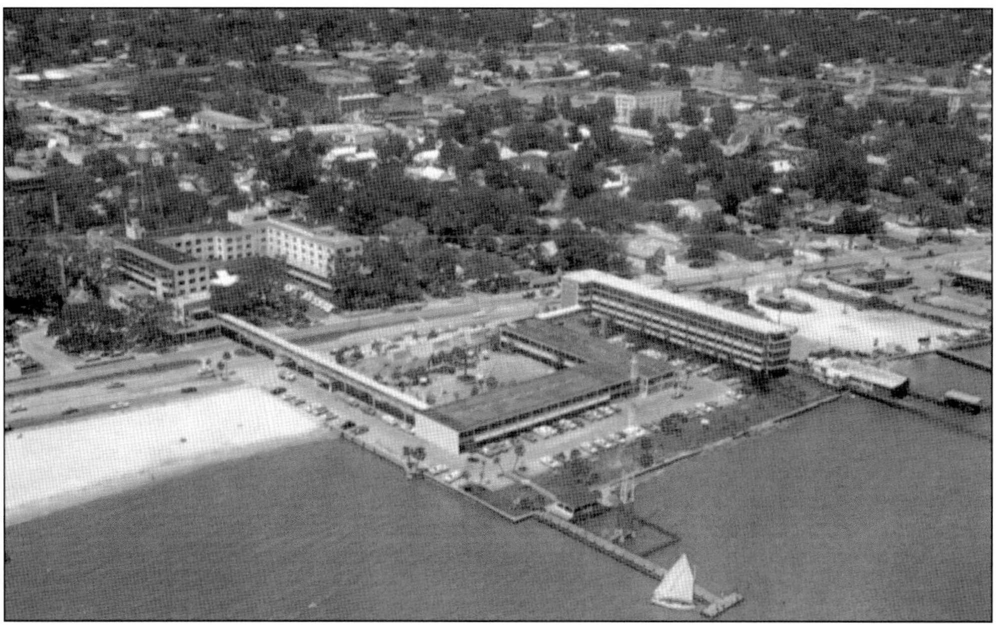

THE BUENA VISTA HOTEL AND MOTEL, C. 1965. The late 1950s and 1960s brought many welcome changes to the property, including a motel, elevated highway walkover, and WLOX radio and television stations. The Buena Vista flourished prior to Hurricane Camille (August 1969). The hotel survived but never quite made it back and was sold to several times before eventually closing. It was destroyed by fire in 1991. (Not Mailed; SC.)

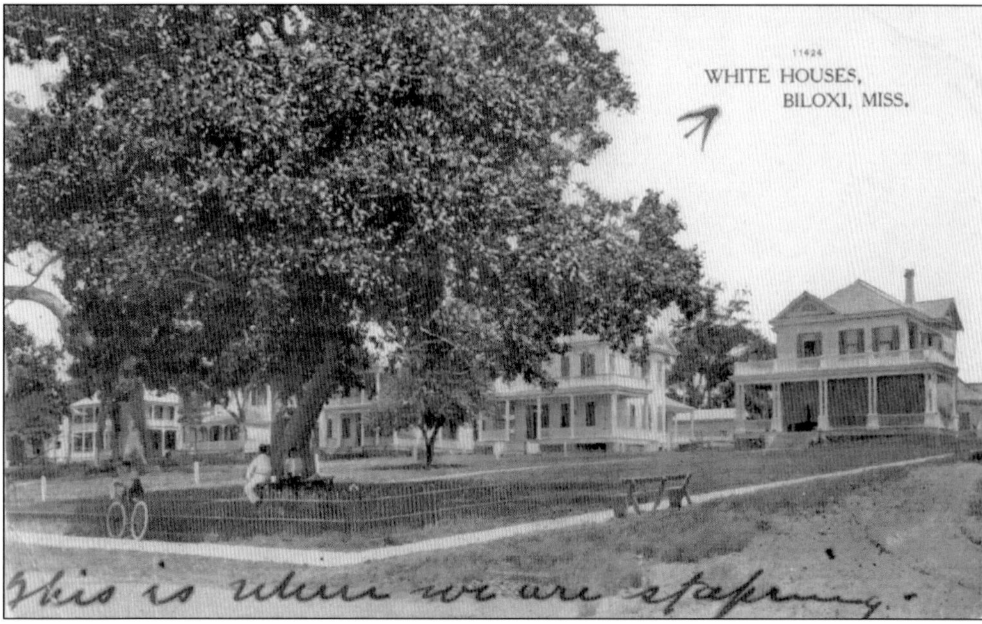

WHITE HOUSES, 1908. Walter White's family home on Highway 90 was completed in 1895, and his attention turned to building his law practice. His resourceful, energetic wife, Cora, began accepting boarders, mostly teachers, and some tourists. Since Biloxi had many visitors but few rooms, Cora seized the opportunity. She began purchasing adjacent houses until she owned seven in a row, creating a very successful business. (Postmarked 1908, SC.)

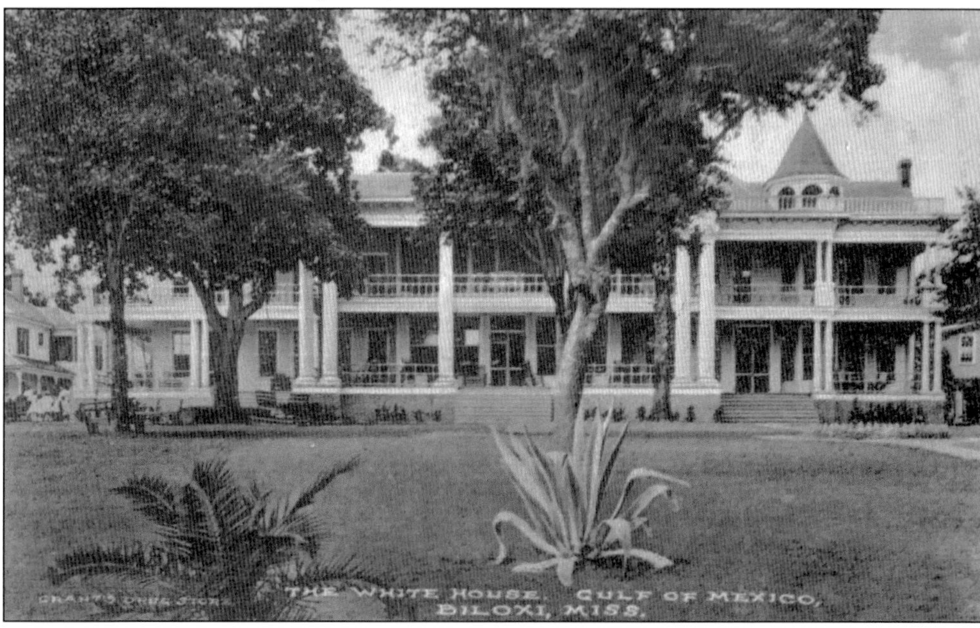

THE WHITE HOUSE, GULF OF MEXICO, C. 1920. The first two houses were joined in 1911, and by 1915, talented musicians, dressed in white linen suits, were playing for the guests three times a day. The grand ballroom, classical pillars, and second-floor balcony were featured. The hotel boasted "Home Comforts, Good Cooking, and Southern Hospitality." Fresh milk, eggs, and seafood were featured on the menu. (Not Mailed; SC.)

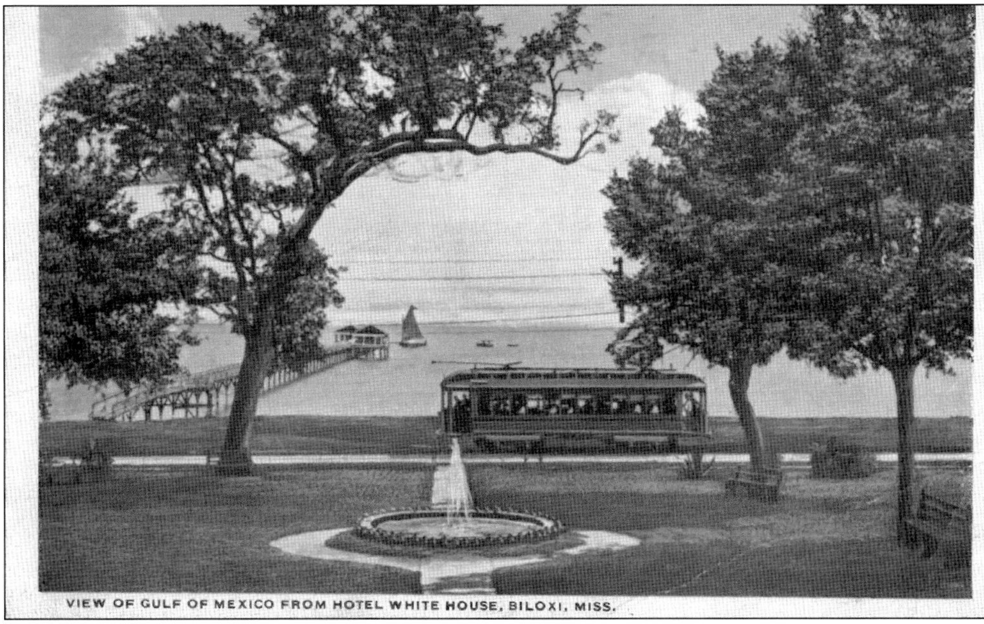

VIEW OF THE GULF FROM THE WHITE HOUSE, 1909. This card depicts the view of the White Pier, the passing trolley, and boats beyond the large oak trees. Thousands of visitors delighted in viewing the fountain's multicolored lights and manually controlled sprays of up to 40 feet high. Today, the fountain is located in the median of Highway 90 and is owned by the City of Biloxi. (Postmarked 1919, SC.)

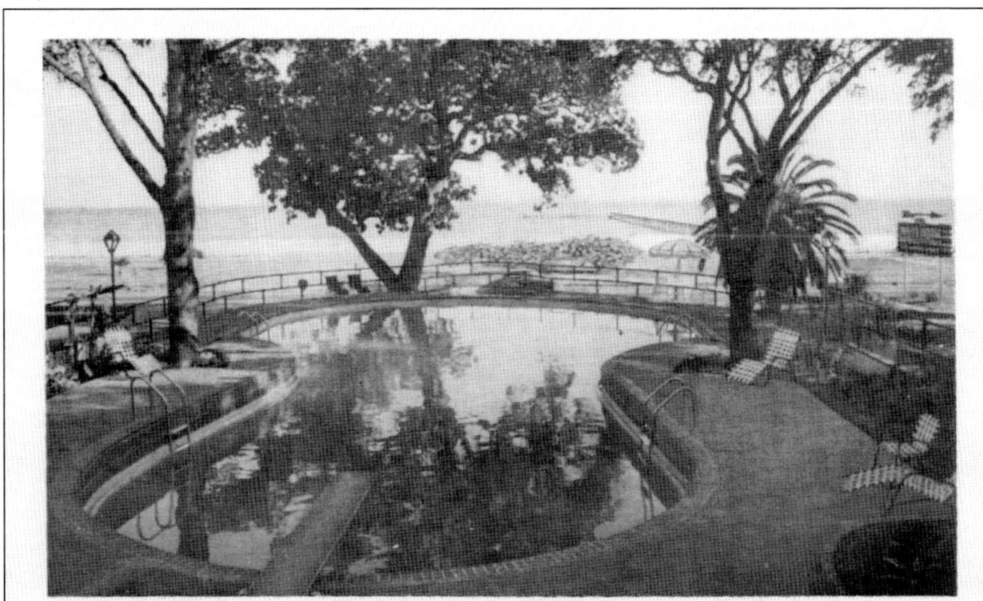

THE WHITE HOUSE TERRACE AND SWIMMING POOL, C. 1950. The hotel property was sold by James S. Love II in 1971. After a succession of financially strapped owners, the hotel closed in 1988. Weeds and an occasional vagrant occupied the property until 1989, when James S. Love III, with hopes of restoration, purchased the property his dad had sold nearly 20 years earlier. It remains closed today. (Not Mailed; SC.)

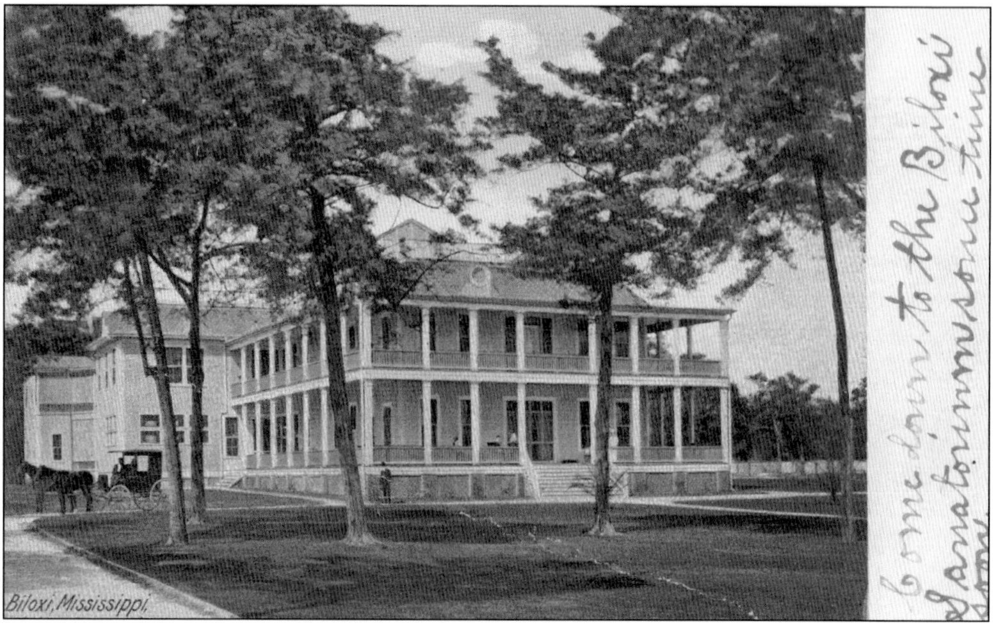

BILOXI SANATORIUM, 1906. About two blocks west of the Biloxi Lighthouse, Dr. H.M. Folkes built this two-story sanatorium in 1904 to replace the structure he had constructed in 1899, which had been destroyed by fire. In 1908, additional rooms were added and its name changed to Gulf Coast Health Resort. In 1909, the facility was changed into a modern hotel, known as the Biloxi Hotel. (Postmarked 1906; SC.)

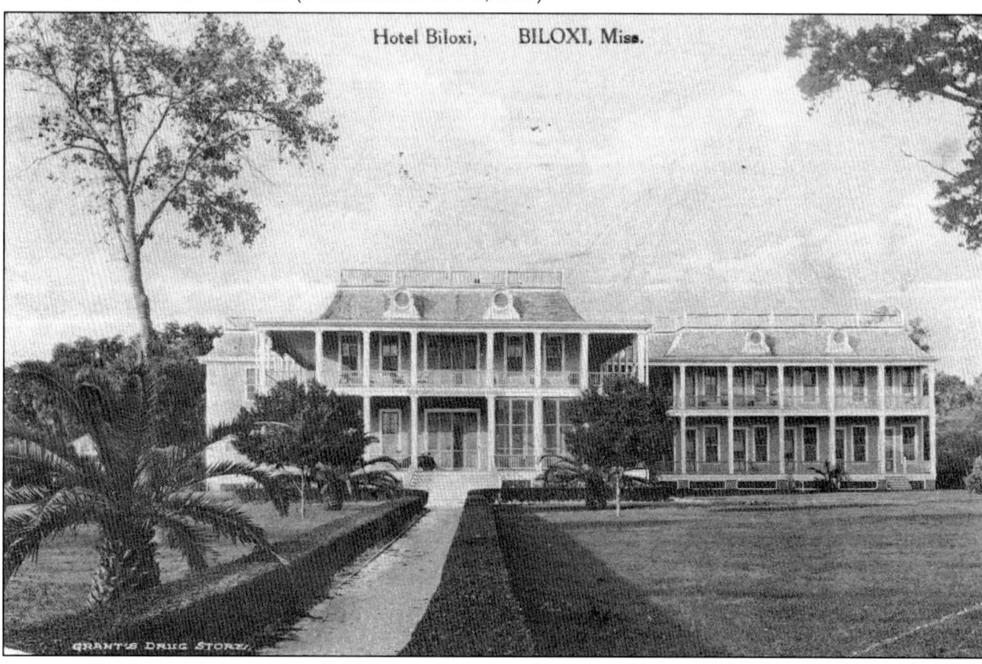

BILOXI HOTEL, 1914. The 1909 transformation of the Biloxi Sanatorium to the Biloxi Hotel was quite easy. With the previous addition of a new wing, the facility moved from a health resort to a hotel that specialized in healthy pursuits of sun, sea breezes, recreation, and a relaxed lifestyle. (Postmarked 1914; SC.)

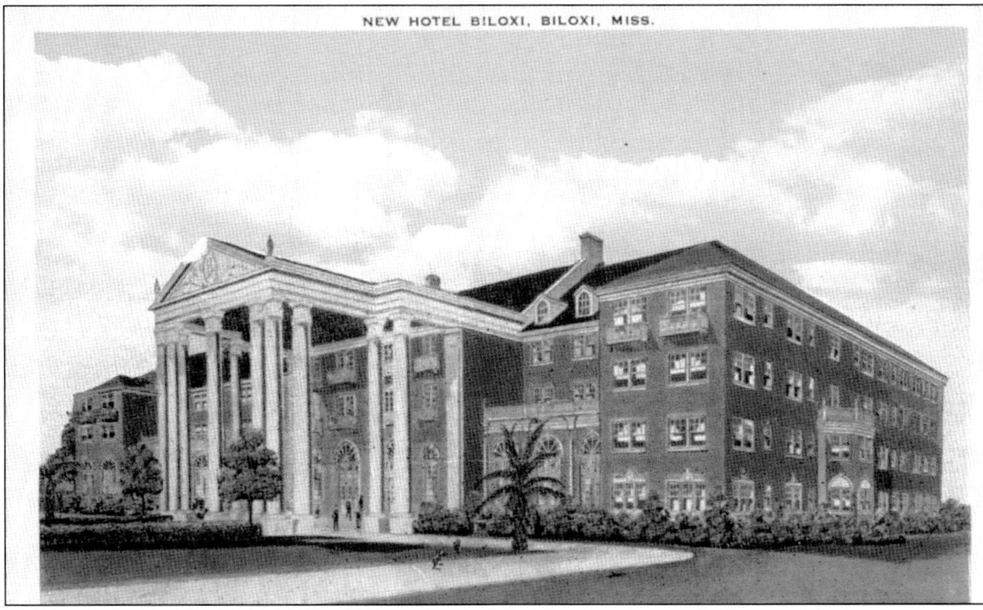

BILOXI HOTEL, C. 1930. In 1928, the wooden structure of the Biloxi Hotel was replaced with a white-columned redbrick building. The hotel offered a large playground, magnolia and live oak trees, plus a great view of the Gulf of Mexico. The hotel prospered until motels became more popular in the 1950s and 1960s. It was no longer in use when Hurricane Camille hit in 1969. (Not Mailed; BL.)

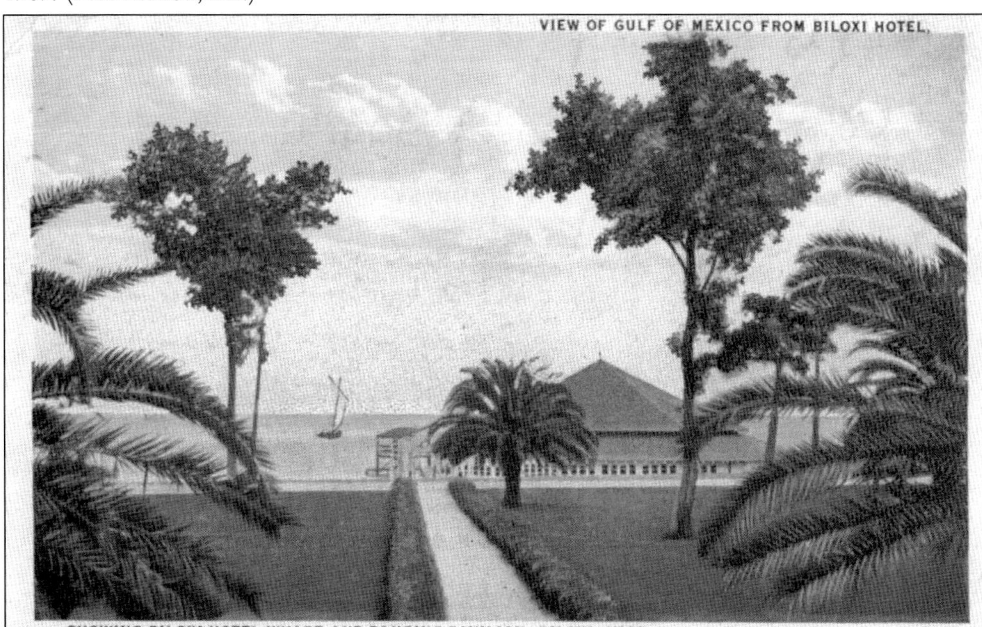

VIEW OF GULF OF MEXICO FROM BILOXI HOTEL, 1923. The pier and dancing pavilion depict a happy, booming time for the tourist business in Biloxi during the mid- to late 1920s. The pavilion held large crowds of locals and tourists that came to party along Biloxi's beaches. Time and hurricanes took their toll on the hotel. After a total refurbishment, it is now the Chateau LeGrand Condominiums. (Postmarked 1925; SC.)

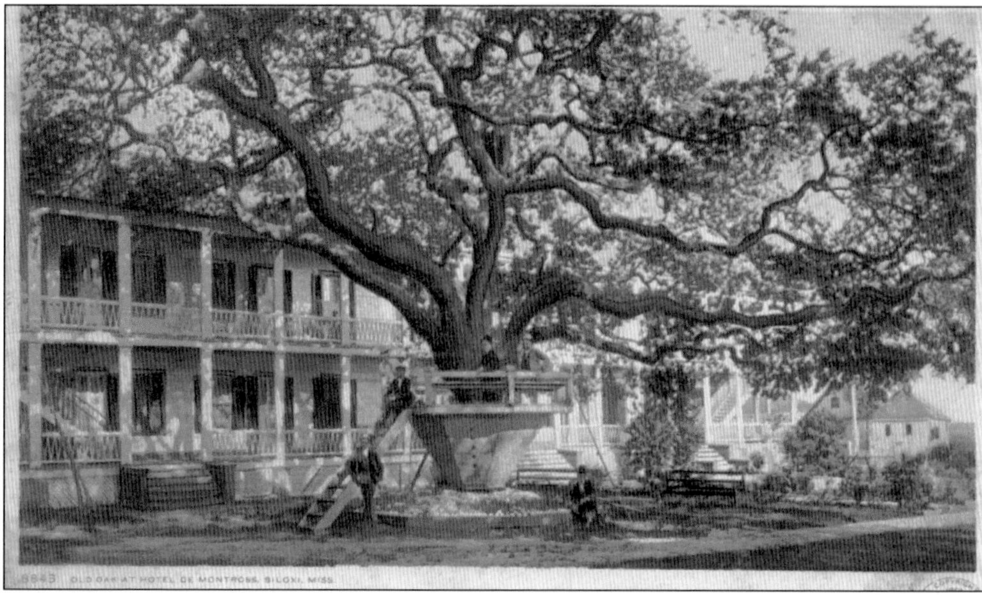

OLD OAK AT HOTEL DE MONTROSS, 1901. On the northeast corner of Lameuse Street and Beach Road was the Shady Grove Hotel. The hotel, which later became the Montross, was one of the early watering holes, as they were known, in the center of Biloxi. The facility served as a gathering place for many events, including the organization of the Biloxi Fire Company in 1883. (Postmarked 1908; SC.)

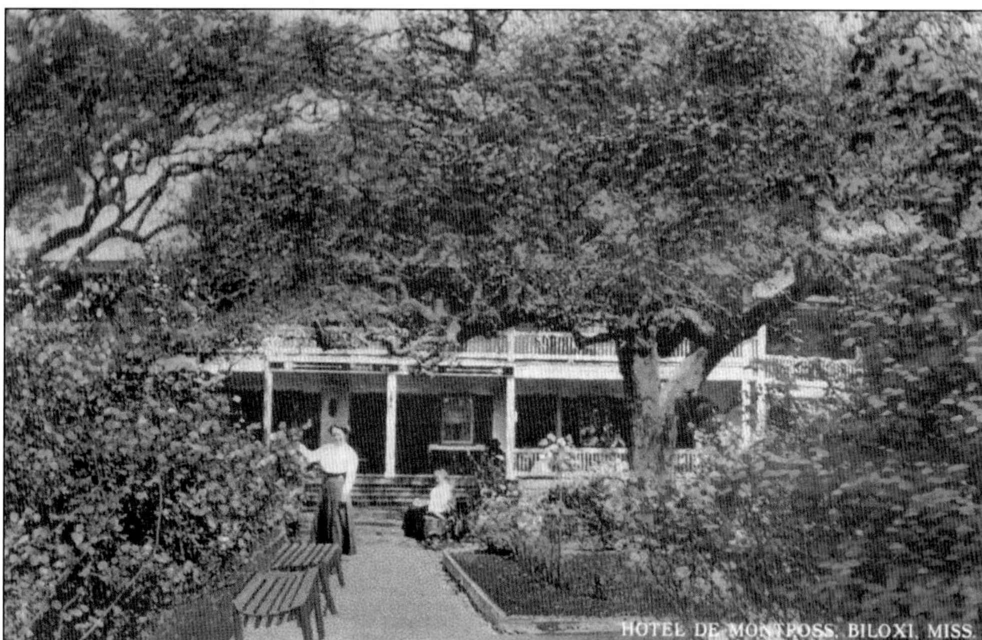

HOTEL DE MONTROSS, 1908. Although one of the hurricanes must have destroyed the shoofly previously located around the oak tree, the Montross boasted of its fine gardens, electric lights, full-dress dinners, and elegant parties. People of wealth from Memphis, Chicago, and other points in the Midwest made early seasonal reservations to stay in this warm resort town. (Postmarked 1914; SC.)

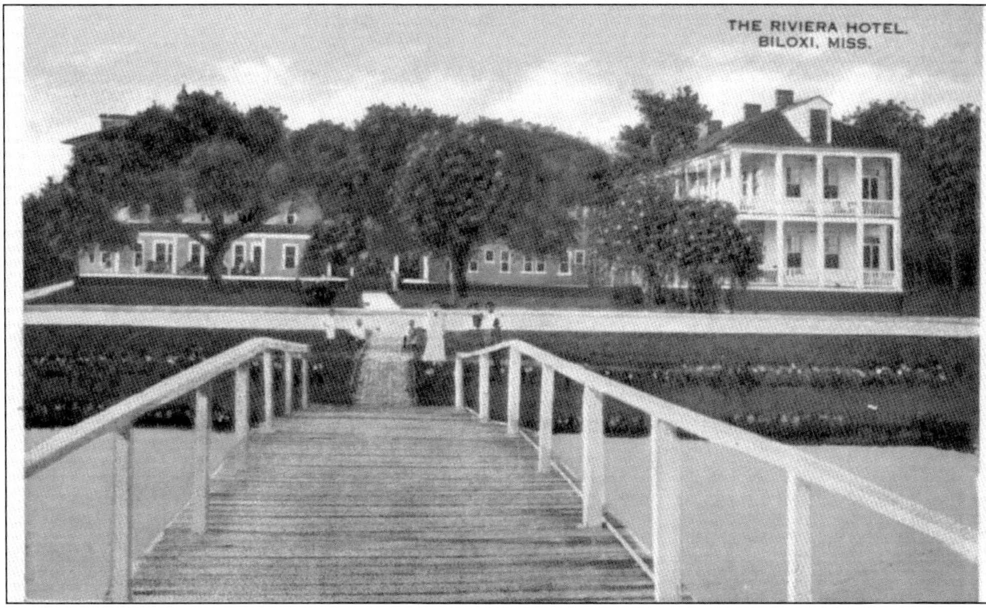

HOTEL RIVIERA, 1920S. The former Hotel De Montross, now remodeled and refurbished, had a new name, the Hotel Riviera. Hoping to capture its share of the booming tourist business of the 1920s, with a prime location in the center of Biloxi, the hotel was a hotbed of entertainment activity. The hotel pier was located across Beach Road, which was home to the Biloxi Yacht Club and the summer boat races. (Not Mailed; SC.)

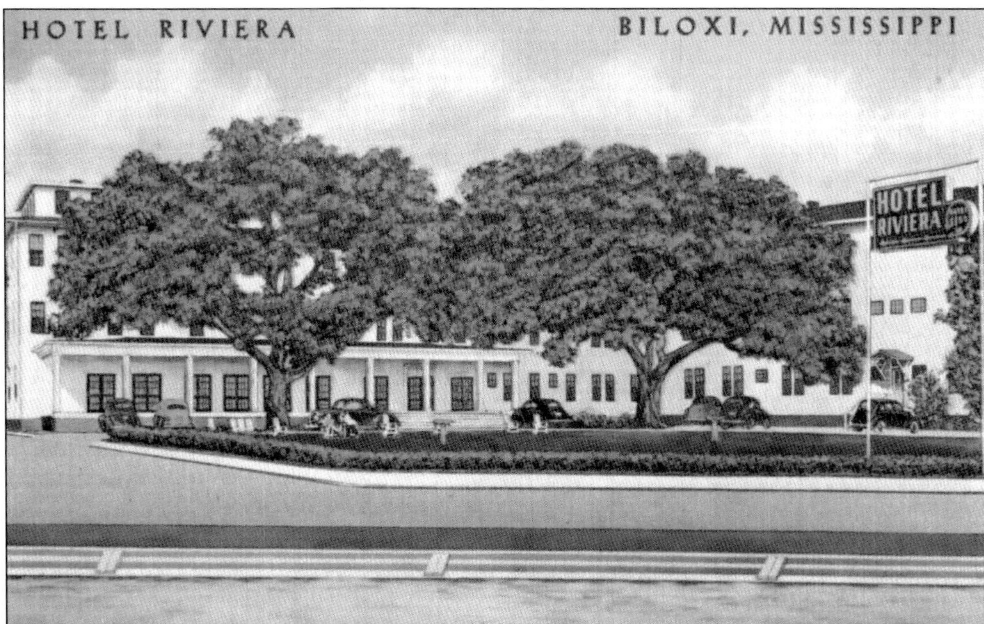

HOTEL RIVIERA, 1946. One hundred air-conditioned rooms, fine dining, and its prime location in the heart of downtown Biloxi kept the Hotel Riviera active as the mid-20th century approached, but age was taking its toll. The newer properties, tourist courts, and motels were outstripping the hotel. Hurricane Camille destroyed the Hotel Riviera in 1969. The property is now the Biloxi Town Green. (Postmarked 1946; SC.)

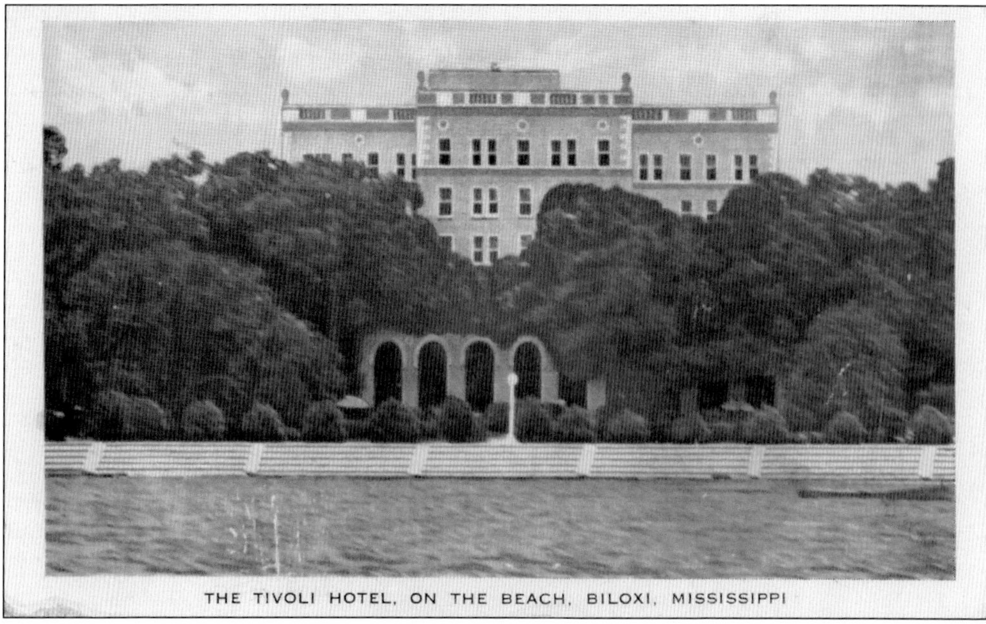

THE TIVOLI HOTEL, C. 1940. Designed by Carl E. Matthes, the designer of the Buena Vista Hotel, the Tivoli was a good fit in the city of Biloxi. The hotel was not nearly as elaborate as the Edgewater or the Buena Vista but featured gardens facing the Gulf of Mexico and a stunning barrel-vaulted lobby ceiling. The modern, fireproof building contained 64 rooms and 24 apartments. (Not Mailed; SC.)

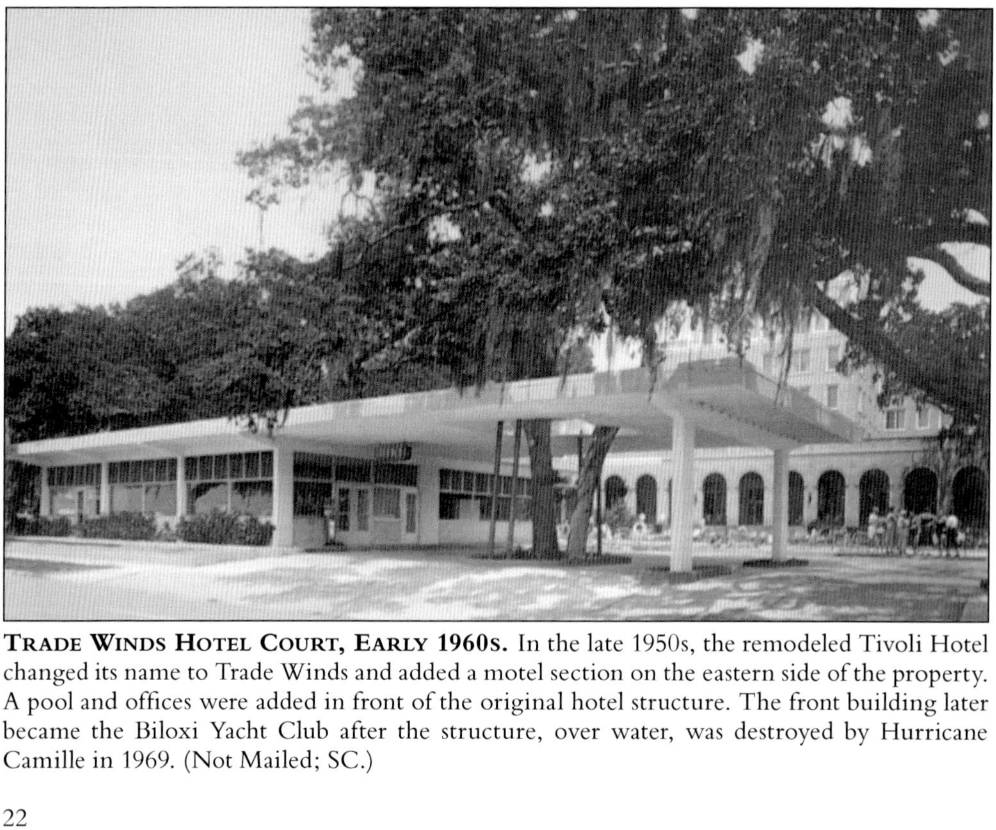

TRADE WINDS HOTEL COURT, EARLY 1960S. In the late 1950s, the remodeled Tivoli Hotel changed its name to Trade Winds and added a motel section on the eastern side of the property. A pool and offices were added in front of the original hotel structure. The front building later became the Biloxi Yacht Club after the structure, over water, was destroyed by Hurricane Camille in 1969. (Not Mailed; SC.)

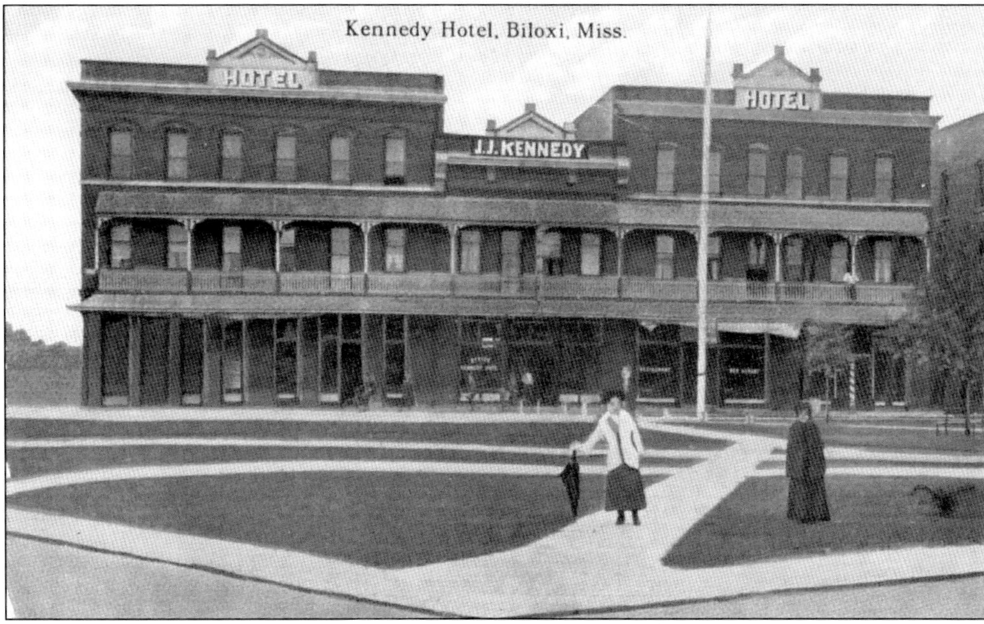

KENNEDY HOTEL, 1913. The great Biloxi fire of November 1900, which destroyed most of the downtown, gave birth to a building boom in 1901, which continued for a few years. The contract was let in 1901 for the two-story Kennedy Hotel at the corner of Reynoir Street and the railroad, across from City Park. An addition was added in 1904 to accommodate increased visitors arriving by train. (Postmarked 1914; SC.)

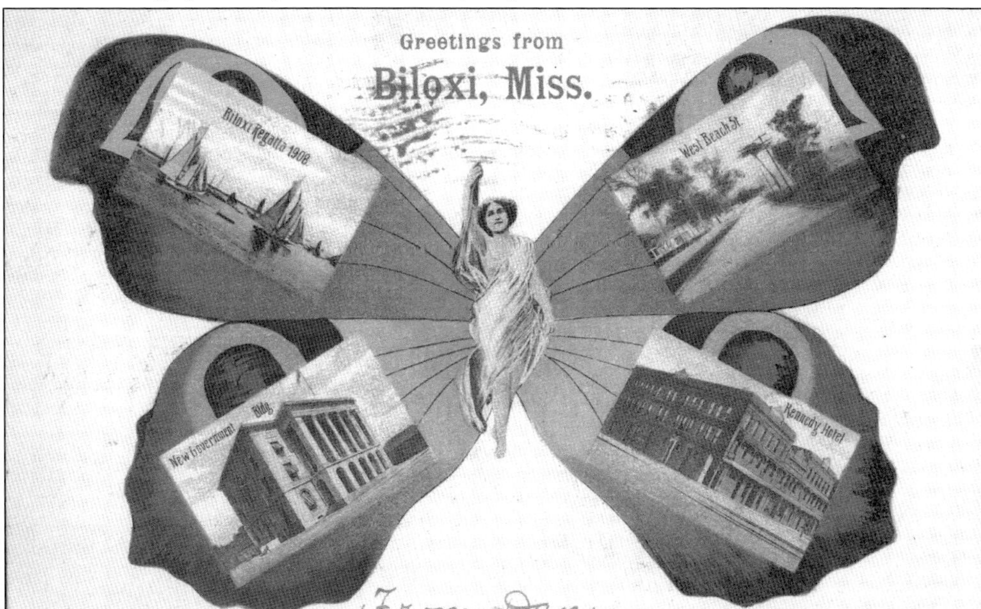

BUTTERFLY MULTI-VIEW, 1910. This classic 1910 postcard was published by the Kennedy Hotel and was printed in Germany. Adorning the wings of the butterfly were schooner races, the new Government Building, West Beach Boulevard, and of course, the Kennedy Hotel. Other similar cards of the time depicted the petals of flowers, fruit, vegetables, or leaves of a plant. (Postmarked 1910; SC.)

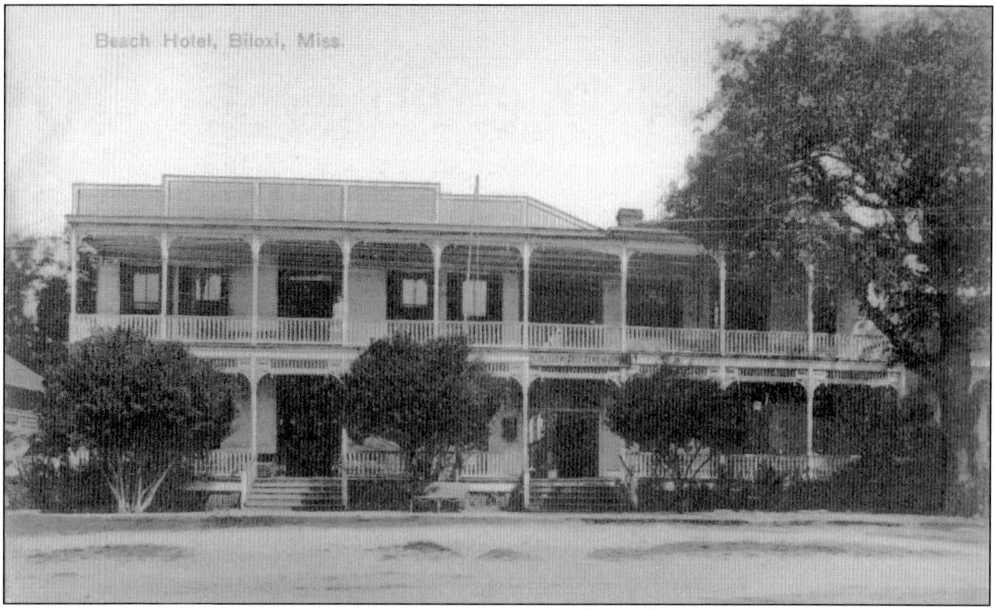

Beach Hotel, Pre-1910. Although hotels and rooming houses existed and flourished in Biloxi prior to the turn-of-the-century, few postcards remain today. This pre-1910 view of the Beach Hotel, which was located just west of Main Street on the beach, is a grand example. The card was distributed by Kimbrough & Kimbrough Pharmacists in Biloxi (later Kimbrough & Quint) and printed in Germany. (Not Mailed; SC.)

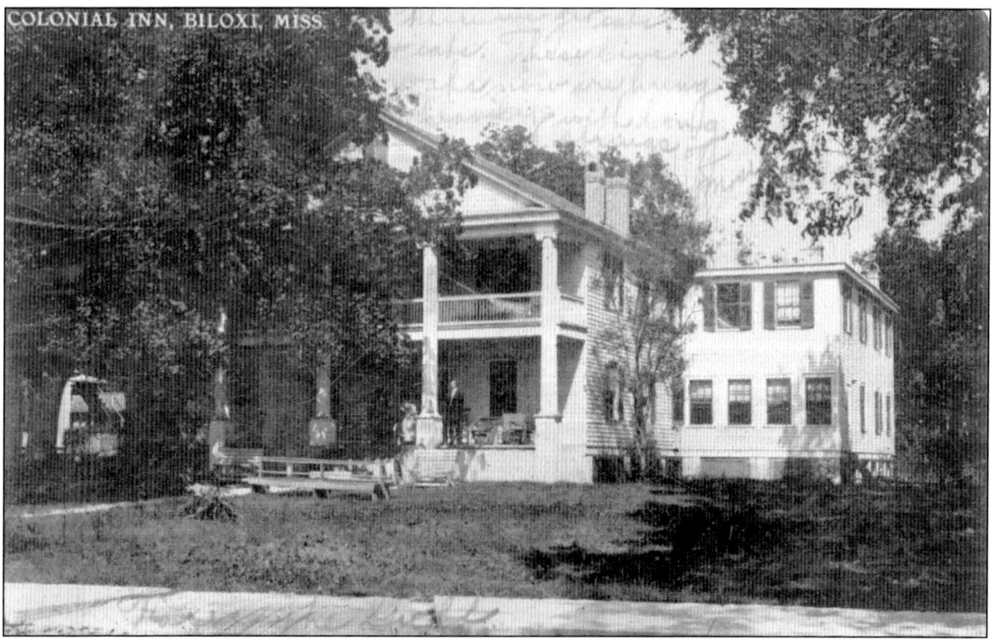

Colonial Inn, 1909. In the early 1900s, hotels were built fronting the Mississippi Sound, overlooking the water and receiving gulf breezes. The beach, as it now appears, did not exist until mid-century when sand was pumped in to create the beach. The Colonial Inn, located at 418 East Beach Boulevard, featured a massive front porch and a long pier with a bathhouse for its patrons' enjoyment. (Postmarked 1913; SC.)

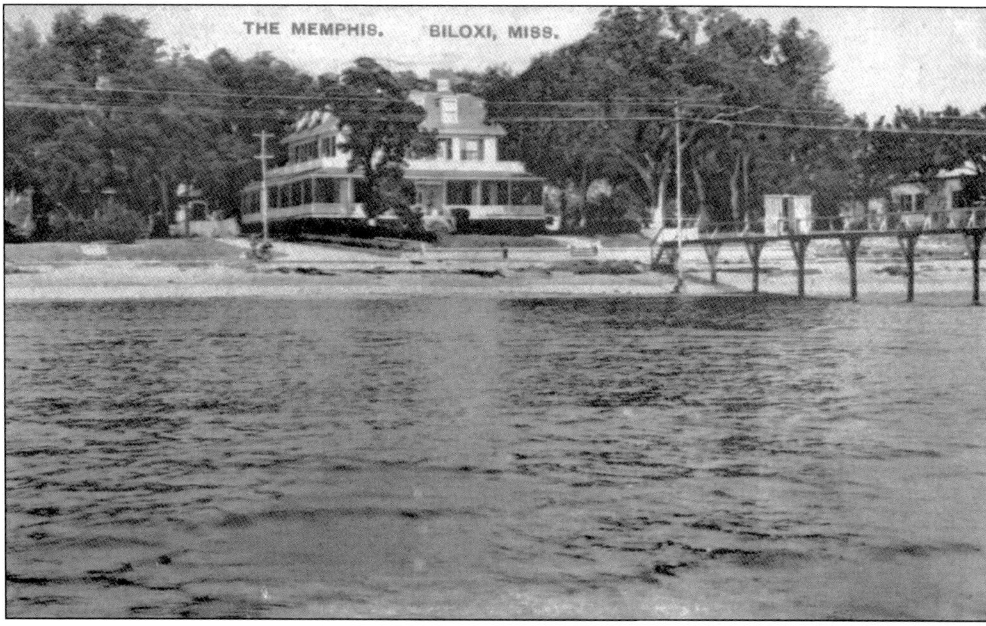

THE MEMPHIS, 1914. In 1913, Col. John W. Apperson (later manager of the new Buena Vista Hotel) became the owner of the former Gulf View Hotel and named it The Memphis. The property was basically a rooming house hotel, located at 433 East Beach Boulevard, on the northeast corner of Seal Avenue and the beach. Apperson did not own it very long; it changed hands twice before 1920. (Postmarked 1914; SC.)

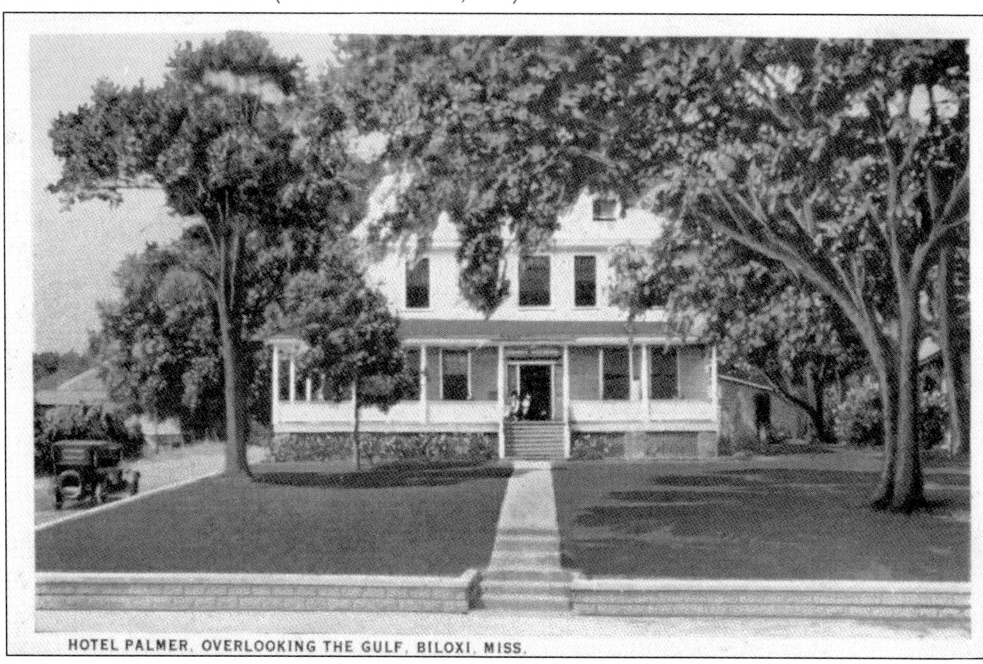

HOTEL PALMER, 1924. Prior to 1920, The Memphis was sold to Charles and Elizabeth Palmer and the name was changed to Hotel Palmer. The Palmer house remained in the ownership of the Palmer family until the late 1930s. With several other owners, it remained in business until 1968. The facility was destroyed by Hurricane Camille in 1969. (Not Mailed; SC.)

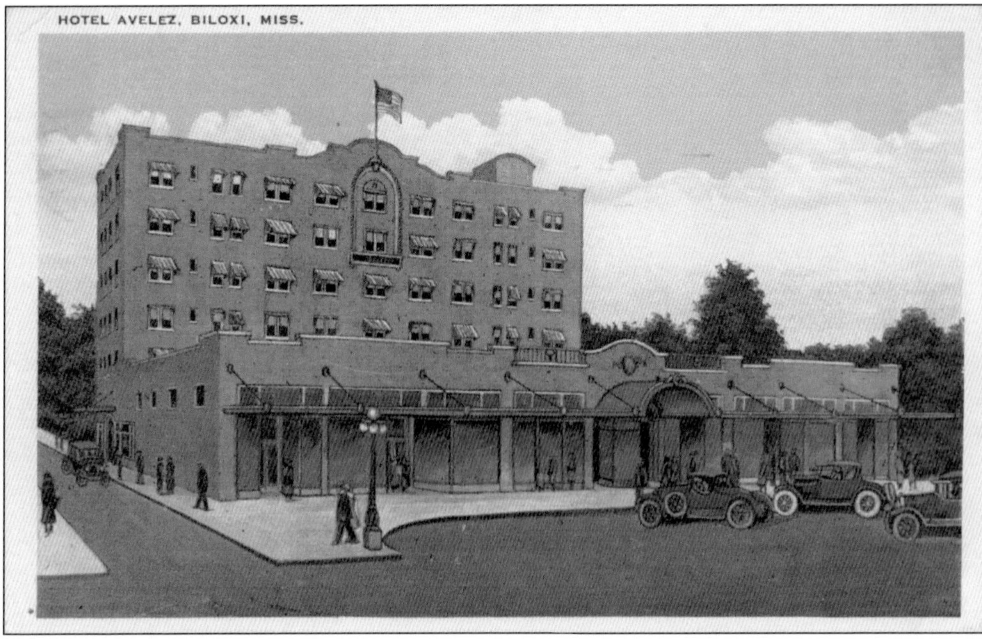

HOTEL AVELEZ, LATE 1920S. This downtown hotel was located at 301 West Howard Avenue, midway between the railroad and the beach. Single rooms were featured in 1942 for $1.50 to $2.50, with a European plan (meals not included). In the late 1950s, Butler's Shoes and Lerner's Dress Shop were located in the Howard Avenue portion of the building front and a gambling operation was part of the lounge. (Postmarked 1930; SC.)

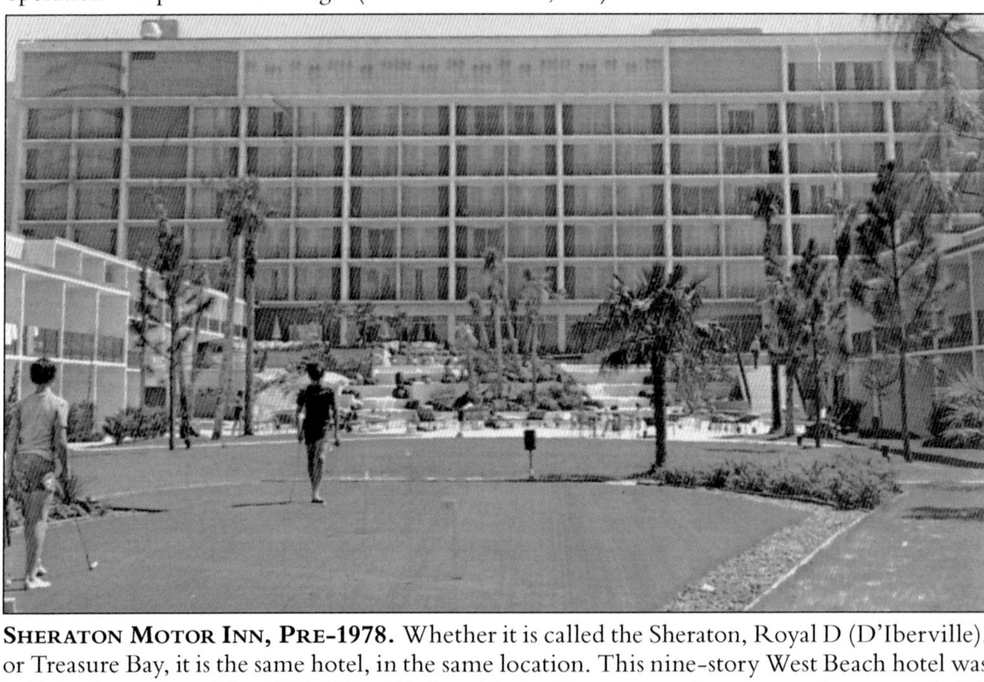

SHERATON MOTOR INN, PRE-1978. Whether it is called the Sheraton, Royal D (D'Iberville), or Treasure Bay, it is the same hotel, in the same location. This nine-story West Beach hotel was built in the center of the 1970s Biloxi Strip with the Fiesta across the street and many nightlife attractions nearby. Like many other hotel properties, it went from feast to famine with the tourism industry. (Postmarked 1978; SC.)

Two

Eat, Drink, and Stay

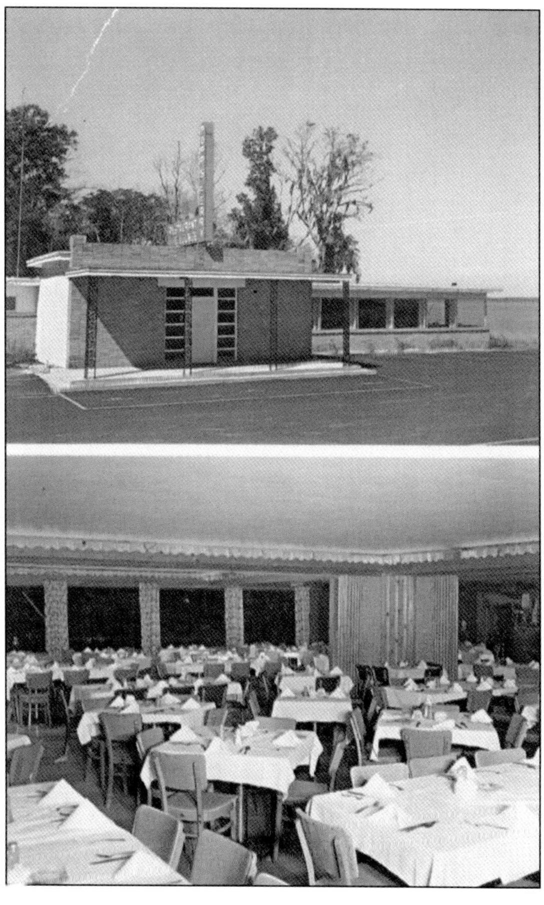

Sinopoli's Popps Ferry Restaurant, c. 1960. In the mid-19th century, Biloxi became a destination for summer visitors as one of the infamous watering holes on the coastal maritime routes. Food, drink, a place to stay, and games of chance became interwoven into the fabric known as Biloxi. Sinopoli's Popps Ferry Restaurant and Lounge was a great place to eat in the late 1950s and 1960s. (Not Mailed; SC.)

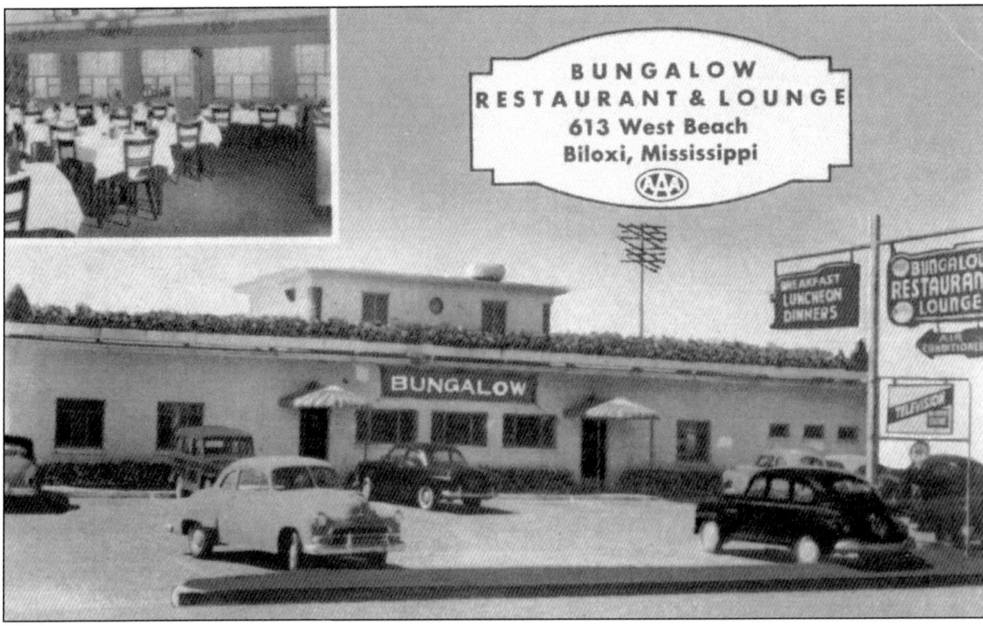

Bungalow Restaurant and Lounge, c. 1955. Twenty-four-hour service was a hallmark of this popular local seafood restaurant and lounge. Three meals were served daily, and it was rumored that, in the early days, other tables were available. Established in 1938 and located on the present site of the Beau Rivage, this attraction was one of the mainstays of the Biloxi Strip. (Not Mailed; SC.)

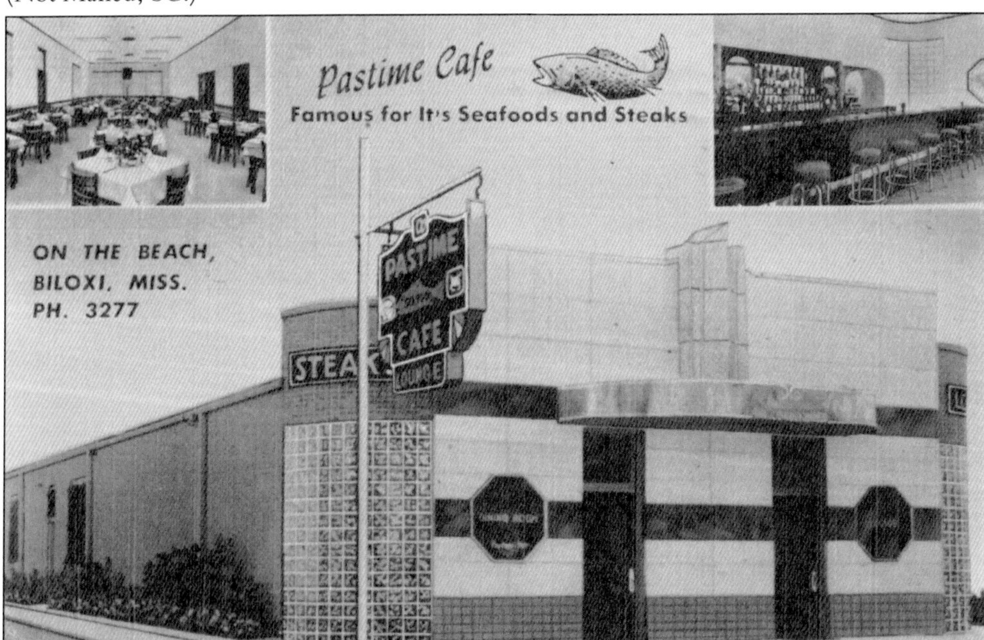

Pastime Café, c. 1950. On this postcard, the Pastime Café claimed to be the oldest seafood restaurant on the Mississippi Gulf Coast. It is said that this Central Beach landmark offered some of the finest local cuisine available. The owners of the café also advertised their tourist court on West Beach on the reverse side of the card. (Postmarked 1951; SC.)

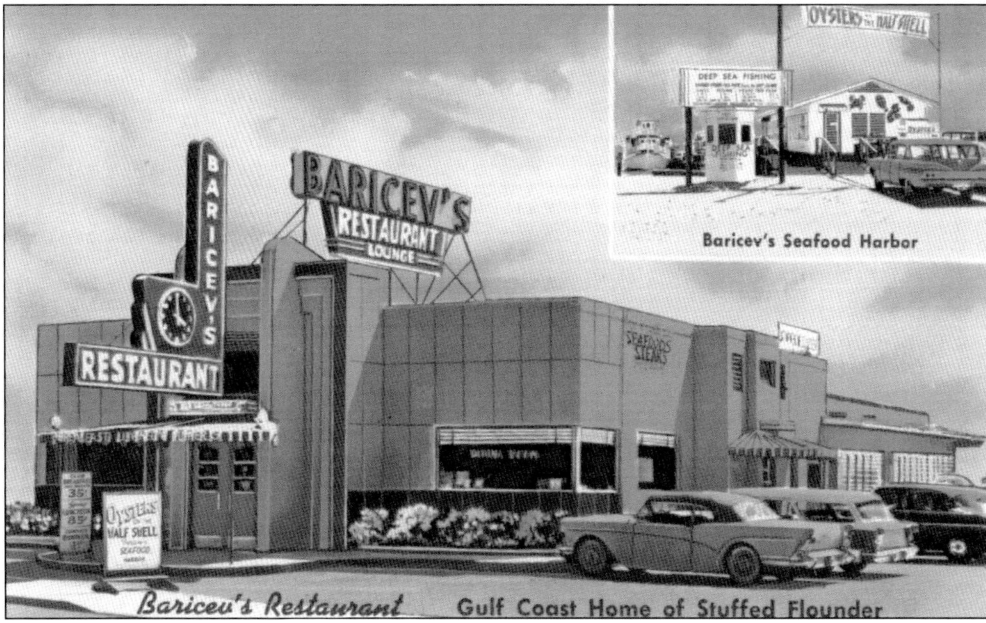

BARICEV'S RESTAURANT, C. 1956. "Gulf Coast Home of Stuffed Flounder" was the motto of Baricev's Restaurant and Lounge. Oysters Baricev, creole dishes, southern fried chicken, and oysters on the half shell helped round out the menu of this local restaurant. A club breakfast for 35¢, a special luncheon for 85¢, and a complete dinner for $1 helped lure visitors to this Central Beach location. (Not Mailed; SC.)

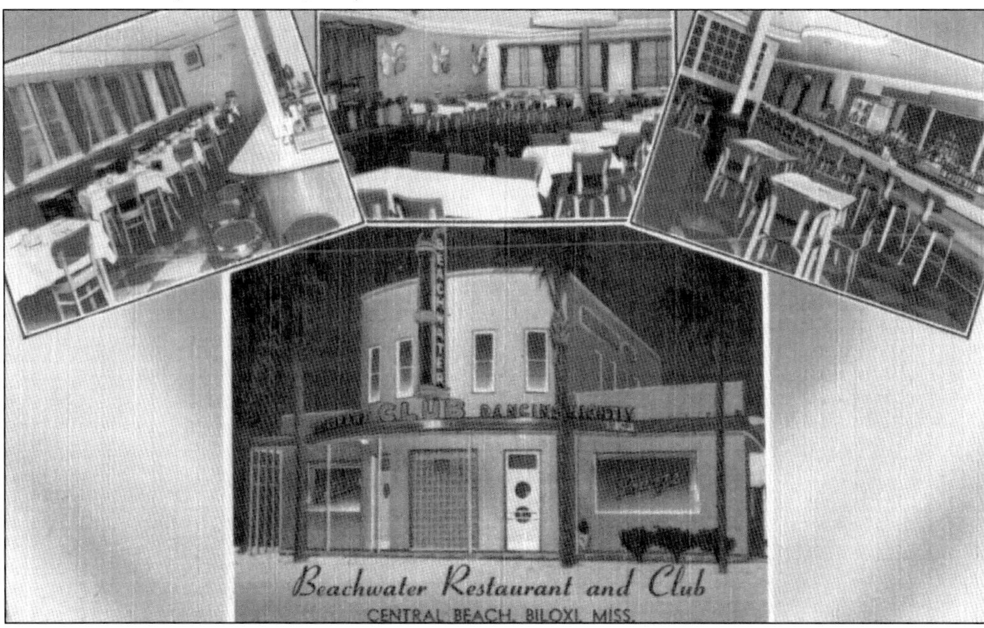

BEACHWATER RESTAURANT AND CLUB, C. 1950. This Central Beach nightclub and restaurant offered visitors dancing nightly, fine food, and year-round entertainment. The Art Deco style of the building ensured that the excitement of the club's exterior would match the excitement of the interior of the facility. The Beachwater was located east of Reynoir Street on the south side of Highway 90. (Not Mailed; SC.)

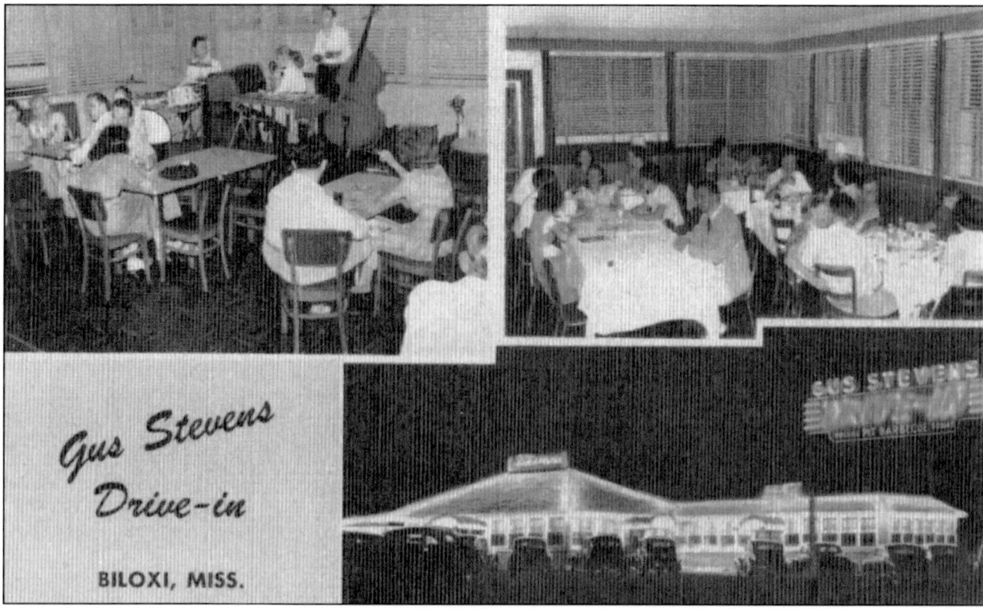

Gus Stevens Drive-In, c. 1950. Located on the corner of Highway 90 and what is now Veterans Avenue, this local hot spot was nothing like what people consider a drive-in today. Over the years, this restaurant and lounge was home to literally hundreds of traveling entertainers. Dining, dancing, and floor shows were highlights of every evening's entertainment at this 24-hours-a-day establishment. (Not Mailed; SC.)

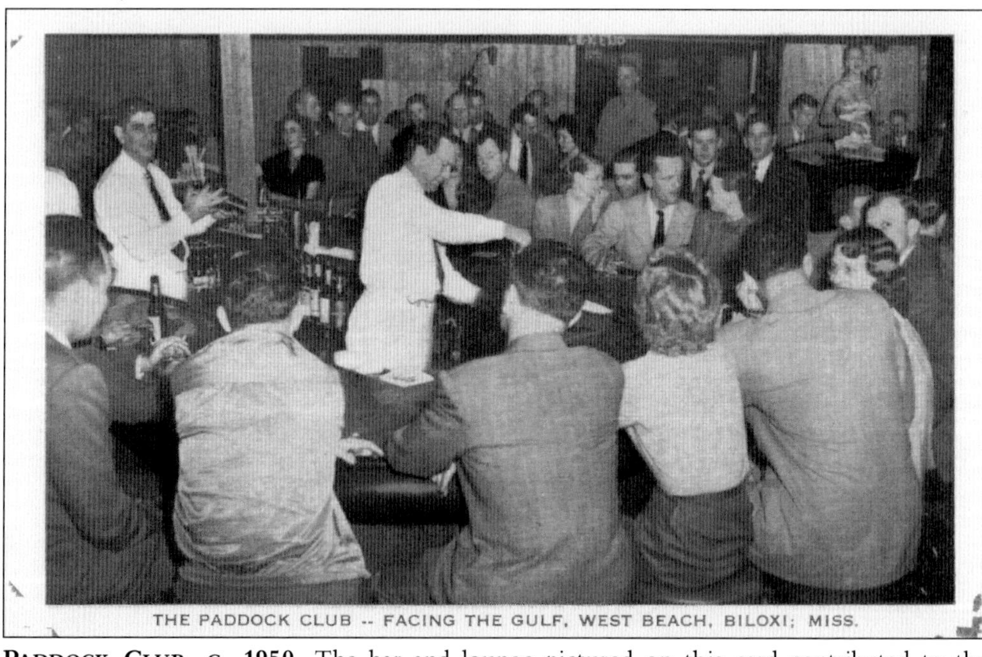

Paddock Club, c. 1950. The bar and lounge pictured on this card contributed to the reputation of Biloxi being wide open in the early 1950s. The advertising on the reverse of the postcard states, "Headquarters for all sports results by direct leased wire." The club also featured nightly entertainment and dancing. In 1952, the club was placed off limits by Keesler Air Force Base for on-premise gambling. (Not Mailed; SC.)

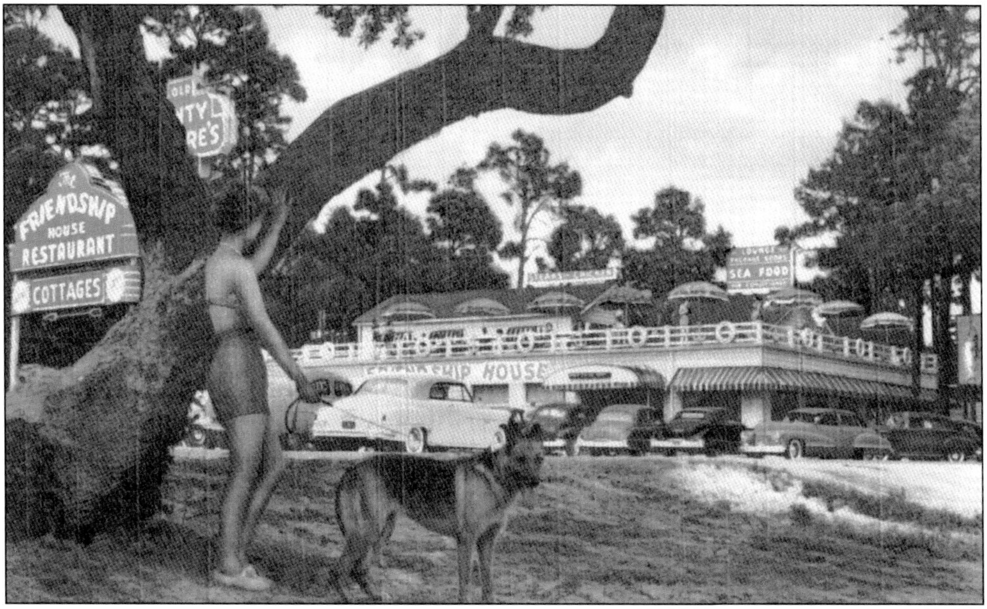

FRIENDSHIP HOUSE, 1950. Known as Beasley's, Dinny Moore's, or the Friendship House, this landmark was the "Host of the Coast" for decades. Located on the east side of DeBuys Road on Highway 90, this famous restaurant and lounge featured menu items that are still talked about today. The hospitality of the owners and waitstaff complimented the great food available at the restaurant. (Not Mailed; SC.)

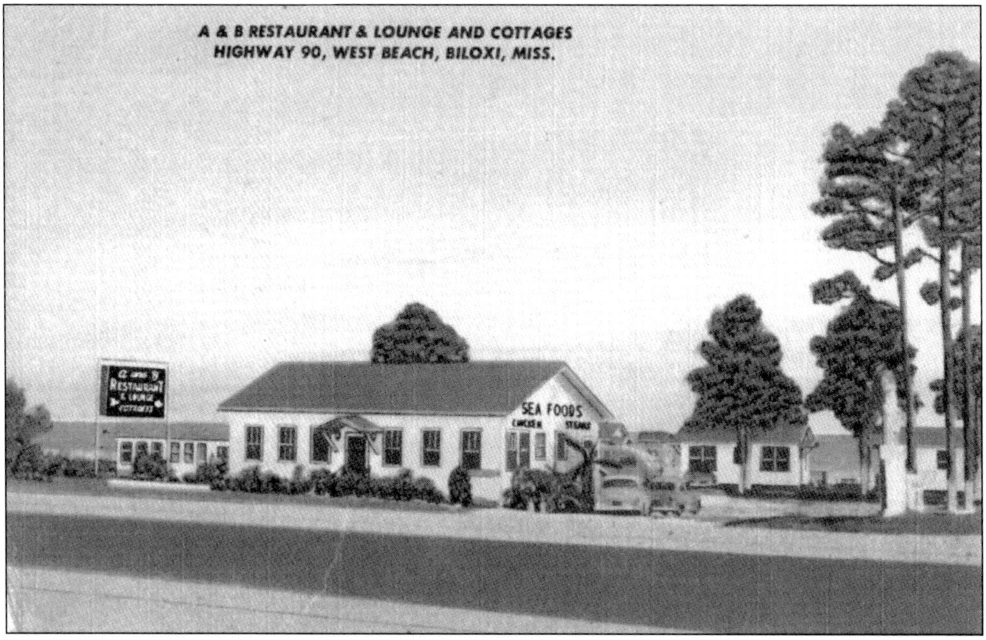

A&B RESTAURANT, LOUNGE AND COTTAGES, C. 1950. This West Beach tourist establishment, owned and operated by the same Barnes family for many years, offered visitors a little bit of everything. Besides the home-style cooking of the restaurant, the beachfront facility included a lounge and cottages with a private beach and pier available for the swimming enjoyment of the visitors. (Not Mailed; SC.)

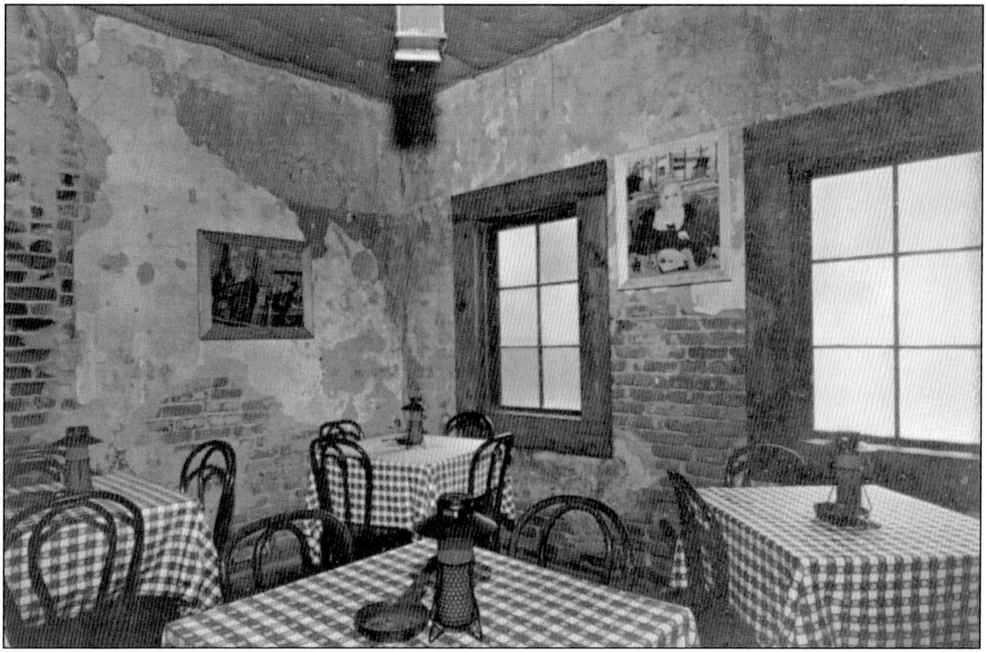

MARY MAHONEY'S OLD FRENCH HOUSE, C. 1970. This view of the Slave Quarters Room in the Old French House building, which was constructed in 1737, is now a part of the Mary Mahoney's Restaurant complex. This fine dining restaurant also features an intimate cocktail lounge and café courtyard. The oak tree located in the courtyard, "known as the patriarch," is estimated to be over 2,000 years old. (Not Mailed; SC.)

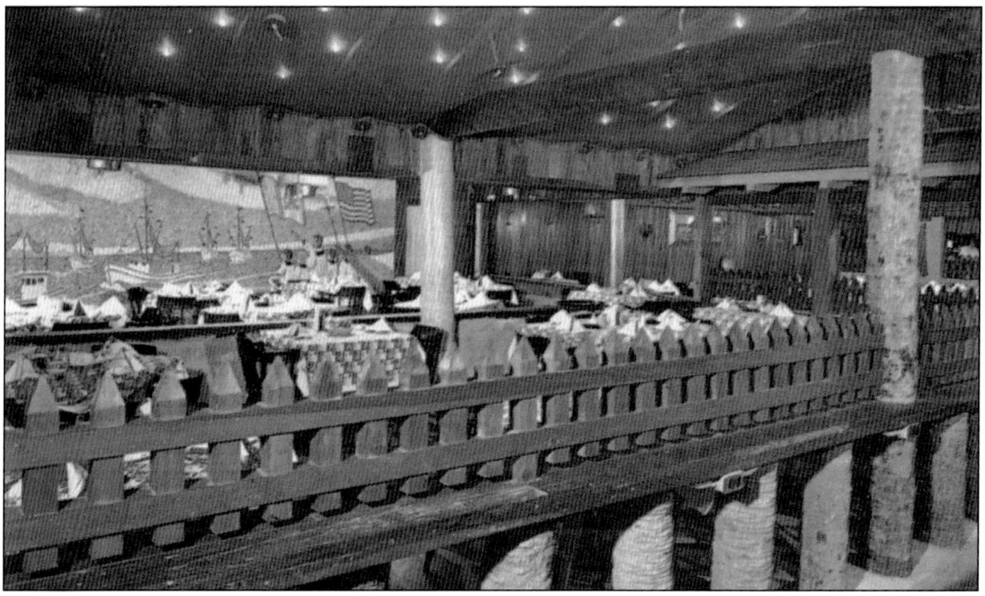

SUN-N-SAND RESTAURANT AND LOUNGE, C. 1960. This pre-Camille view of the restaurant in the Sun-N-Sand featured a beautiful Italian marble chip mosaic depicting Biloxi's colorful Blessing of the Fleet. In its heyday, this facility, located on the south side of Highway 90 at Camellia Street, offered a breakfast, lunch, and dinner buffet. An adjacent lounge provided nightly entertainment. (Not Mailed; SC.)

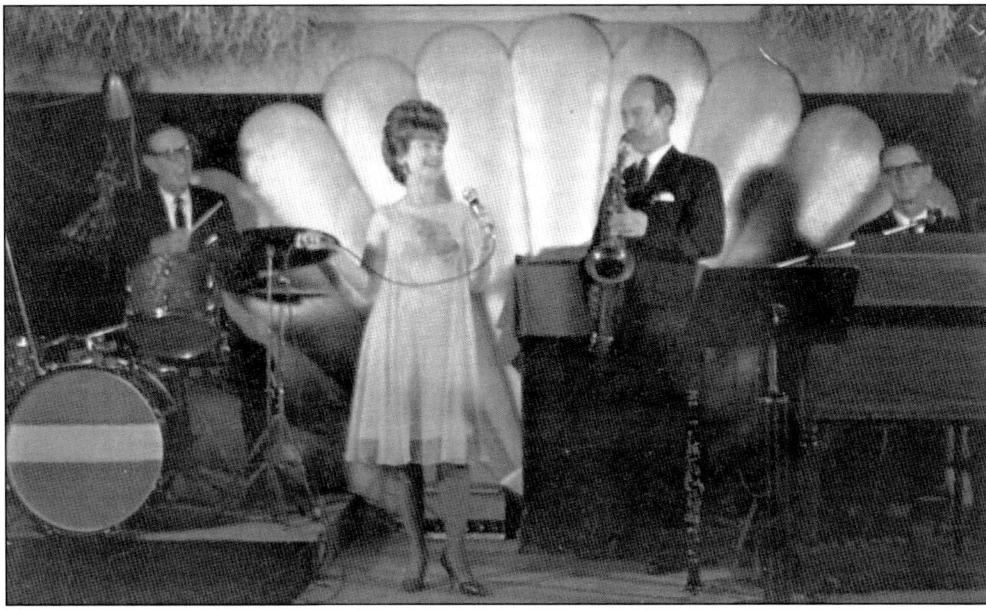

FIESTA AT THE FIESTA, C. 1970. From the mid-1950s through the mid-1980s, this nightclub was one of the bright spots with live entertainment on the Biloxi Strip. It was known for its adaptability to the changing times, featuring machines and tables, Latin music, cage dancers, and straw hats on the ceiling. Owned by the Mladinich family, it was one of several enterprises in the complex. (Not Mailed; SC.)

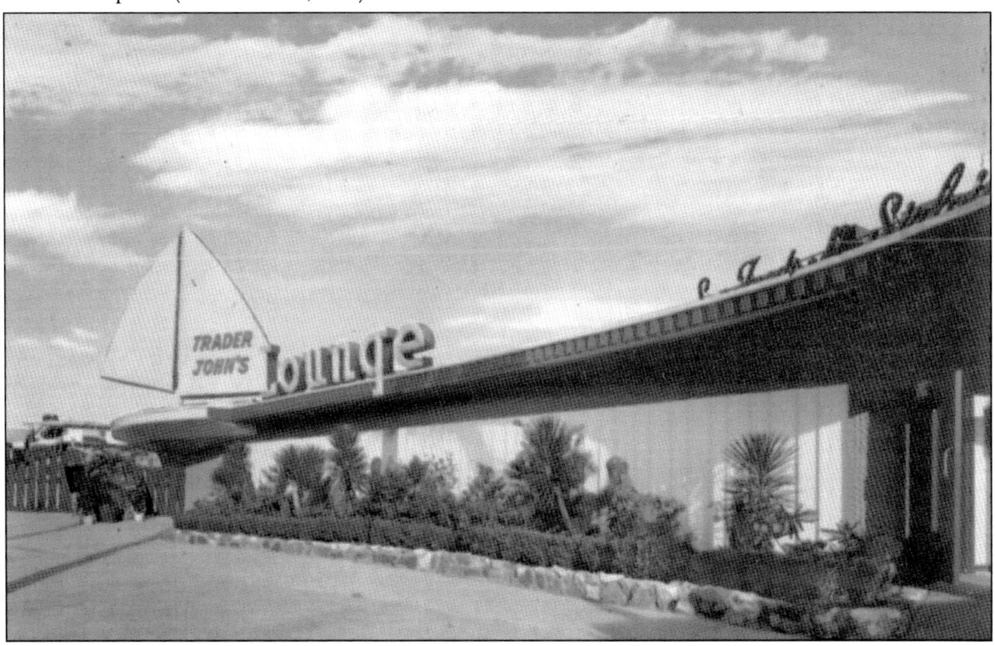

TRADER JOHN'S LOUNGE, C. 1960. "Never a dull moment" was a motto of this West Beach lounge. The tropical island atmosphere of this facility featured exotic mixed drinks, nationally famous performers such as Jimmy Buffet and Johnny Mathis, and hootenannies every Monday night. Located on the south side of Highway 90, west of the Fiesta, this lounge provided entertainment for the younger crowd. (Not Mailed; SC.)

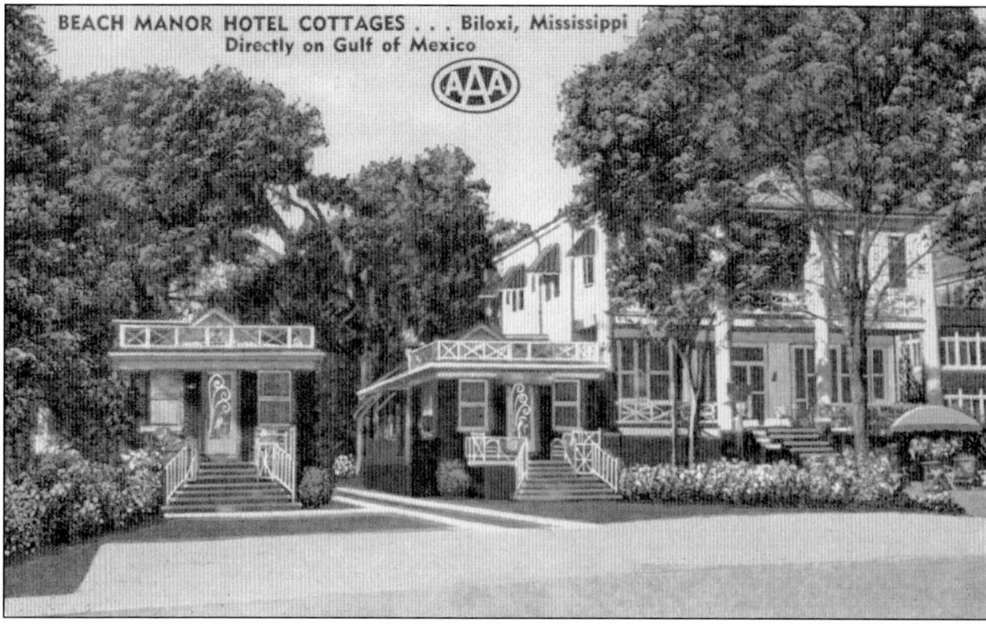

BEACH MANOR HOTEL AND COTTAGES, C. 1950. Located on Highway 90 between the Biloxi Community Center and the Biloxi Hospital, the Beach Manor offered its guests exclusive, but not expensive, accommodations. In close proximity to the Central Biloxi of the day, just across from the Biloxi Small Craft Harbor, the facility featured air-conditioning and was approved by the American Automobile Association (AAA). (Not Mailed; SC.)

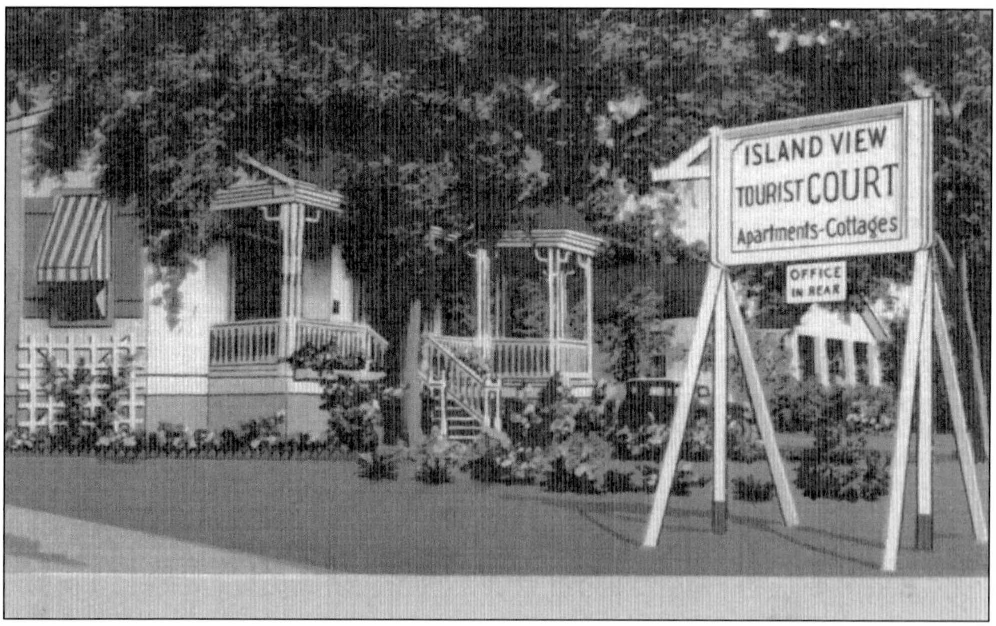

ISLAND VIEW TOURIST COURT, C. 1935. The furnished apartments and cottages of this establishment were truly typical of the Biloxi cottage industry in the 1930s. Small, family-owned and operated facilities dotted many locations along the beachfront roadway. This location west of Oak Street gave its visitors a great look at Deer Island and of the boats traveling the Biloxi Channel. (Not Mailed; SC.)

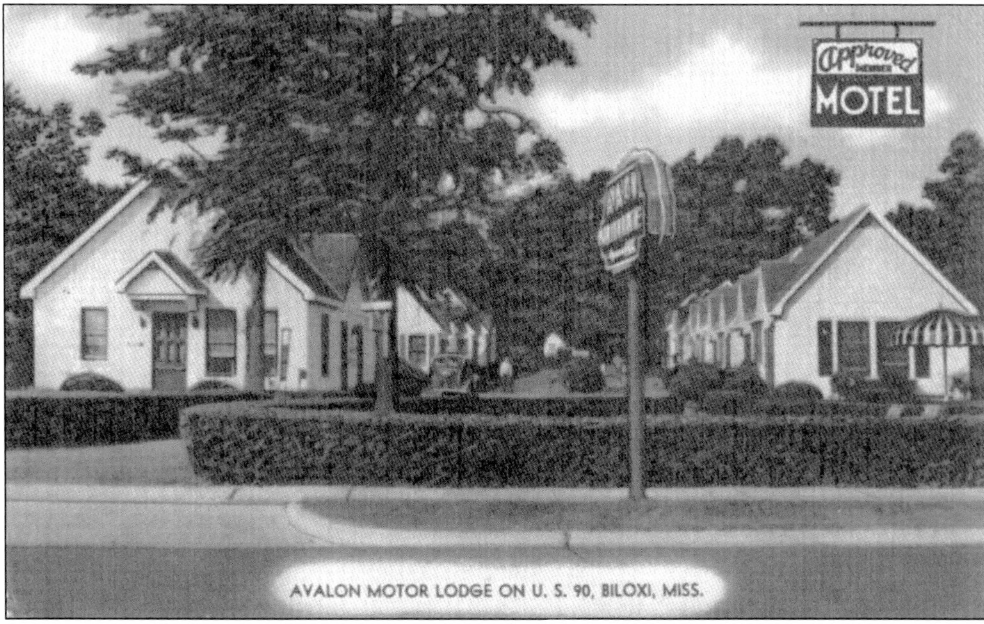

AVALON MOTOR LODGE, C. 1950. The buildings that lined the Avalon beachfront property were called lodges, rather than cabins or cottages, by the owners. This new, modern, and clean facility offered bathing, boating, and deep-sea fishing amenities to its guests. Located one mile west of the lighthouse on West Beach, this property remained locally owned and operated for many years. (Not Mailed; SC.)

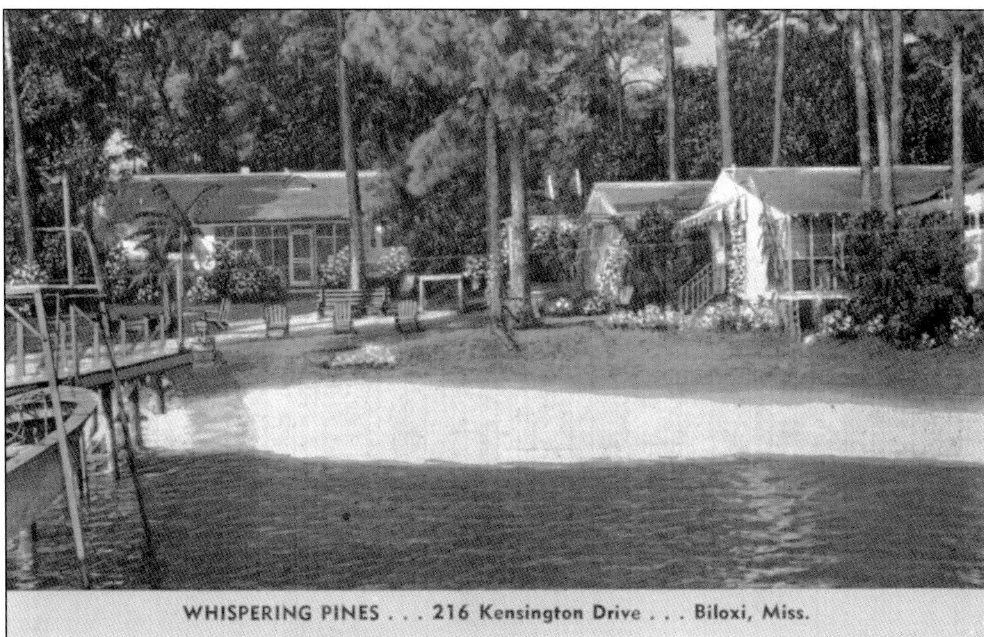

WHISPERING PINES, C. 1955. Hotels, motels, and tourist cottages in Biloxi were not solely located on Highway 90 during the 20th century. Whispering Pines' apartments, cottages, fishing pier, and boating facilities were located on Kensington Drive, situated on beautiful Back Bay. (Postmarked 1955; SC.)

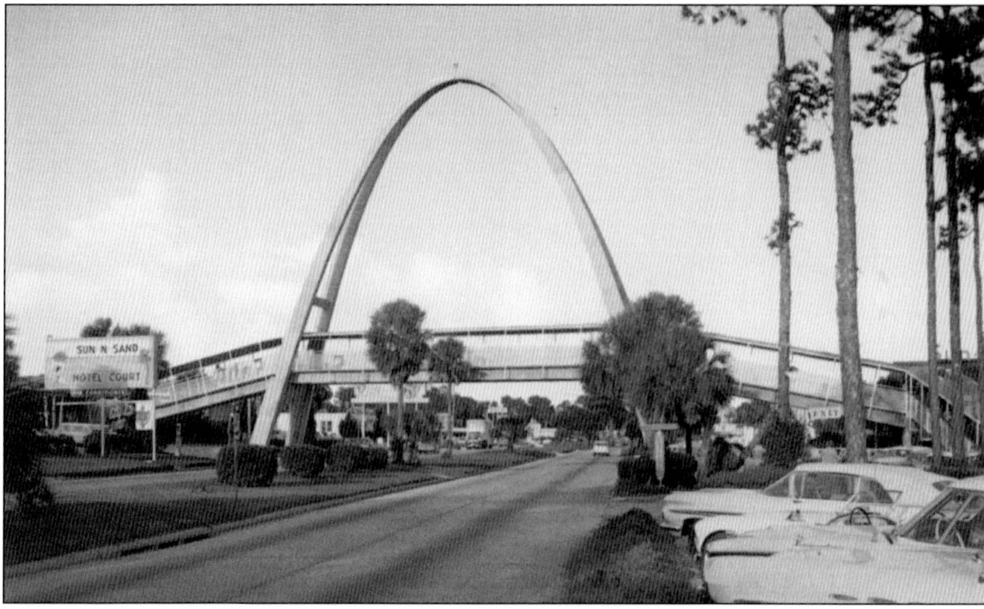

SUN-N-SAND HOTEL COURT, C. 1960. This view shows the archway and walkover that joined the two sections of the Sun-N-Sand Motel Court across Highway 90 in West Biloxi. With half of the rooms located north of the highway and the restaurant, lounge, and additional rooms located south of the highway, the walkway provided a passage for pedestrians to cross busy Highway 90 without the worry of traffic. (Not Mailed; SC.)

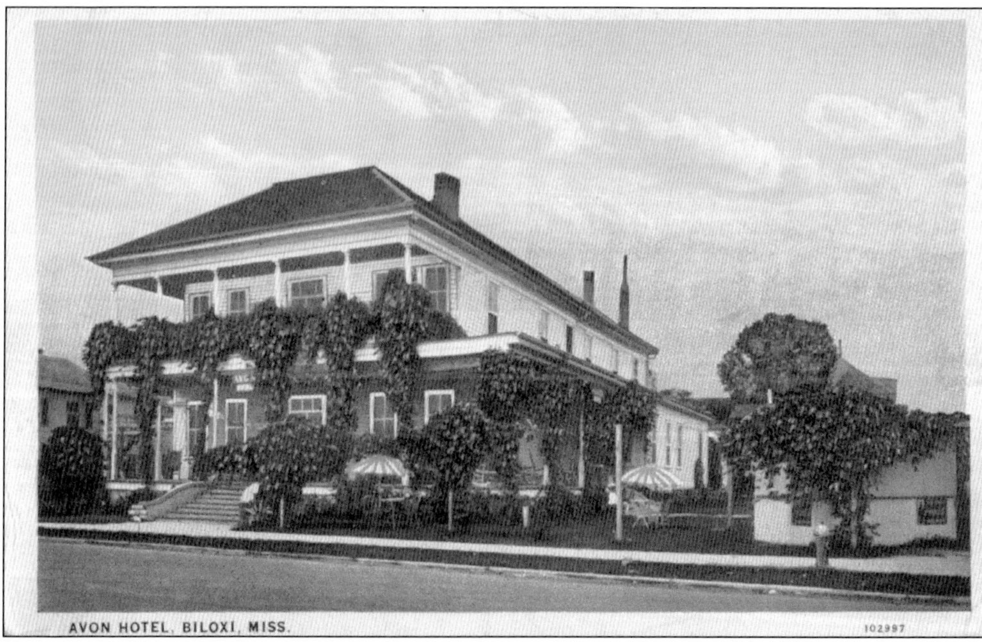

AVON HOTEL, 1925. This property was near downtown Biloxi, on the beach west of Lameuse Street. Although it was called a hotel in its day, it was actually more a boardinghouse, which included meals and drinks for its guests. The proprietors advertised rooms for $1 per night and a very convenient location for traveling salesmen and vendors who came to the area. (Postmarked 1925; SC.)

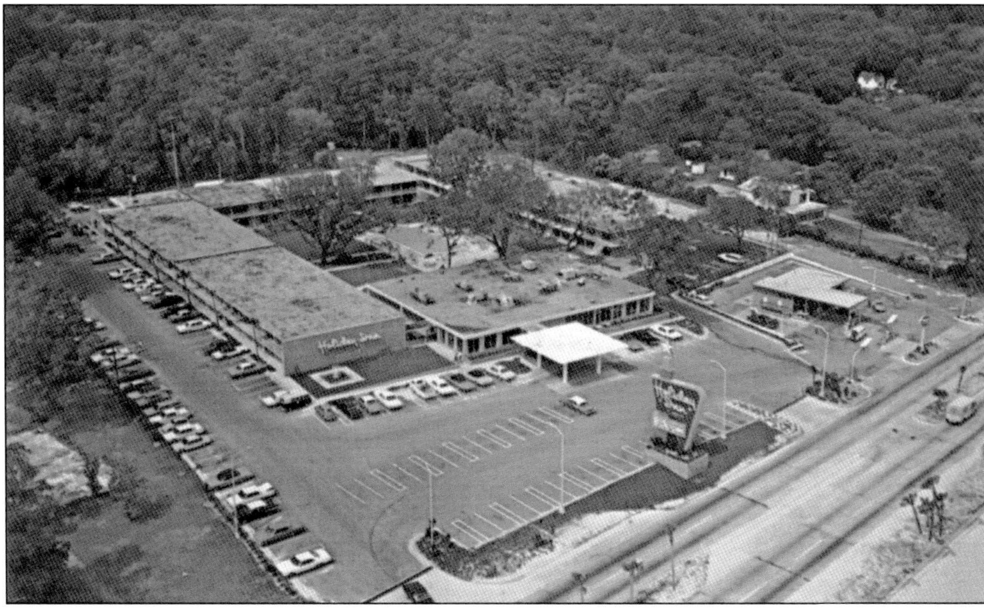

HOLIDAY INN MOTEL, C. 1965. This card provides a great view of the Holiday Inn and the adjacent Gulf station, located in the heart of the Golden Gulf Coast resort area, west of Beauvoir Road on the beach. However, missing from this landscape are the Mississippi Coast Coliseum and Convention Center and the Howard Johnson Hotel, which were both constructed at a later date. (Not Mailed; SC.)

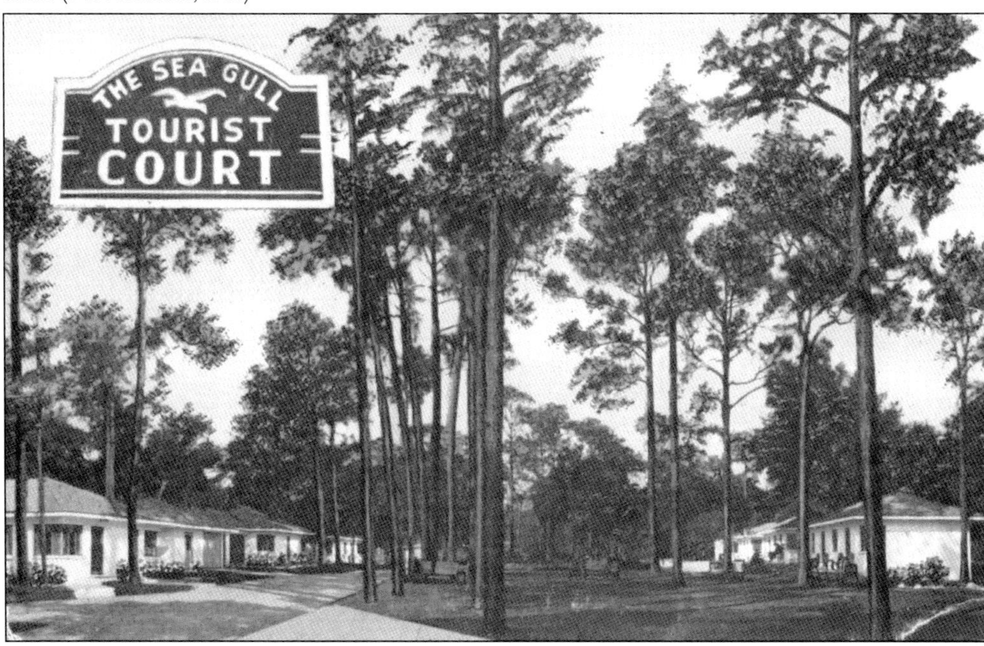

SEA GULL TOURIST COURT, C. 1960. Built prior to the establishment of the adjoining corporate limits of Biloxi and Gulfport, this motel, located just east of the Friendship House on the beach and DeBuys Road, featured a Biloxi address and a Gulfport telephone number. The 18-unit facility featured fireproof cottages, nine with kitchenettes. Later, the owners of the property constructed a large swimming pool overlooking the Gulf of Mexico. (Not Mailed; SC.)

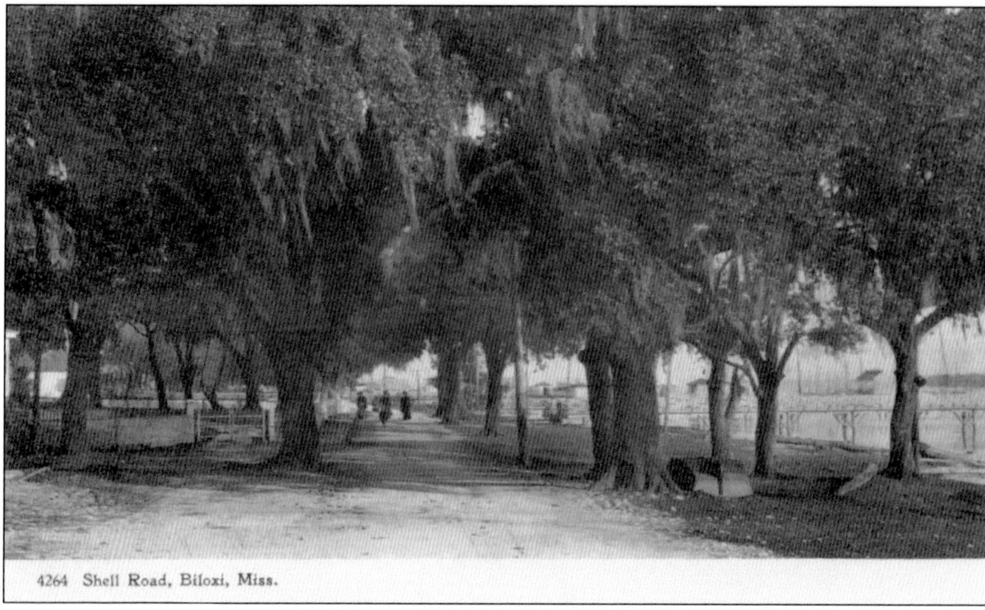

SHELL ROAD, C. 1907. In the early 20th century, Highway 90 looked far different than it does today. Moss-draped trees shade the roadway, a skiff is pulled up along the shoreline, and long piers with bathhouses make up this waterfront view. Current traffic would not allow ladies to stroll down the middle of the thoroughfare. (Not Mailed; SC.)

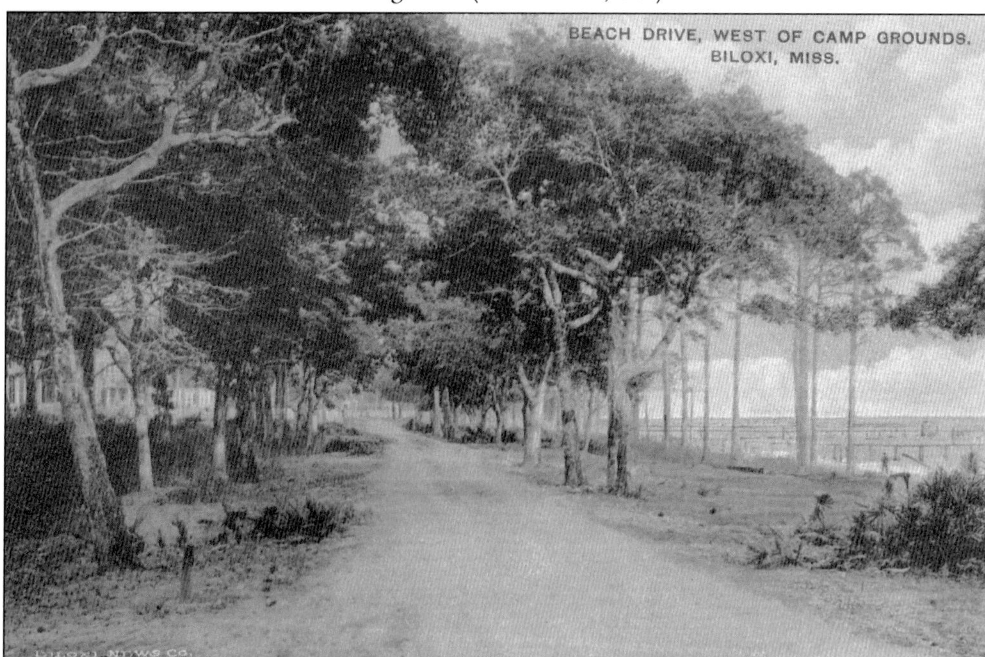

WEST BEACH DRIVE, C. 1910. Long piers jetting out into the Mississippi Sound were part of the view and activities of Seashore Campground and the daily lives of Biloxi citizens and visitors. This view, with its moss-draped oaks and pine trees, was very familiar along the shoreline in the early 20th century. A man walking along the sand beach is also featured on this early postcard. (Not Mailed; SC.)

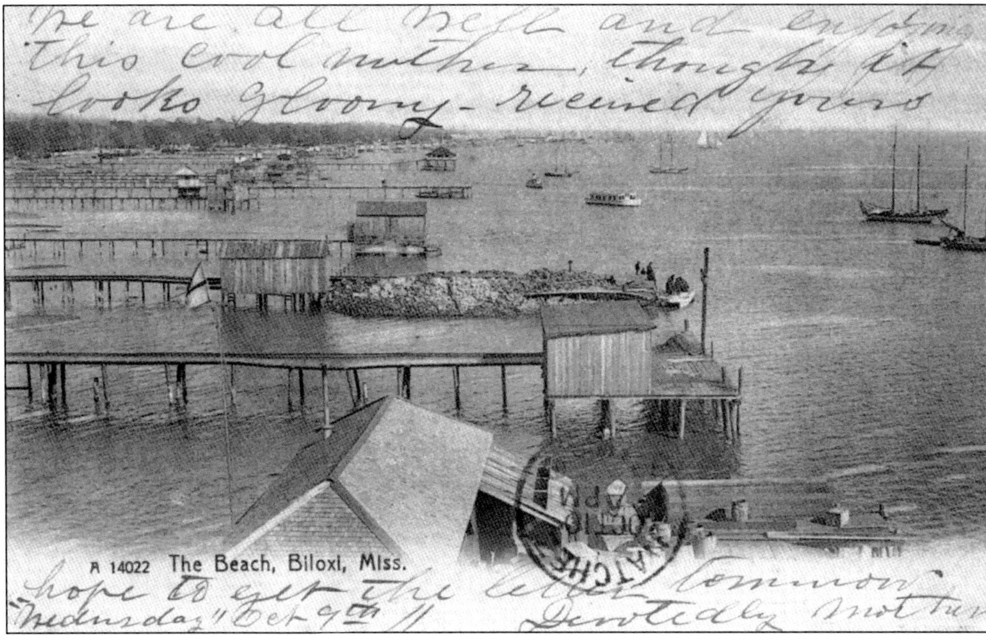

The Beach, c. 1905. From atop the Biloxi Lighthouse, this aerial photograph of the Biloxi channel shows the view from Porter Avenue east to Caillavet Street. People are making a living along the waterfront, among long piers and shell piles. Small boats and schooners dot the waterway. (Postmarked 1907; BL.)

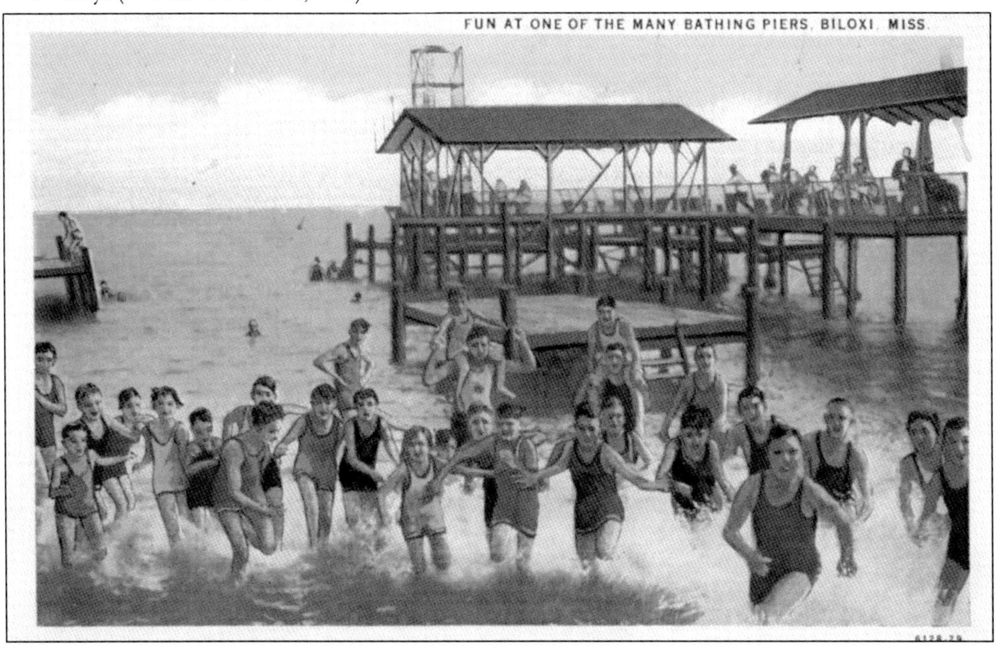

Bathing Piers, 1929. Water sports have long been popular along Biloxi's beachfront. The piers along the waterfront have provided locals and visitors with many opportunities to enjoy the tropical climate. In the 1920s, swimming races were common, and it was not unheard of for participants to swim from the mainland to Deer Island, pause to enjoy the island treasures, and then swim back to the mainland. (Postmarked 1934; SC.)

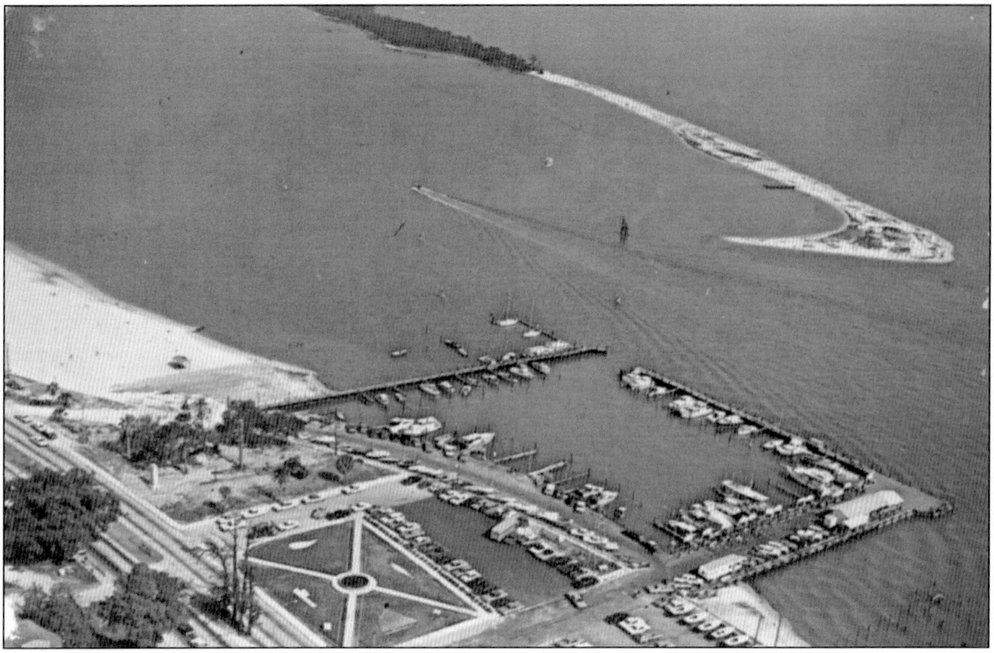

Small Craft Harbor, c. 1960. In the days prior to Hurricane Camille, the Biloxi Small Craft Harbor was home to a deep-sea charter fishing fleet. This aerial view of Guice Park, Glennen Park, and Deer Island compliment the view of many boats in the area. This photograph was taken prior to the construction of McElroy's Seafood Restaurant and the Port Commission facilities. (Not Mailed; BL.)

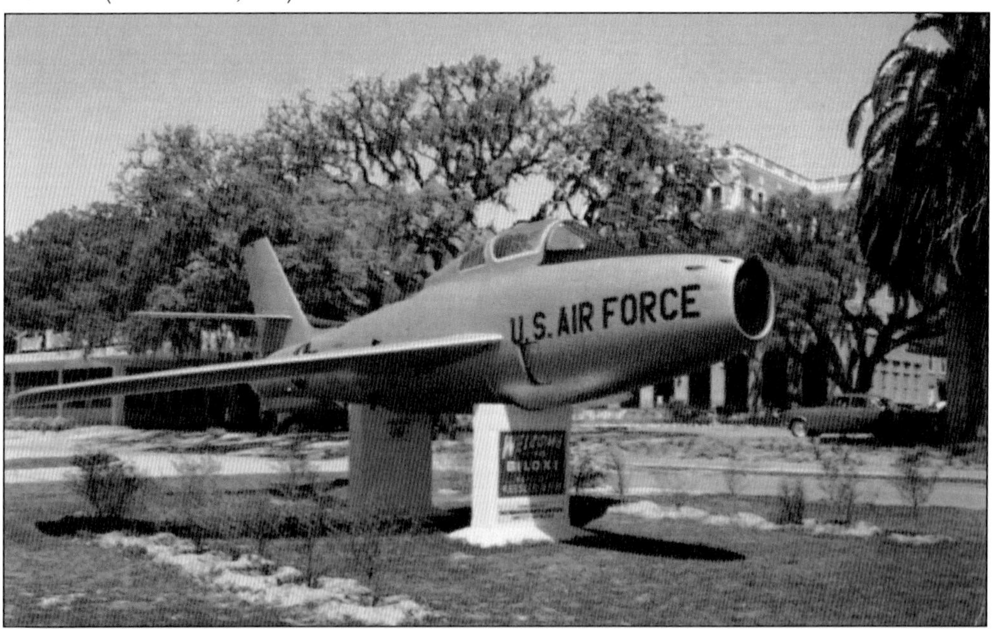

Thunderjet at the Tivoli, c. 1960. Air Force planes were placed in the median of Highway 90 near the Tivoli Hotel and the White House Hotel, as welcoming beacons to visitors to the Mississippi Gulf Coast and Keesler Air Force Base. Both planes were heavily damaged during Hurricane Camille in 1969, and the one at the Tivoli was not replaced. (Not Mailed; SC.)

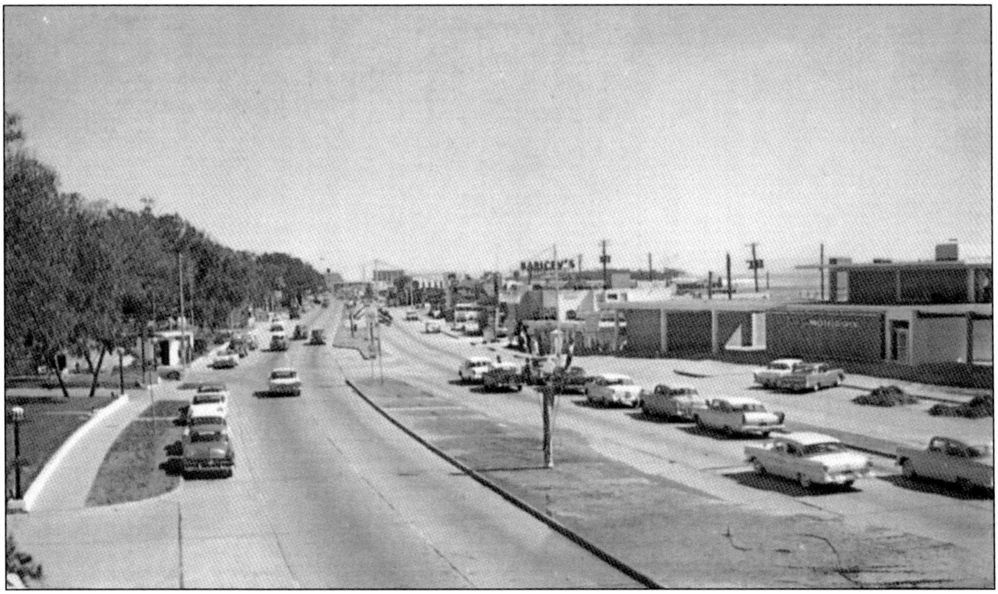

JEFFERSON DAVIS HIGHWAY, C. 1958. The stretch of Highway 90 in Biloxi is called by many names. This photograph was taken from the Buena Vista Hotel walkway over the beachfront highway in the late 1950s. The Buena Vista Motel and Baricev's Seafood Restaurant are shown here along with vintage cars and the line of restaurants, lounges, and shops that made up Biloxi's downtown strip. (Postmarked 1959; BL.)

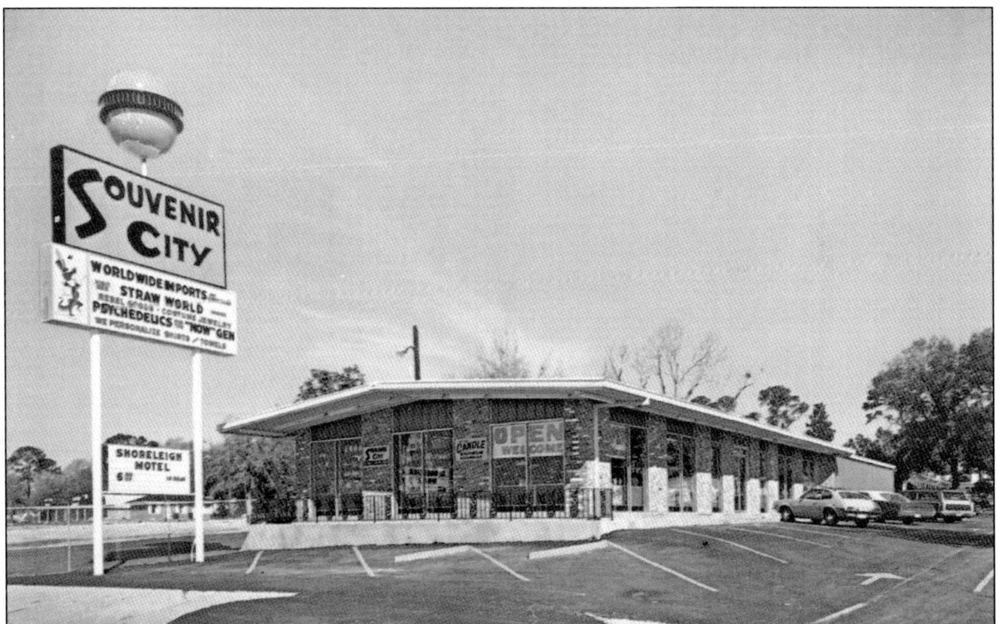

SOUVENIR CITY, C. 1970. Owners change and hurricanes damage and destroy buildings but roots are deep. The alligator head, which now adorns the building, is missing from this 1970s postcard. However, Souvenir City, between the Broadwater Hotel and the Sheraton Inn on Highway 90, still exists today. This facility and its sister business Sharkheads are signs of the resiliency of the local business community. (Not Mailed; SC.)

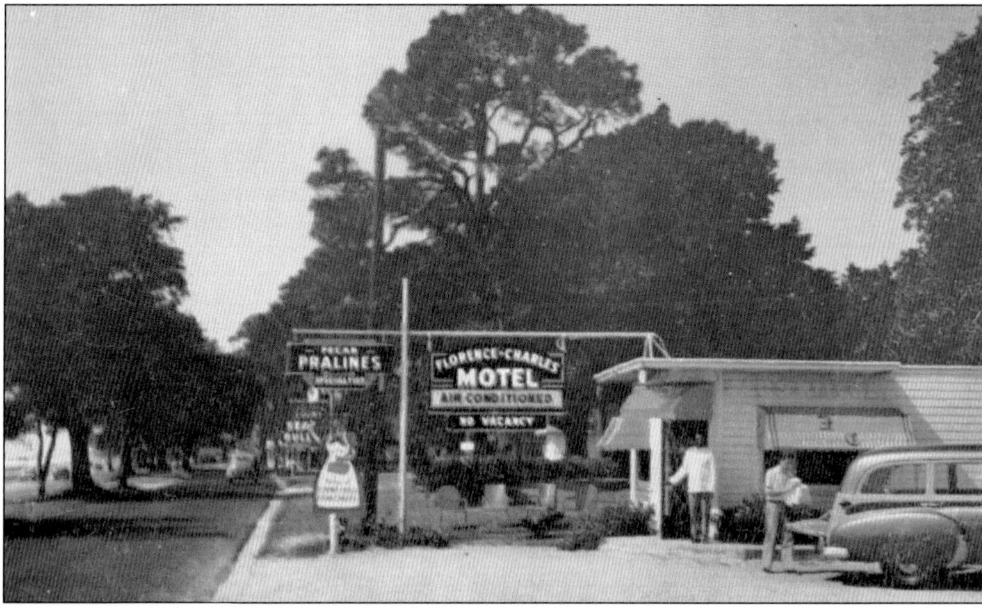

PECAN PRALINES, C. 1955. It was not uncommon in West Biloxi in the early 1950s for a business to have a Biloxi address and a Gulfport telephone number; this was the case of the Florence-Charles Motel and Candy Store. Located east of DeBuys Road, mom-and-pop business operations dotted Highway 90 and often combined their beachfront rooms with other tourism-related enterprises. (Not Mailed; SC.)

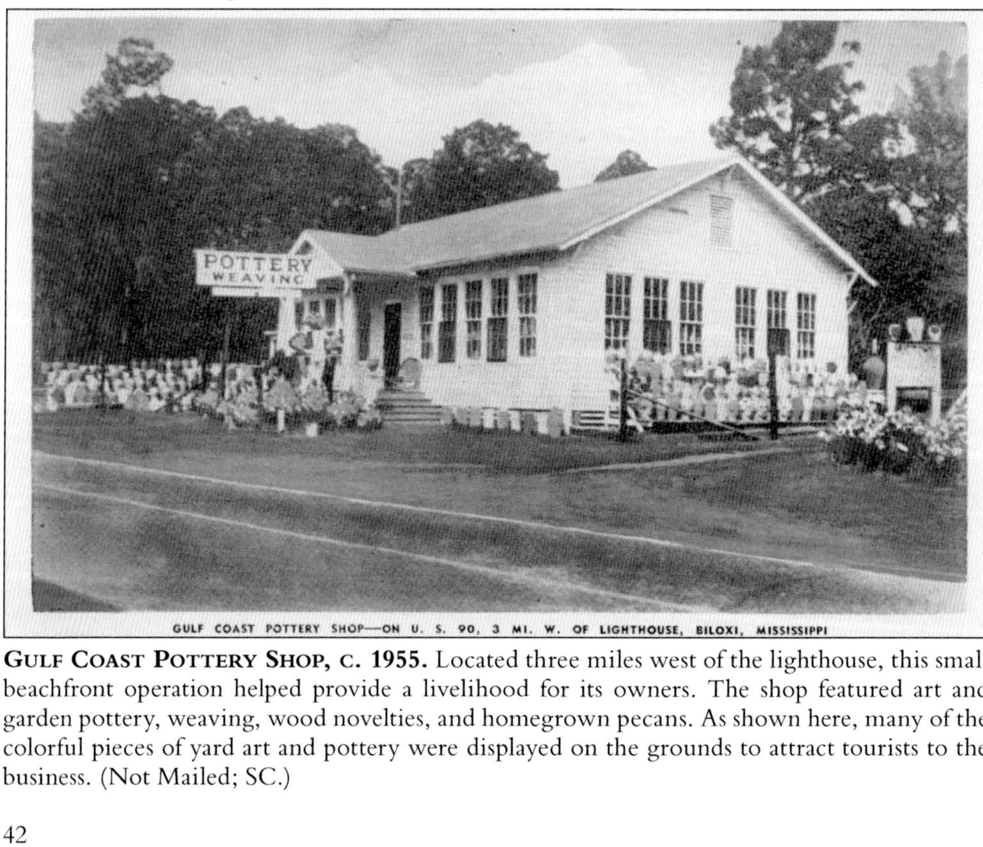

GULF COAST POTTERY SHOP, C. 1955. Located three miles west of the lighthouse, this small beachfront operation helped provide a livelihood for its owners. The shop featured art and garden pottery, weaving, wood novelties, and homegrown pecans. As shown here, many of the colorful pieces of yard art and pottery were displayed on the grounds to attract tourists to the business. (Not Mailed; SC.)

Three

NATURE'S BOUNTY

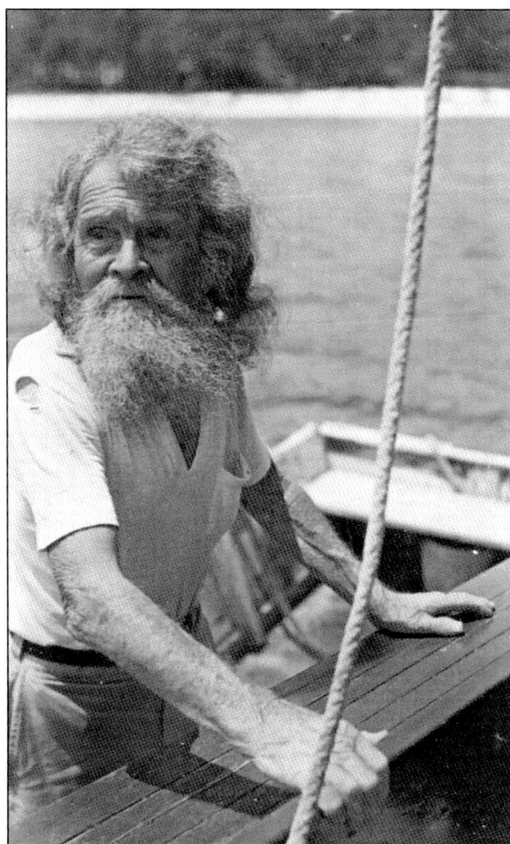

HERMIT OF DEER ISLAND, C. 1950. Waters surrounding the Biloxi peninsula have provided a plentiful food source to the residents and visitors of the area for centuries. Actual history and stories of the seafood and maritime way of life have become a major factor in the development and its people. This postcard features John Guilhot, "the Hermit of Deer Island," who is part of that development story. (Not Mailed; SC.)

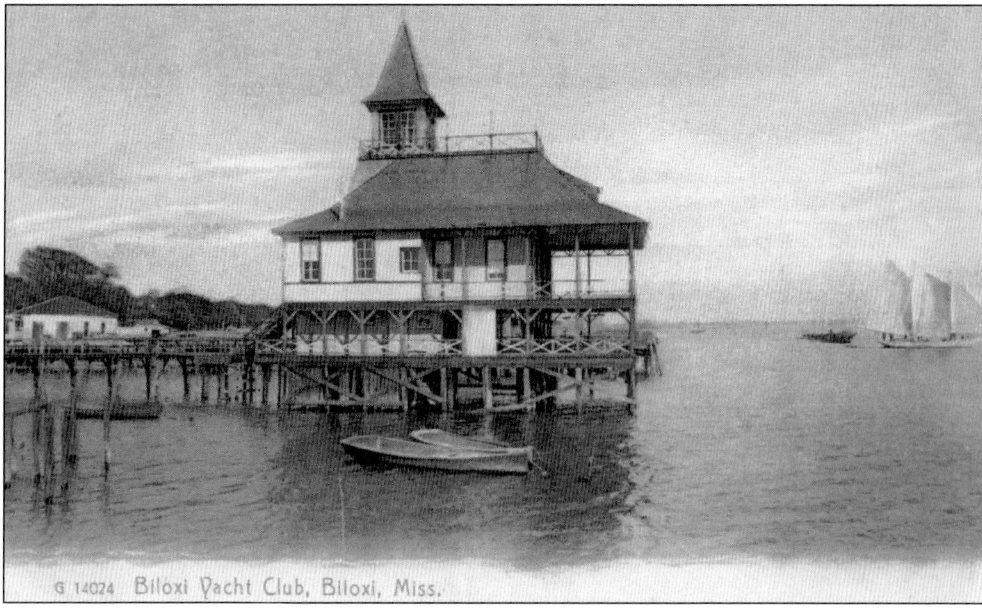

Biloxi Yacht Club, 1902. Designed by Theodore Brune, this clubhouse was connected to the shore by a long pier directly across from the Montrose Hotel on Highway 90. Its gallery accommodated 500 observers with a full view of the club's annual regatta, a 15-mile course in the Mississippi Sound. Secretary of the Navy Franklin D. Roosevelt was entertained here during his 1913 visit to Biloxi. (Postmarked 1908; SC.)

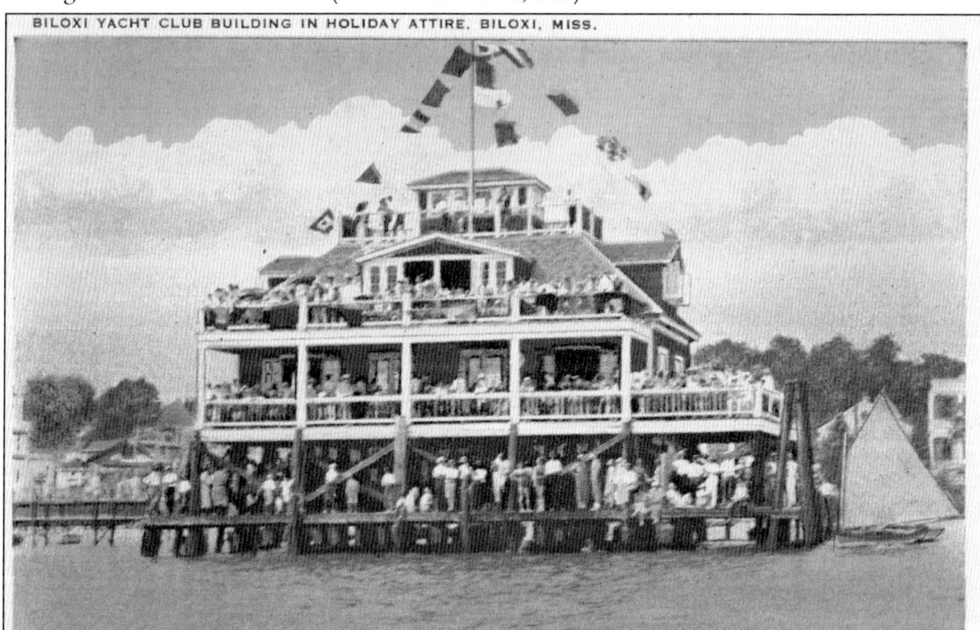

Biloxi Yacht Club in Holiday Attire, 1927. Sailing and sailing races have long been a part of the fiber of Biloxi. This postcard depicts the Biloxi Yacht Club that was constructed in 1916 to replace the club's building, which was destroyed in the hurricane of 1915. It did not take the organization long to rebuild and get back into their summertime Sunday afternoon races. (Not Mailed; BL.)

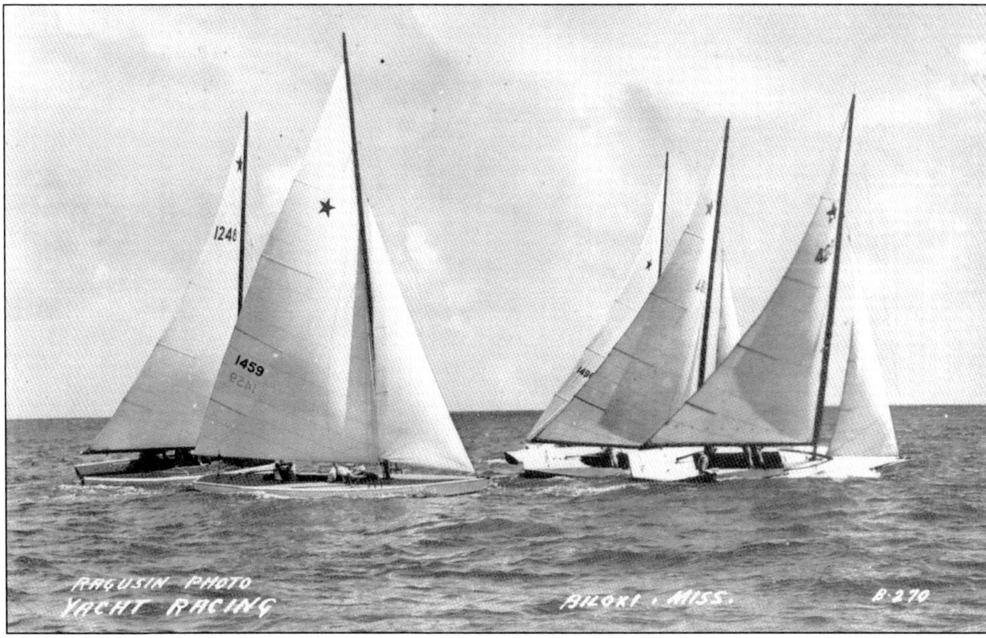

YACHT RACING, C. 1940. This local postcard shows one of the many classes of sailing competitions featured in water off the Biloxi coast. Throughout the 20th century, the Biloxi Yacht Club, along with others, offered a variety of sailing races and regattas of various distances for local competitors and vessels from other yacht clubs along the Gulf Coast. (Not Mailed; SC.)

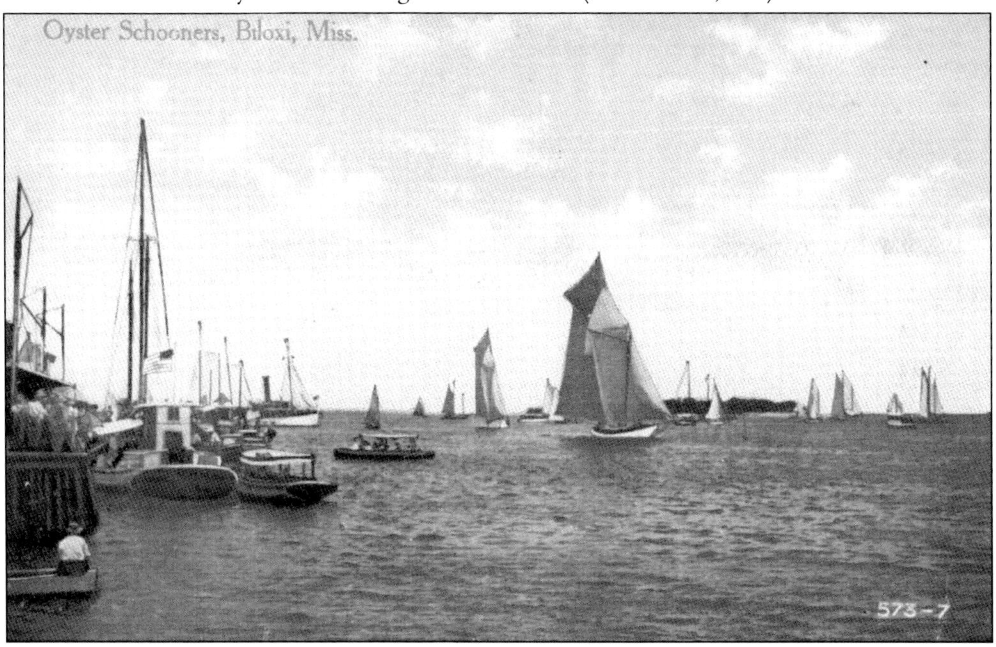

OYSTER SCHOONERS, C. 1930. Motorized skiffs and small boats are shown in this postcard sailing next to the oyster schooner fleet in the Biloxi channel. With Deer Island in the background, it appears that the Biloxi Yacht Club was having one of their traditional Sunday afternoon summertime races where the winning crew received $100 and a keg of beer for the prize. (Not Mailed; SC.)

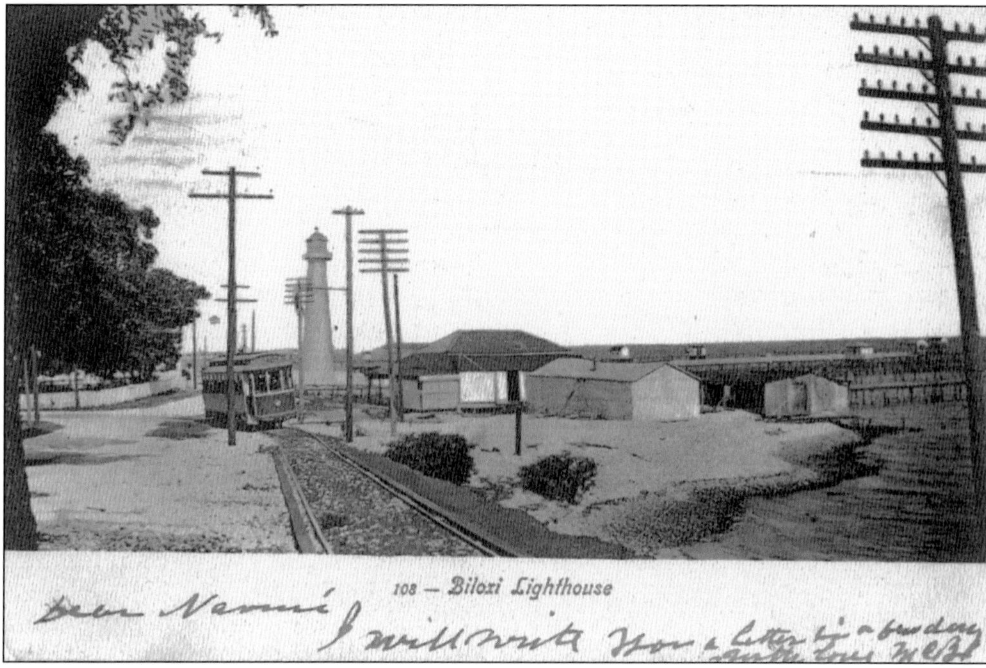

BILOXI LIGHTHOUSE, C. 1907. Many remember the seafood industry and their factory locations as being on the point and east of Caillavet Street on Back Bay. Here, the John Clark Oyster House is visible adjacent to, and immediately west of, the Biloxi Lighthouse. Piles of oyster shells and seafood sheds occupy the land that is now Highway 90. (Postmarked 1907; SC.)

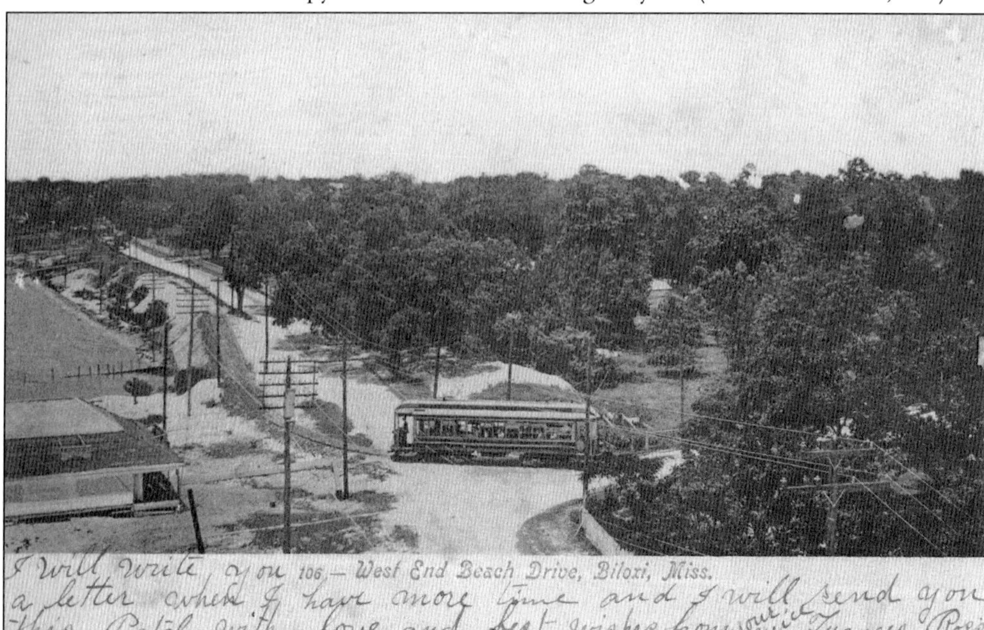

PORTER AVENUE TROLLEY, C. 1907. This view of West Beach Drive, taken from atop the Biloxi Lighthouse, features a trolley turning west from Porter Avenue heading down the beach, a beach shell road, the Oyster House, and a small drainage bridge going under the trolley tracks and the roadway. (Postmarked 1907; SC.)

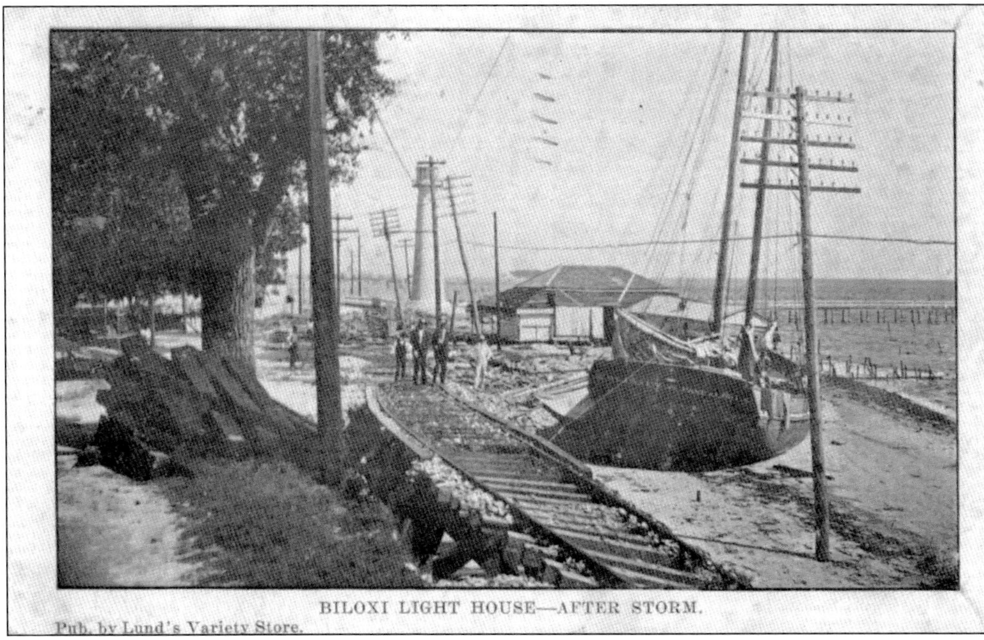

BILOXI LIGHTHOUSE AFTER STORM, C. 1910. This picture was taken from the roadway west of the Biloxi light looking east shortly after one of the many storms that hit the coast between 1905 and 1912. The photograph depicts displaced trolley tracks and utility poles and a damaged oyster shed. The schooner *Classey*, out of Pascagoula, washed ashore and almost reached the trolley tracks. (Postmarked 1913; SC.)

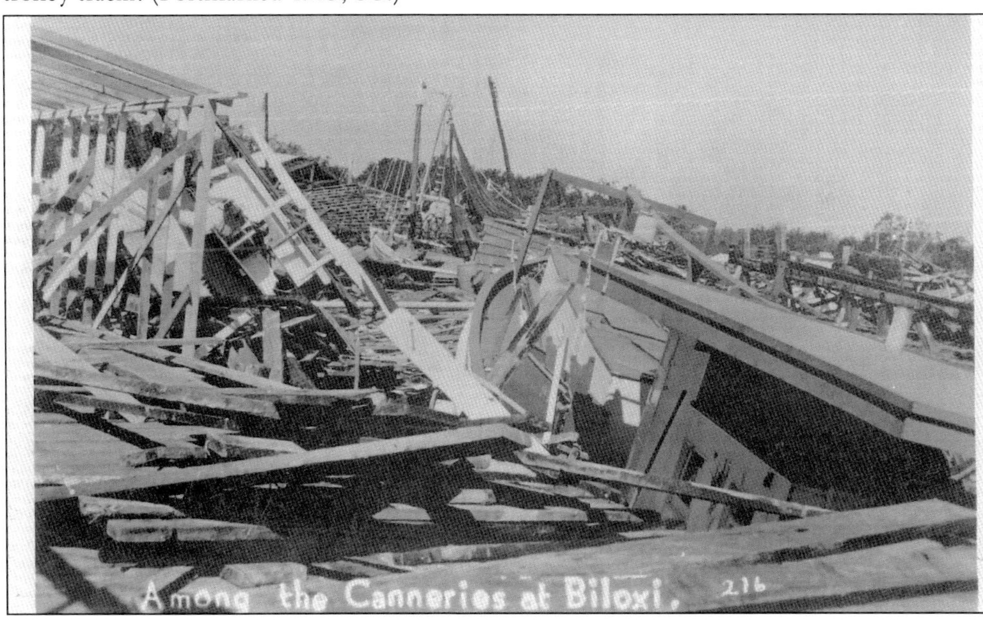

AMONG THE CANNERIES, 1947. Parts of boats, buildings, and piers shown soon after the devastation caused by the 1947 hurricane sent a signal to the seafood industry that it was time to rebuild (again). The winds and rising water of this storm caused severe damage not only to the seafood industry, but also to the community infrastructure, buildings, and the entire population. (Not Mailed; SC.)

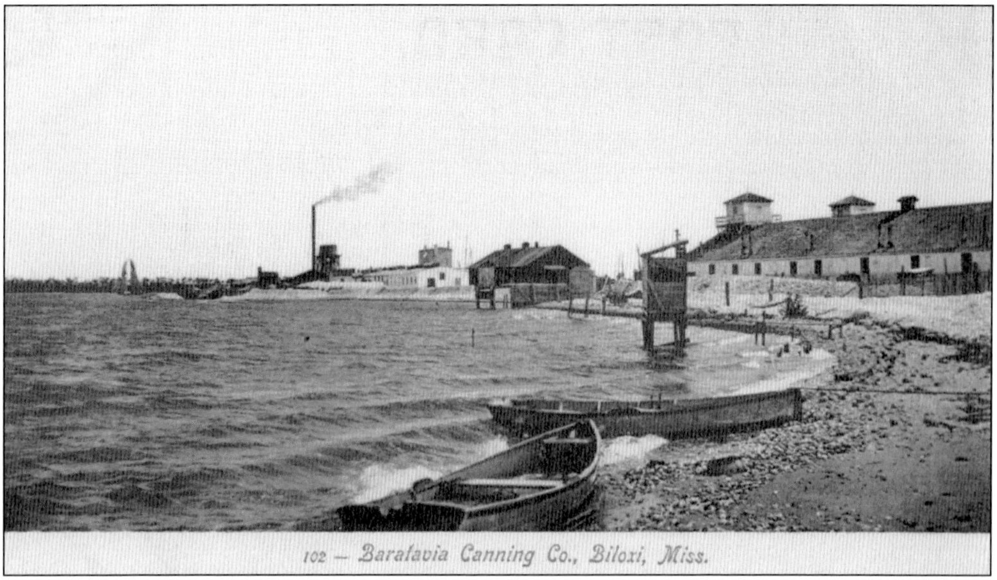

BARATARIA CANNING FACTORIES, 1905. The buildings of Barataria Canning Company were located on the very eastern end of the Biloxi peninsula. Several oyster and shrimp processing buildings and a large schooner fleet called this east end location home. The factory opened in 1885 and was a major processer of seafood until the buildings were destroyed in the 1915 hurricane. (Not Mailed; SC.)

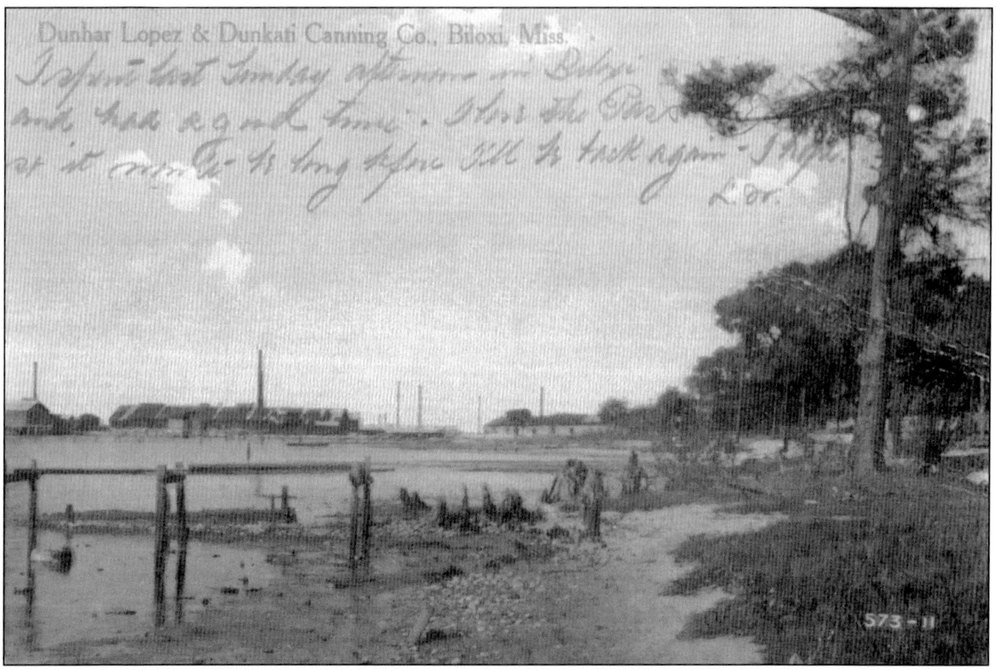

DUNBAR, LOPEZ & DUKATE CANNING COMPANY, C. 1910. Located on the beach just east of Oak Street, this Biloxi seafood factory would become one of Biloxi's giants. The combination of local seafood pioneers, Lopez and Dukate, with the New Orleans food processors, the Dunbar Brothers, led the company to become one of the largest of its kind in the world. (Postmarked 1911; SC.)

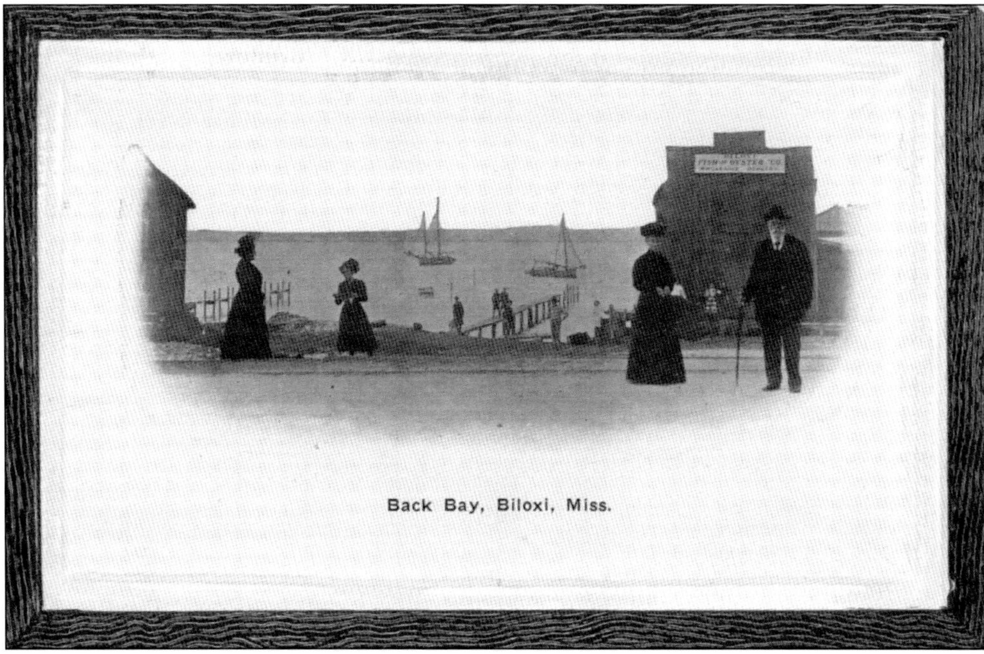

BILOXI FISH AND OYSTER COMPANY, C. 1910. This postcard of one of Biloxi's wholesale seafood dealers depicts their small buildings, located on Back Bay east of Lameuse Street. Several seafood workers are seen near the building and on the pier leading out to where schooners are docked in the peaceful bay. Adults show the fashion of the day, and children are visible on the porch. (Not Mailed; SC.)

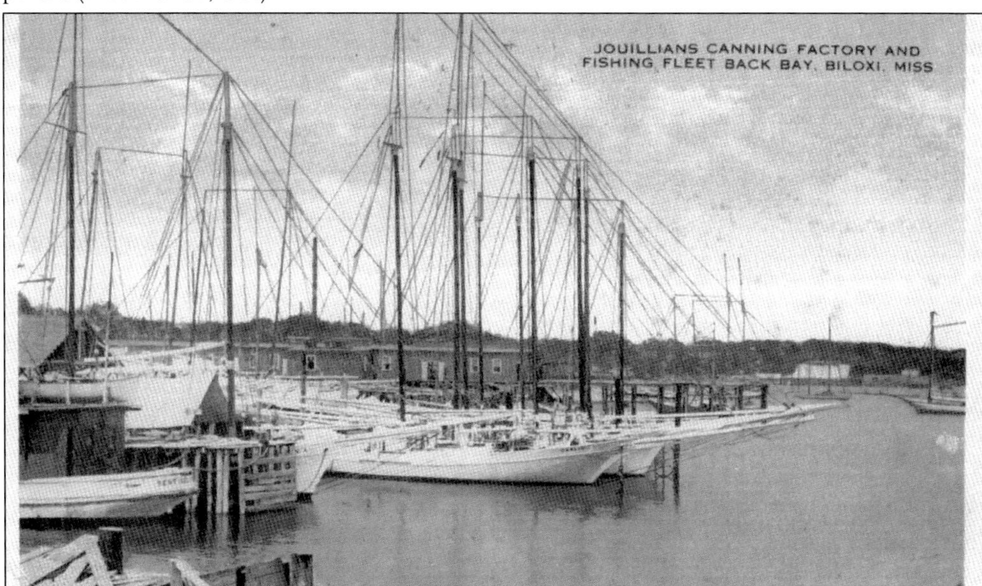

JOULLIAN CANNING FACTORY AND FLEET, C. 1915. E.C. Joullian, one of Biloxi's seafood pioneers, opened his factory in the late 1800s. This Back Bay factory was located near the junction of Bay View and Lameuse Street. This early postcard shows the working schooners in the early 20th century. The picturesque vessels with their full riggings fascinated the writer of this card. (Postmarked 1917; SC.)

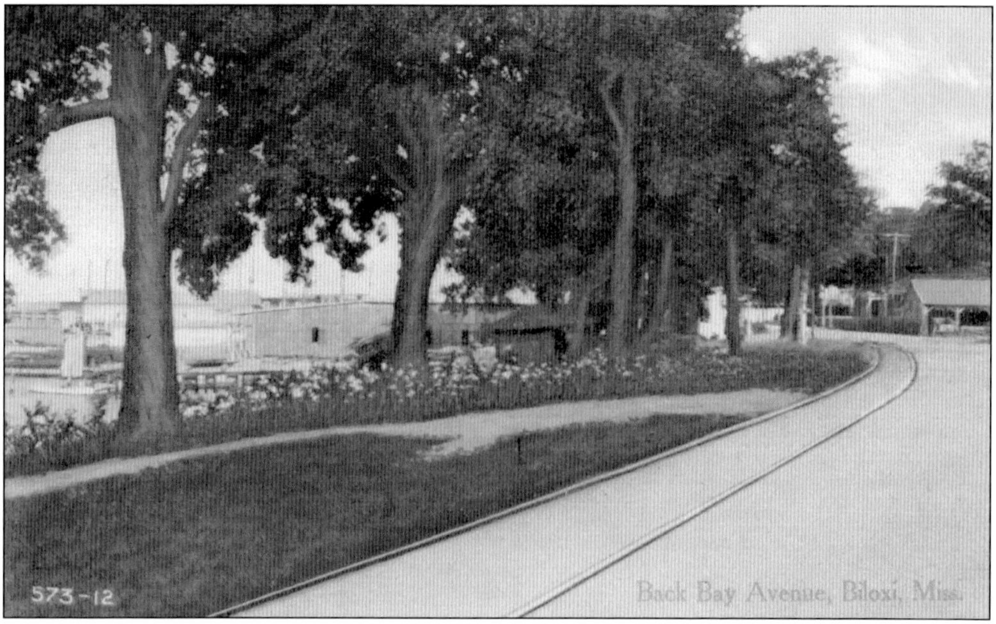

Back Bay Avenue, c. 1910. The trolley tracks are the featured item in this card showing the avenue and some of its seafood factories. Today, trolleys transport people, but when the trollies were used along the bay, they moved both people and freight. Driving along Bay View Avenue today, near Lameuse Street, it is easy to imagine this scene. (Postmarked 1911; SC.)

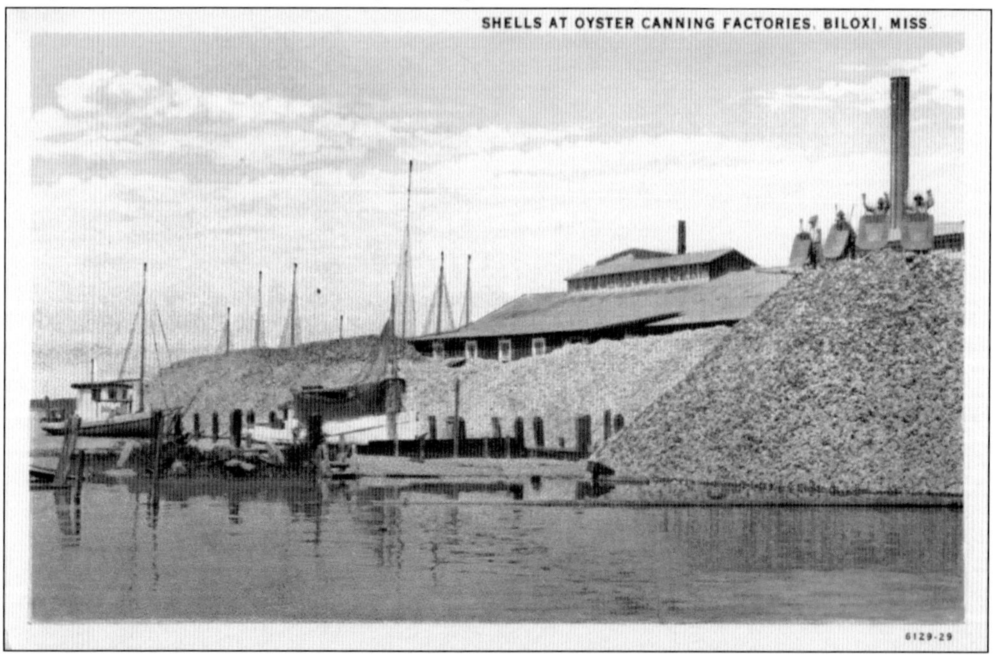

Shells at the Oyster Canning Factories, 1929. Four men with wheelbarrows dumping oyster shells are seen at the C.B. Foster Seafood Plant showing the vast amount of shells created annually. Many of the shells were pushed into the water, creating a hard bottom and adding to the saying that locals have heard for years that Biloxi was built on oyster shells. (Not Mailed; SC.)

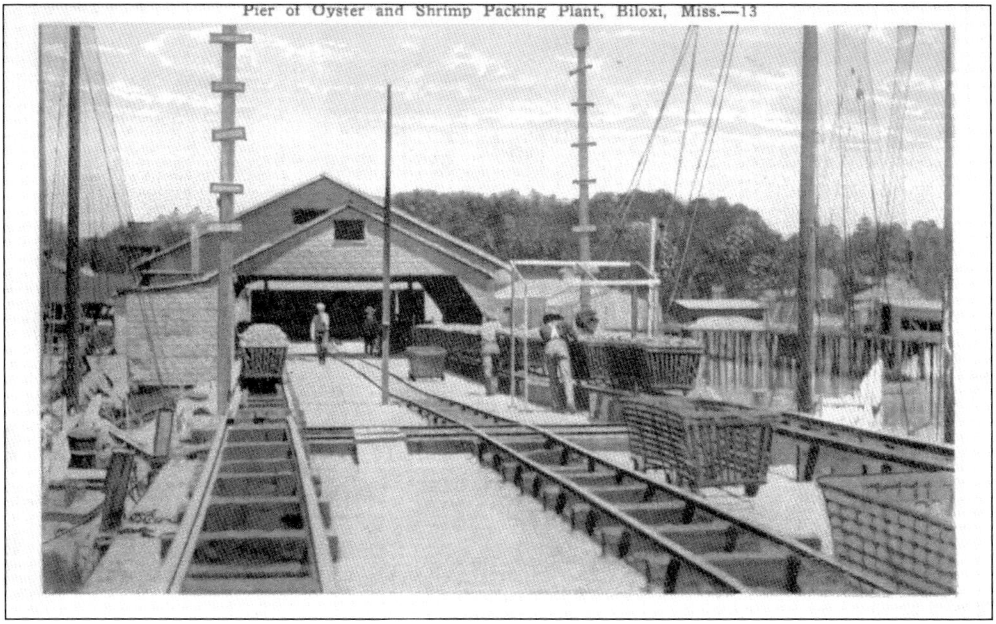

PIER OF SEAFOOD PACKING PLANT, C. 1920. A typical pier of one of the large oyster and shrimp canning factories is shown here with workers rolling oysters just unloaded from boats into the shucking and packing sheds. The oyster-moving steel cart and rail system was one of the many mechanized conveniences used to lighten the physical workload of the people involved in the seafood industry. (Not Mailed; SC.)

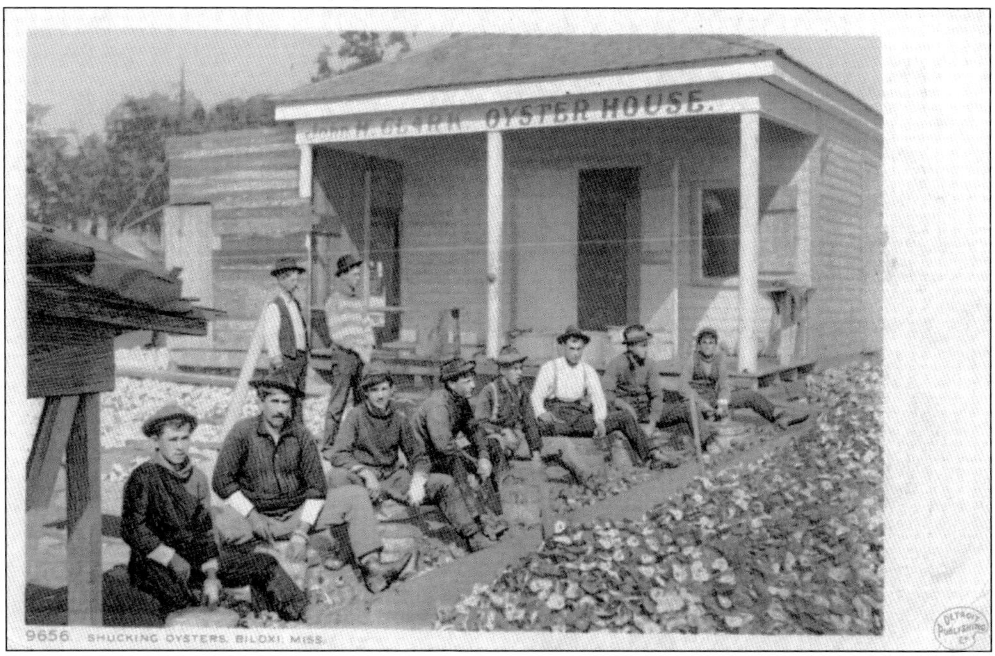

SHUCKING OYSTERS, C. 1905. This early postcard of the John Clark Oyster House featured eight men opening oysters in an area outside the factory building. Oyster processing at this factory was done outside with workers using wooden buckets and sitting on the ground. At that time, oysters were harvested from October through April. (Not Mailed; SC.)

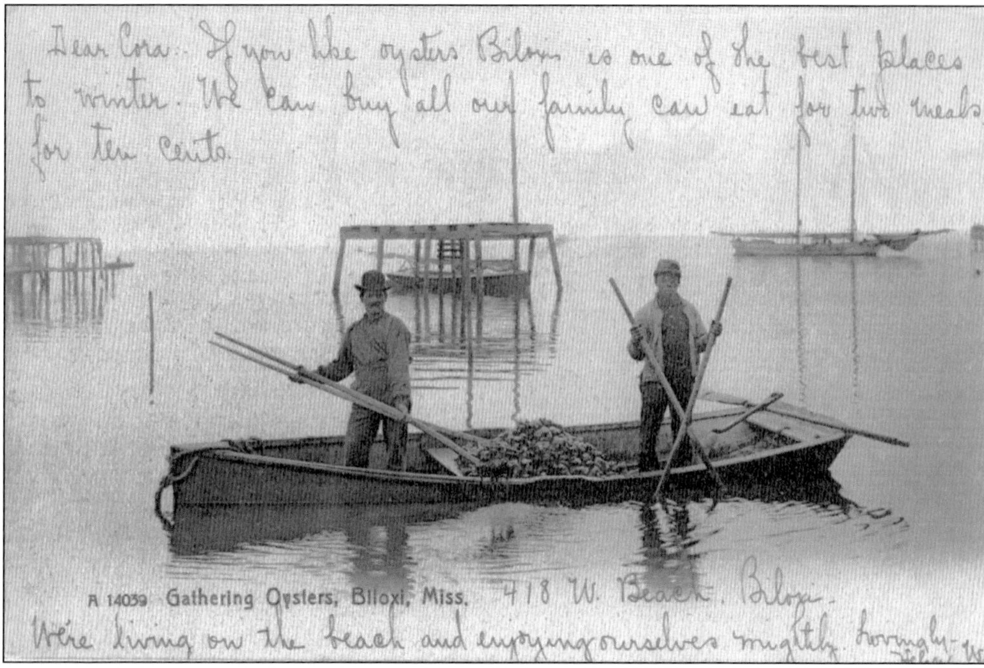

Oyster Gathering, c. 1909. Small skiffs and oyster tongs were used to harvest oysters in the shallow waters of the Mississippi Sound. Many were harvested from inshore reefs and bottomland leases around Deer Island. The writer of this card stated that Biloxi is a good place to buy and eat oysters, and a family can buy enough for two meals for 10¢. (Postmarked 1909; SC.)

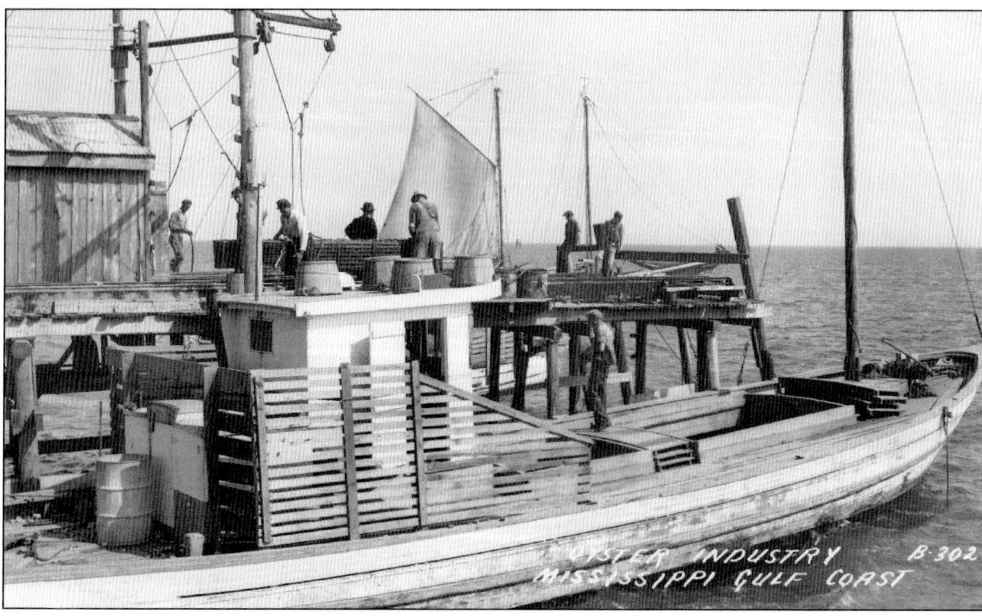

Oyster Industry, c. 1940. This real picture postcard highlights one of Biloxi's motorized schooners. The wooden pens located on the side of the cabin were used to keep the harvested oysters from falling back into the water after being loaded on the boat. A closer look at the card reveals a schooner with its sail raised and similar pens in the background. (Not Mailed; SC.)

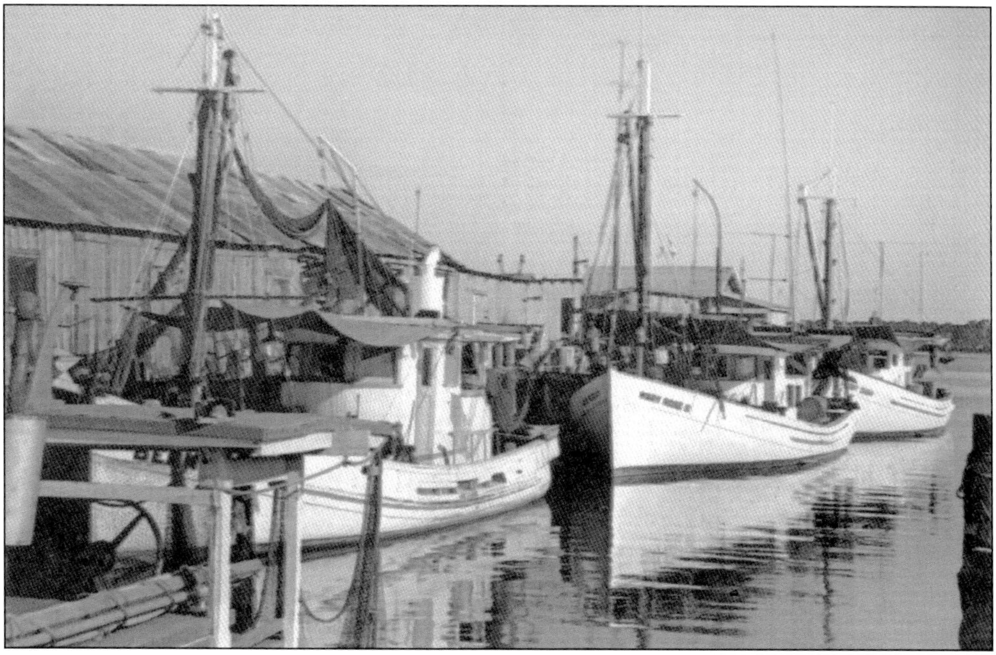

SHRIMP AND OYSTER FISHING BOATS, C. 1970. Part of the Biloxi lugger shrimp fleet is shown on this Point Cadet postcard. The motorized vessels with nets hanging to dry are moored at their docks with Deer Island in the background. *Mary Rose D* and others boats may have been docked at the Dubaz Brothers Seafood factory. (Postmarked 1973; SC.)

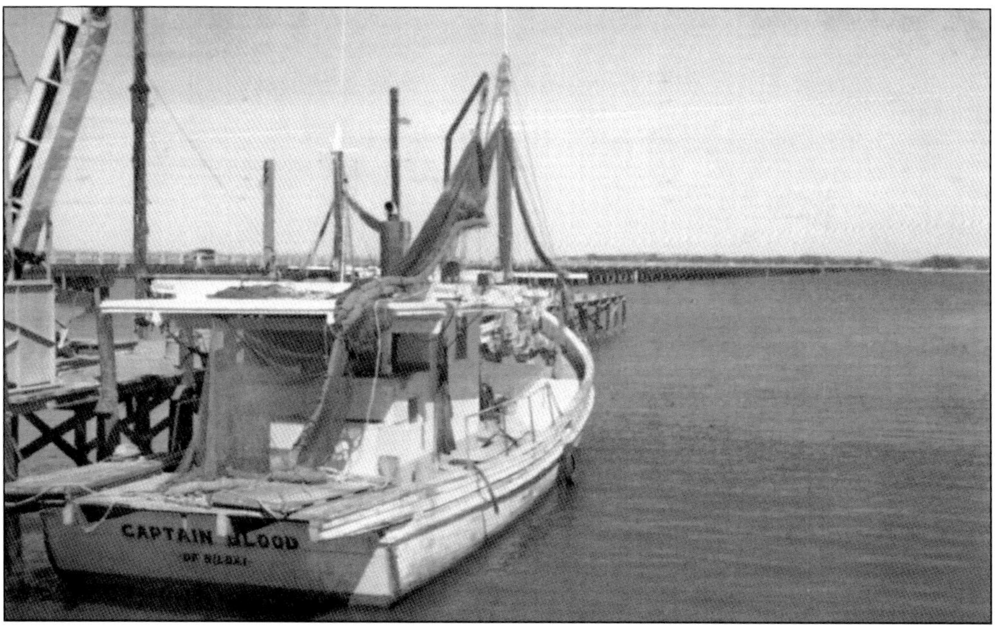

VIEW OF THE BAY, C. 1960. This 1960s postcard pictures one of the legendary wooden shrimp boats of the Biloxi fleet. The *Captain Blood* of Biloxi is shown moored at the dock. This vessel fished oysters and shrimp in the Gulf waters and participated in the annual Blessing of the Fleet for many years. Also shown in the background is the Biloxi Bay Bridge. (Postmarked 1965; SC.)

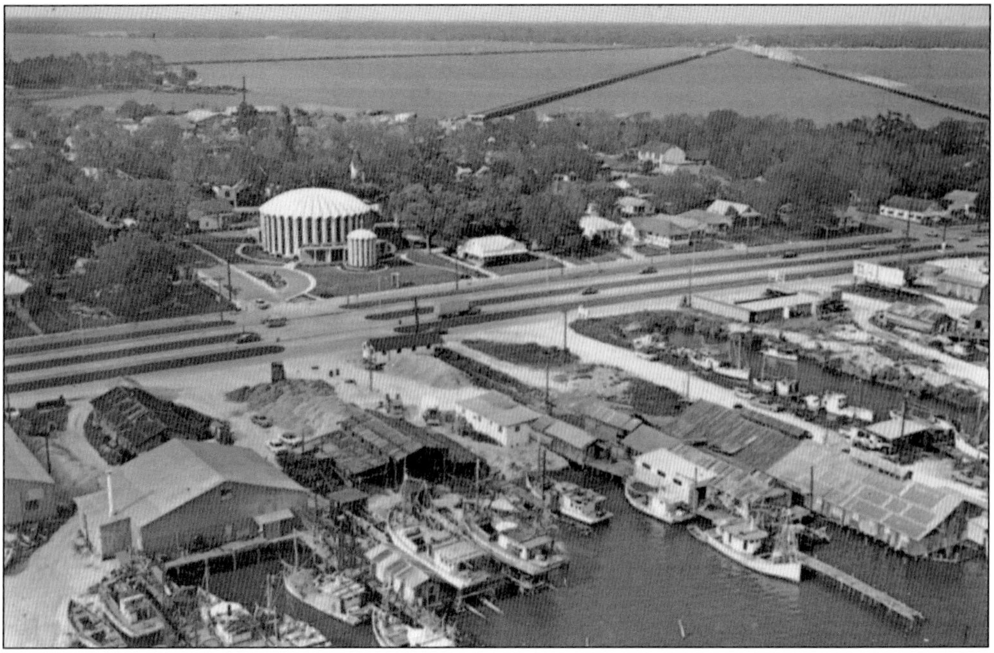

Aerial View St. Michael's Church, c. 1960. Knowing the events of the time determined the dates of this mid-1960s view of Point Cadet. Shown here is the new St. Michael's church, which was erected in 1964. Also seen are the Wentzell family home and the Point Cadet seafood factories, destroyed in 1969 during Hurricane Camille. (Not Mailed; SC.)

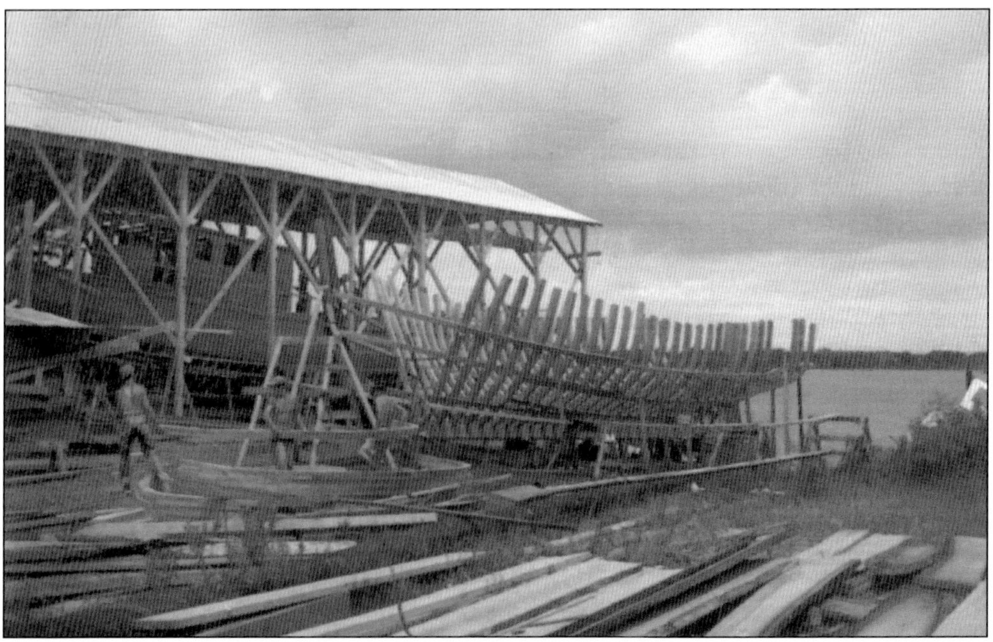

Boatbuilding, c. 1960. Wooden boatbuilding has long been an industry on the Gulf Coast. Boatbuilders brought ideas from their various homelands and adapted them to the local waters and the needs of the industry. (Not Mailed; BL.)

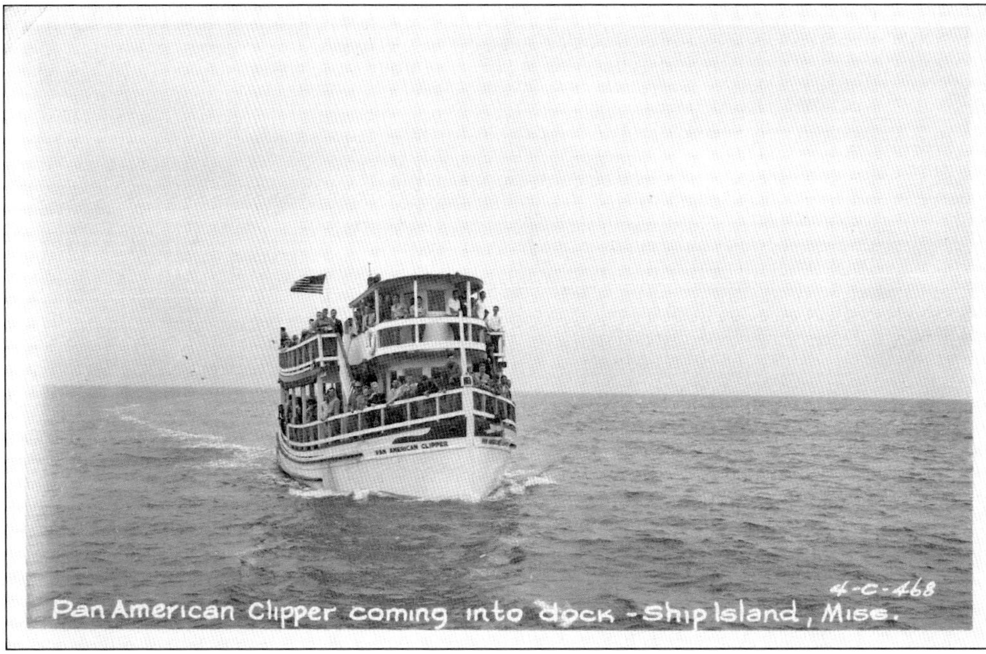

PAN AMERICAN CLIPPER, C. 1960. This excursion boat, which traveled from the mainland to Ship Island, has been in operation for many years. During the 1940s and 1950s, slot machines were included as one of the amenities on the boat. According to the sender of this postcard, the vessel had a 274-passenger capacity and the 14-mile trip took 1.5 hours, costing $1.50 round-trip. (Not Mailed; SC.)

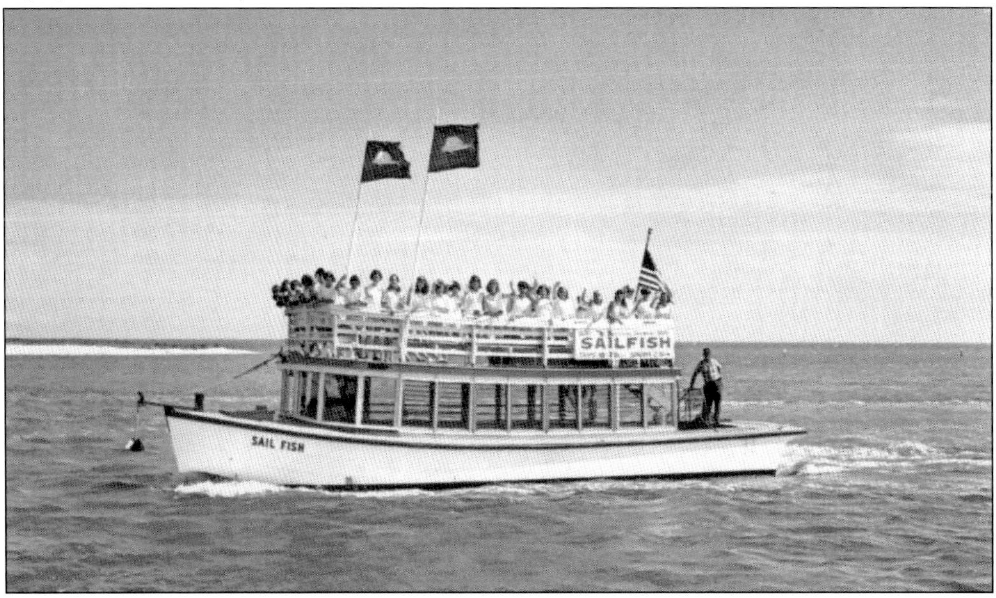

***SAIL FISH*, C. 1965.** Shrimp trawling and views of Deer Island, the seafood industry, and now the casinos are highlights of this famous Biloxi Harbor tour boat's excursions. Although the actual vessels and ownership of the 90-minute cruise have changed, the picturesque trip remains the same. In the 1950s, the Hermit of Deer Island would join the vessel in progress and entertain the visitors. (Postmarked 1972; SC.)

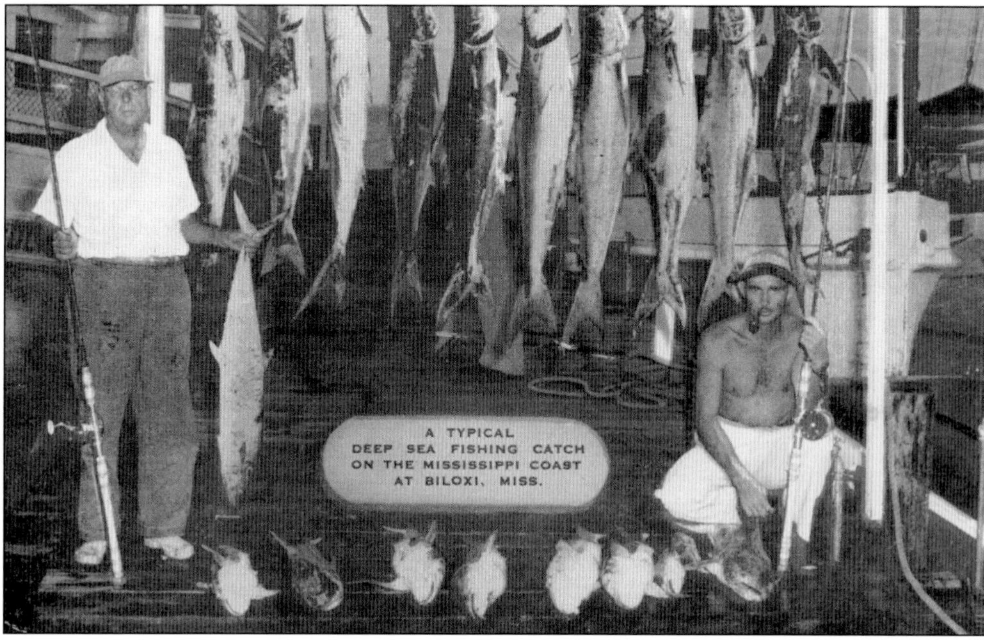

TYPICAL DEEP-SEA FISHING CATCH, 1953. Two boats are seen along a dock in Biloxi as fishermen display their fine catch following their deep-sea fishing trip. Charter boats are still operating today, catching their limit of many species of fish during exciting, fun-filled, daily trips. (Postmarked 1953; SC.)

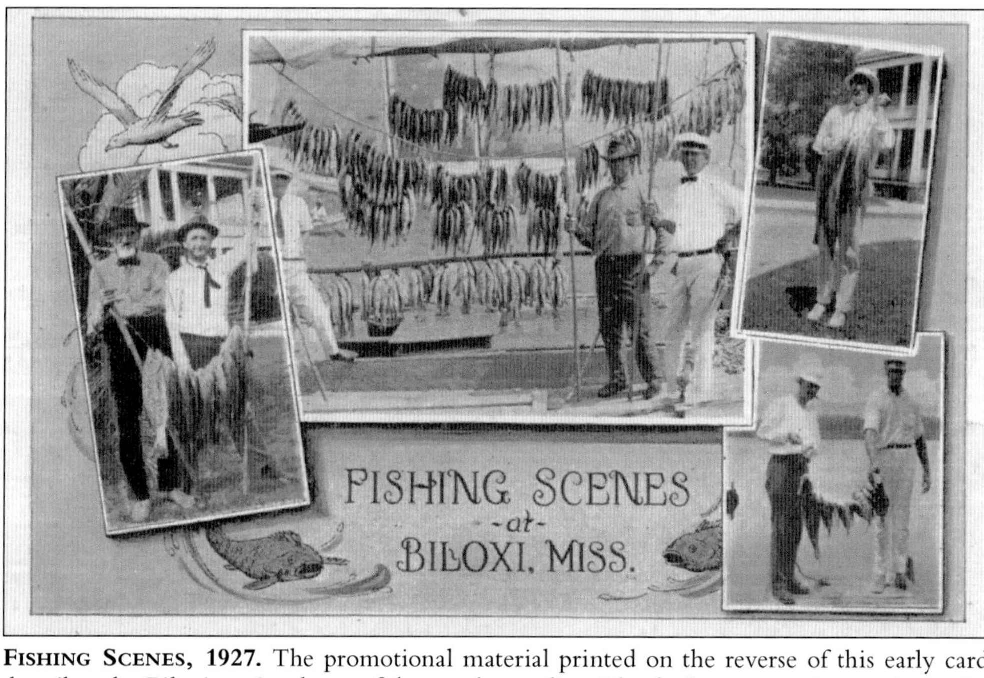

FISHING SCENES, 1927. The promotional material printed on the reverse of this early card describes the Biloxi peninsula as a fisherman's paradise. The freshwater species caught in the rivers and bays and the saltwater species caught in the Mississippi Sound and the Gulf were highlighted. The four scenes shown on the postcard feature local fishermen, fishing guides, and tourists displaying their catches. (Postmarked 1931; SC.)

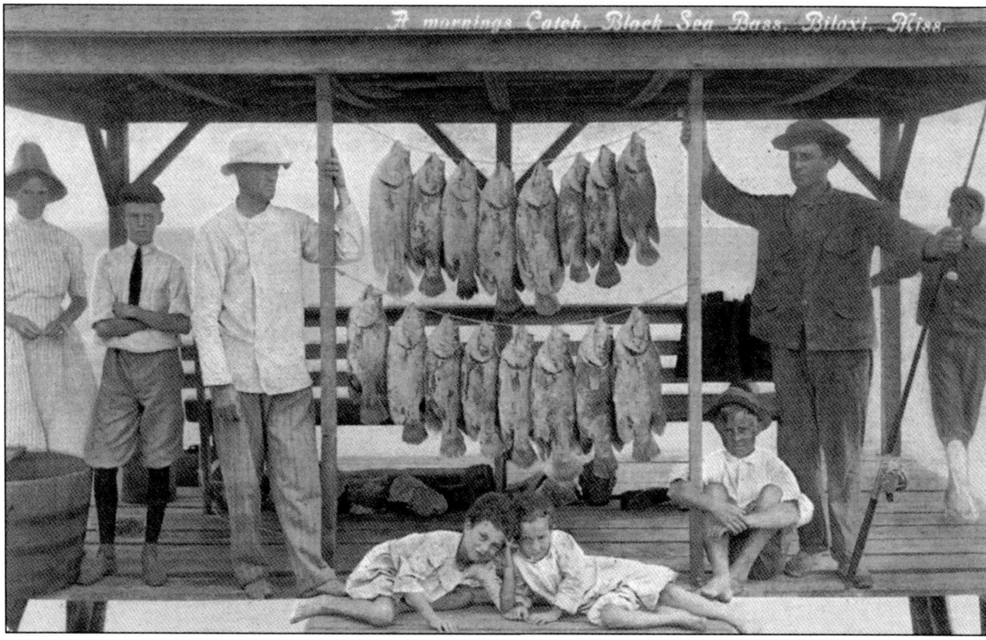

A Morning's Catch, c. 1908. This family fishing photograph shows the men, women, and children of the group displaying their catch of black sea bass on a local pier. The size of the fish caught is remarkable, as are the period costumes worn by the fishermen. Knickers, pajamas, nightshirts, and strange hats are highlighted on the card. (Not Mailed; SC.)

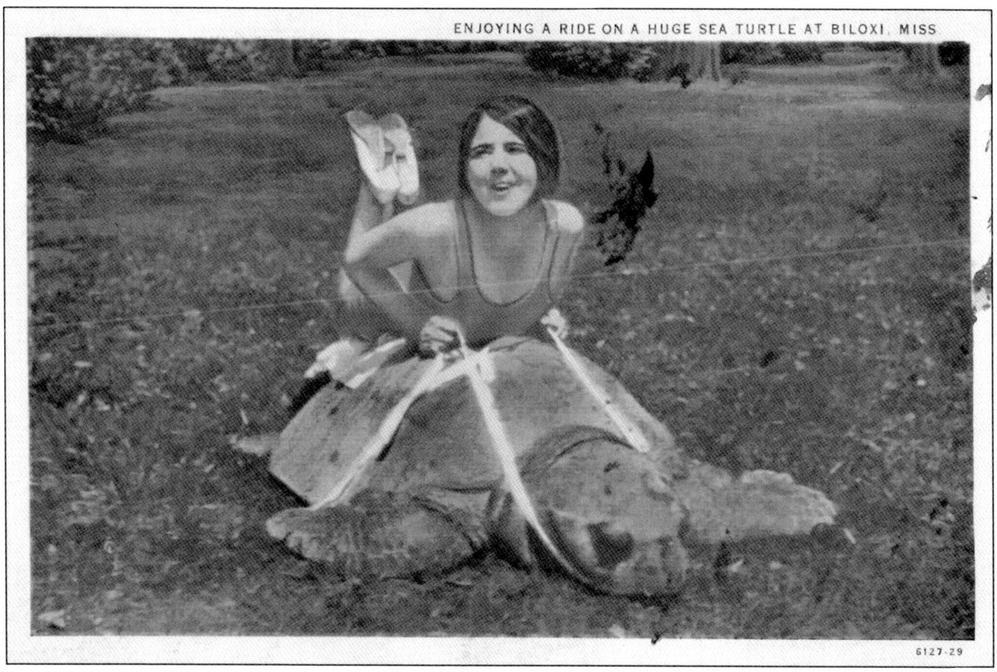

Sea Turtle Ride, 1929. Local beauty Louise Fayard enjoys riding on a sea turtle brought into Biloxi from the Gulf of Mexico. Although sea turtles are an endangered species now, in the early part of the 20th century they were not considered so. The writer of this card noted, "Plenty of these around here." (Postmarked 1933; SC.)

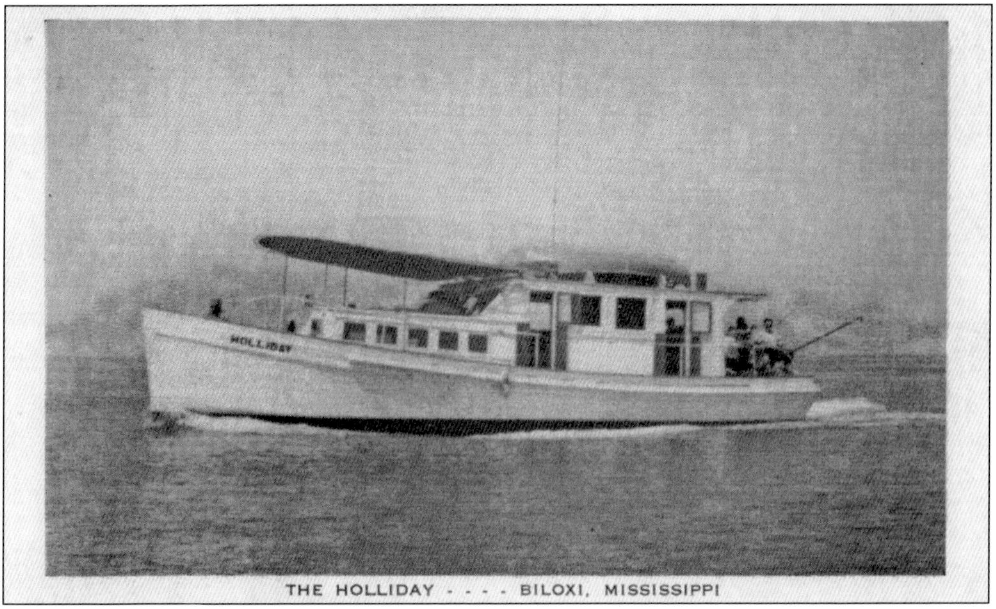

THE *HOLIDAY*, C. 1950. All tackle, ice, and bait were furnished on the 8:00 a.m. to 4:00 p.m. daily fishing trips aboard this early charter boat. Fishermen are shown with their rods and reels and their lines in the water, trying to harvest their daily catch. The boat departed its Baricev's Pier location on Central Beach and included a fish fry onboard during the trip. (Not Mailed; SC.)

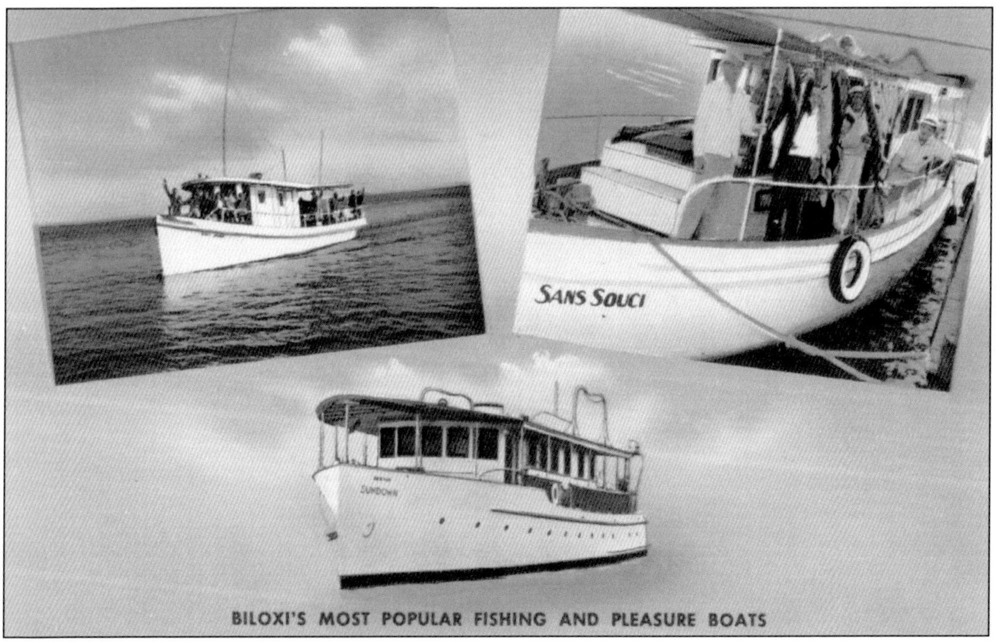

BILOXI'S MOST POPULAR BOATS, C. 1960. Three charter boats are featured on this mid-20th-century postcard. The three vessels were docked at Bolton's Pier, on West Beach, across Highway 90 from the Buena Vista Hotel. The *Sundown* conducted daily fishing trips for $5 per person. The *Sans Souci* conducted charter fishing trips for up to 20 people. The *Aunt Jennie* conducted two-hour harbor sightseeing trips, twice daily. (Not Mailed; SC.)

Four

It is All About Water

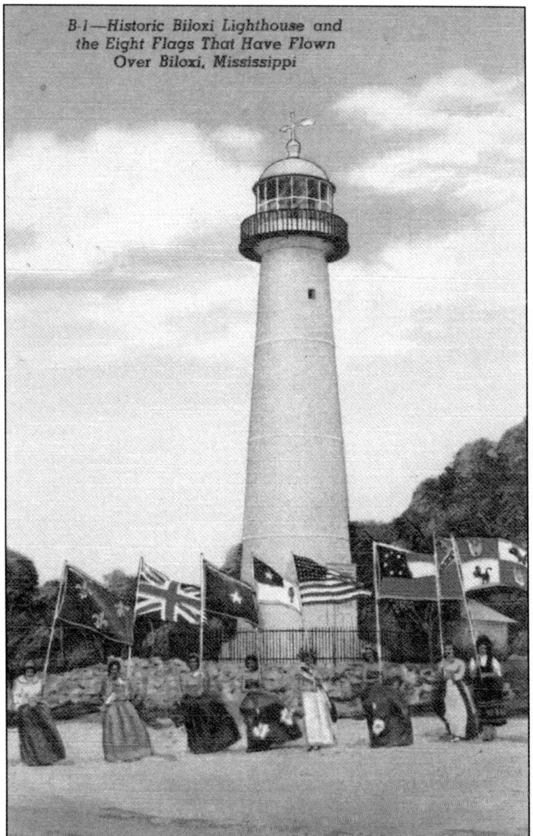

Historic Lighthouse, 1952. This is the most photographed view of the Mississippi Gulf Coast. The lighthouses, seawall, beach, bridges, and parks in and around Biloxi provide accommodations to the waters of the rivers, bays, and bayous, giving life to Mississippi Sound. The water surrounding the Biloxi peninsula adds credence to the old saying, "When it's good, it's very good, and when it's bad, it's terrible." (Not Mailed; SC.)

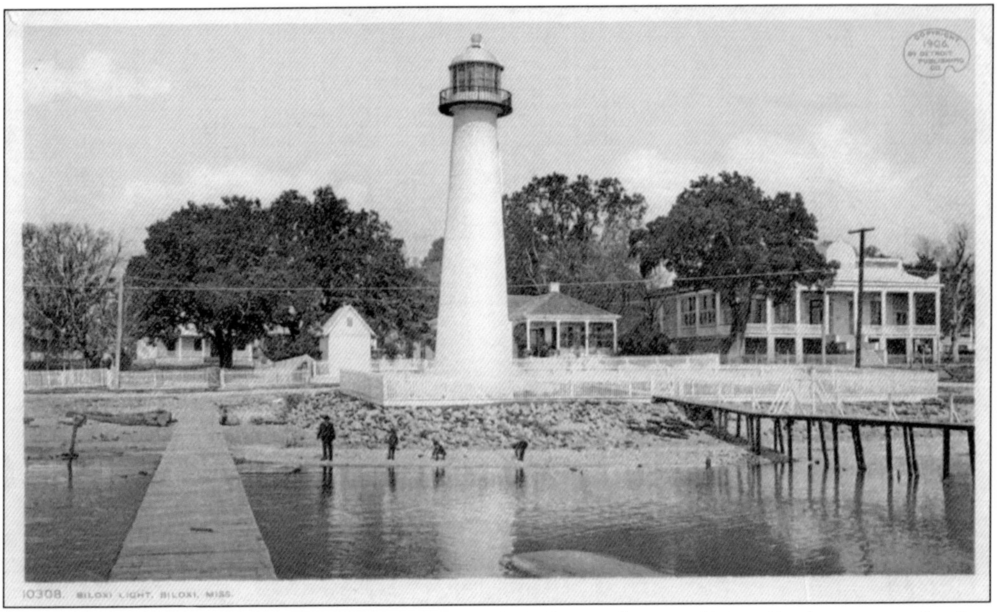

BILOXI LIGHT, 1906. The area around the lighthouse has traditionally been a gathering place for locals and visitors alike. This postcard shows treasure hunters searching the sand for fortunes. The structures in the background include the small building used for storing supplies, the lighthouse keeper's house, and the Dantzler-Maloney House. This is the current site of the Biloxi Visitors Center. (Not Mailed; BL.)

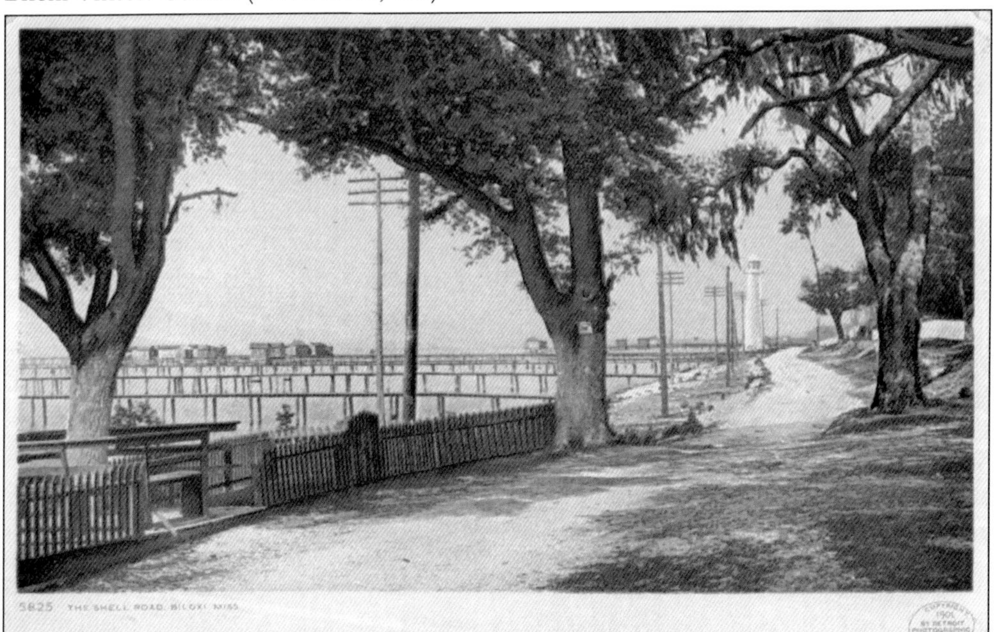

SHELL ROAD, 1901. This photograph, taken east of the lighthouse, shows the oyster shell road, later Highway 90, with power poles south of the roadway, seating around the oaks, and the 1848 lighthouse in the background. The cast-iron lighthouse was forged in Baltimore and then assembled in Biloxi. Its light and powerful lenses guided mariners for over 100 years. (Postmarked 1908; SC.)

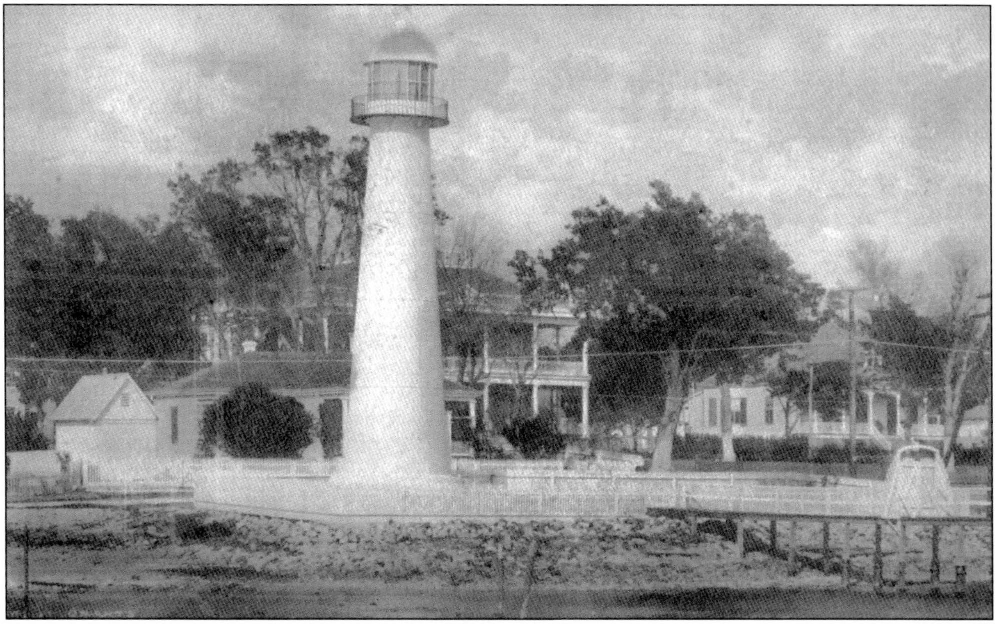

LIGHTHOUSE, C. 1904. Of the thousands of different postcards printed about Biloxi and the area, the number-one image is the Biloxi lighthouse. This iconic structure is the hallmark symbol of the Mississippi Gulf Coast. The waters of the Mississippi Sound touch the stone foundation of the telescoping light and a white picket fence surrounds the lighthouse grounds in this photograph. (Postmarked 1908; BL.)

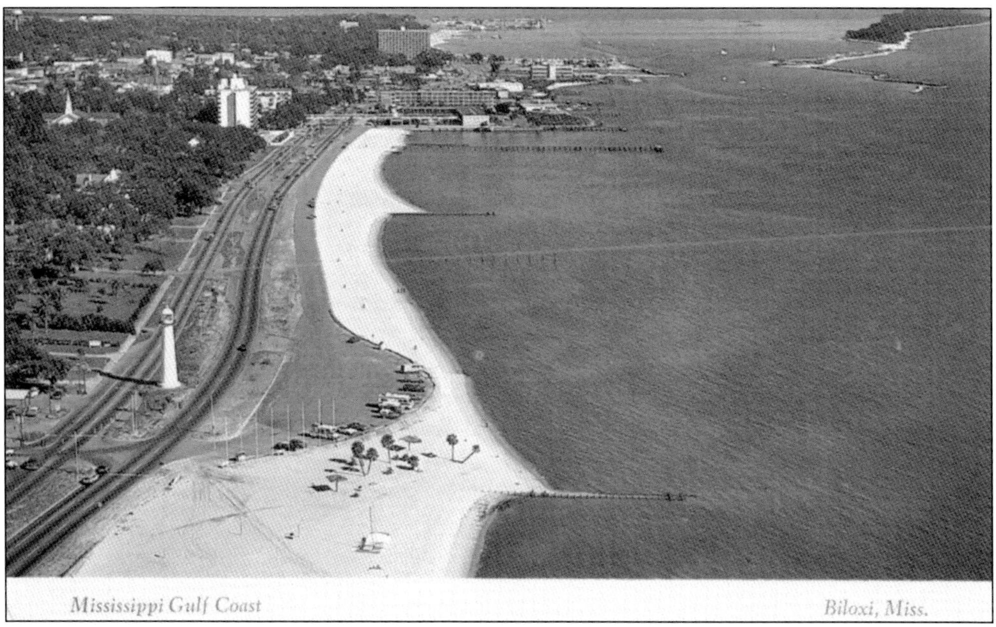

MISSISSIPPI GULF COAST, C. 1965. This aerial view of the lighthouse area and highway shows how the area looked prior to hurricanes Camille (1969) and Katrina (2005). The card features a great view of Deer Island, the white sand beach without the lighthouse pier, and without the I-110 Loop. The Buena Vista Hotel and Motel were standing on both sides of Highway 90. (Not Mailed; SC.)

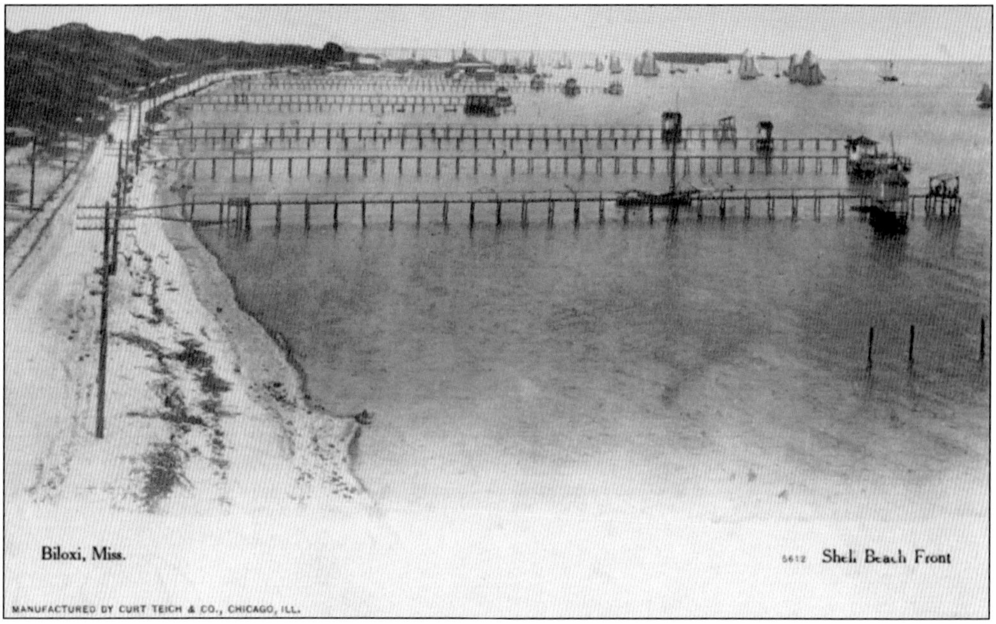

THE SHELL BEACH FRONT, C. 1904. This east-facing photograph, taken from atop the Biloxi Lighthouse, features life on the waterfront during a much simpler time. Working schooners in the Biloxi channel, long piers jotting into the sound, and no seawall or manmade beach are visible. The beachfront is highlighted with trolley tracks and utility poles. (Postmarked 1907; SC.)

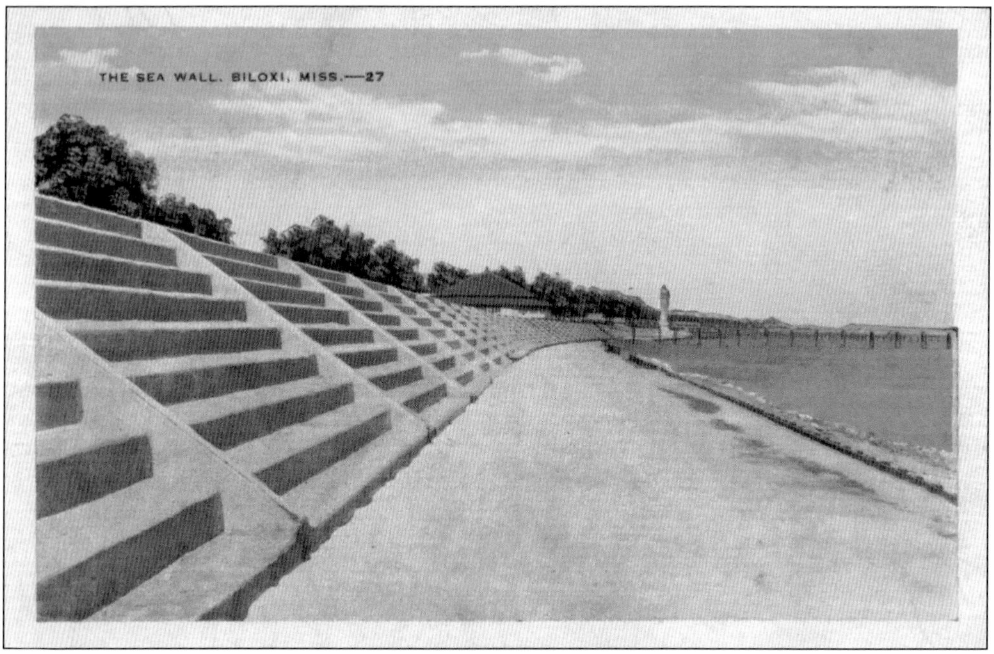

THE SEAWALL, 1930S. West of the Biloxi Lighthouse are the nine concrete steps of the Harrison County seawall. Built for $3.4 million in the mid-1920s to protect Highway 90 (Old Spanish Trail), it was the longest and largest seawall in the world. The beach depicted here is the natural beach. The manmade beach was not created until the 1950s. (Postmarked 1931; SC.)

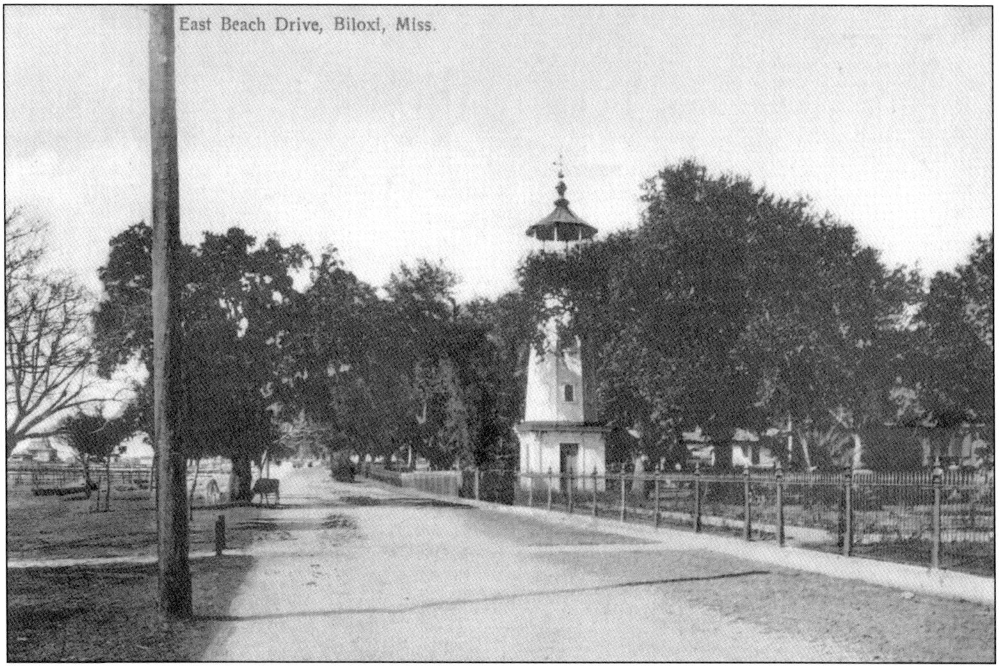

EAST BEACH DRIVE, C. 1920. This lighthouse was constructed in 1875 as a private observation platform on the Howard (Howard Avenue) family property, at the corner of Bellman Street and the beach. In 1912, the property was purchased by Baldwin Wood, the New Orleans inventor of the largest pumps in the world, which were used to reclaim much of the land of the city of New Orleans. (Not Mailed; SC.)

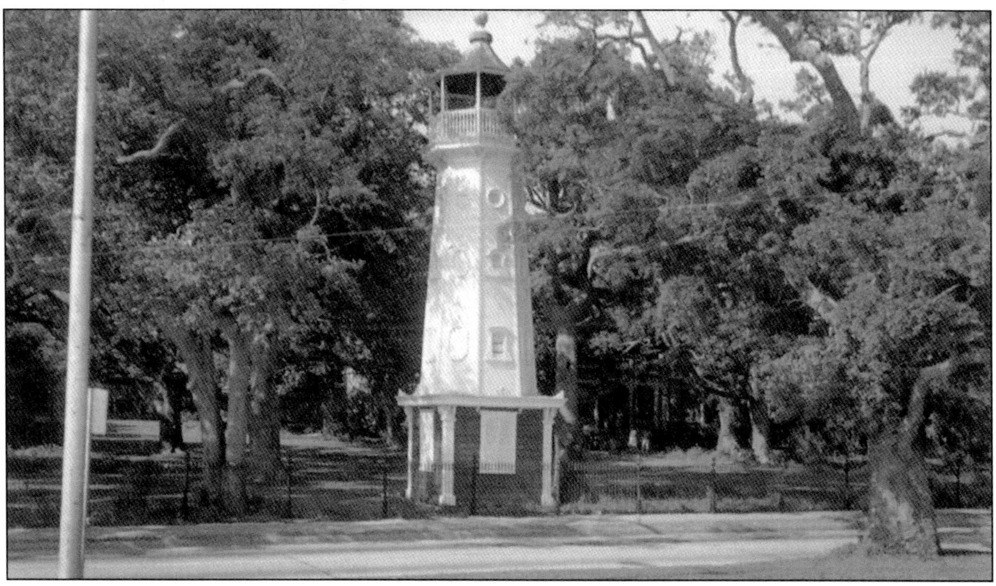

BALDWIN WOOD LIGHTHOUSE, C. 1950. The structure became an actual lighthouse when Baldwin Wood, an avid sailor, purchased a strong light for it and used it to shine on his beloved sloop *Nydia* at night after vandals had ransacked his vessels. The lighthouse was severely damaged during the 1947 hurricane and was later repaired, only to be totally destroyed by Hurricane Camille in 1969. (Not Mailed; BL.)

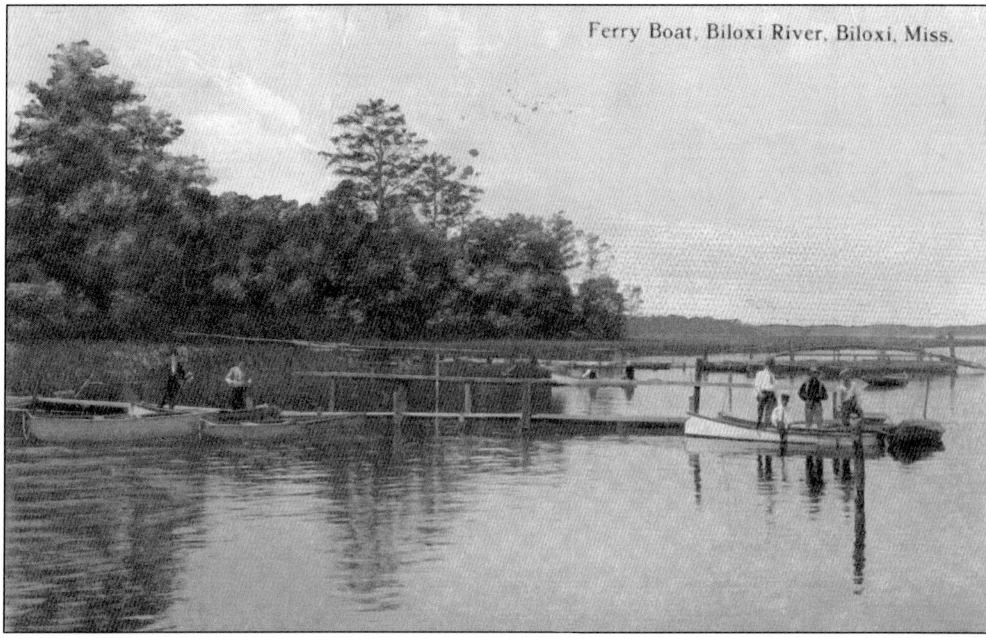

FERRY BOAT, BILOXI RIVER, C. 1909. An early ferryboat operator crosses a wide span of the Biloxi River. John Popp operated one of the many ferries that crossed the rivers and bays of South Mississippi. His ferry operated between the mainland and the Biloxi peninsula; the bridge and roadway that replaced his ferry still bears that name. (Postmarked 1913; SC.)

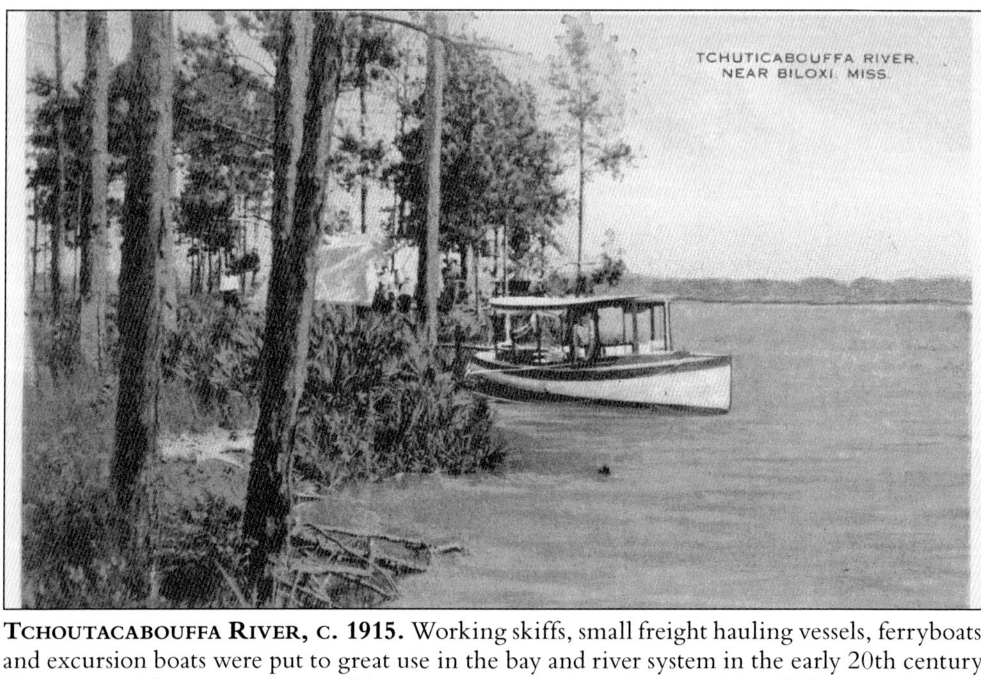

TCHOUTACABOUFFA RIVER, C. 1915. Working skiffs, small freight hauling vessels, ferryboats, and excursion boats were put to great use in the bay and river system in the early 20th century. This postcard features a motorized boat at a campsite along the river. Mrs. Williams, who lived on Cedar Street in Biloxi, mailed this card to a friend who lived in Watson, Massachusetts. (Postmarked 1916; SC.)

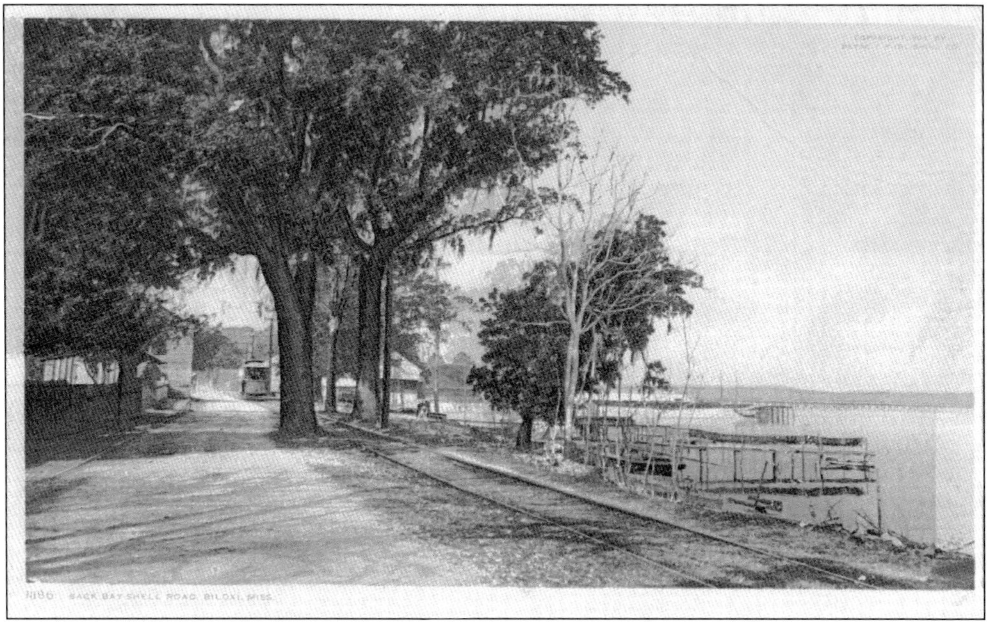

BACK BAY SHELL ROAD, 1906. Closer examination of this 1906 Detroit Publishing postcard of early Bay View Avenue reveals several history lessons about Biloxi. This photograph, taken from the south side of the bay, from a location near Lameuse Street, highlights the bay-side trolley and its tracks, the Biloxi Canning Company factory, small piers and houses, and the Biloxi Bay Bridge in the background. (Not Mailed; SC.)

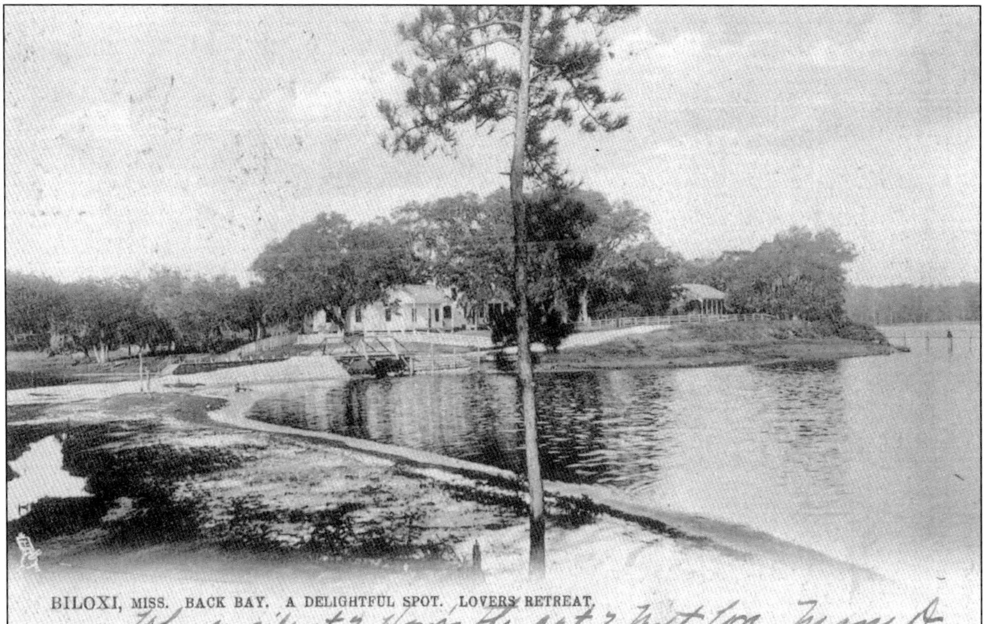

BACK BAY, 1902. Whether it is called Back Bay or Peaceful Bay, the photograph was the same used by three different publishers on three different postcards in the collection. This photograph depicts the entrance to one of the many local bayous and inlets, a small wooden bridge, a pier leading from the house to the bayou, and a boatbuilding shed. (Postmarked 1907; SC.)

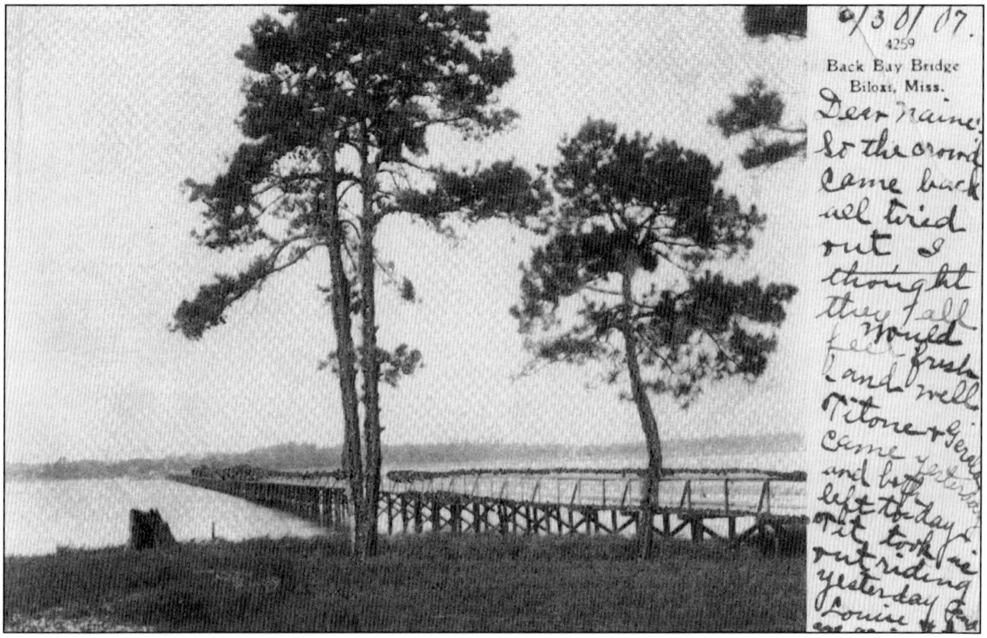

BACK BAY BRIDGE, 1907. This early postcard of the Biloxi Bay Bridge is known as a glitter card, with sparkle to attract attention. Two identical postcards were in the collection, one was mailed to Norway and written in Norwegian. Was the writer an immigrant living or working in Biloxi, a visitor, or a seaman working on a timber ship that visited the Port of Gulfport? (Postmarked 1907; SC.)

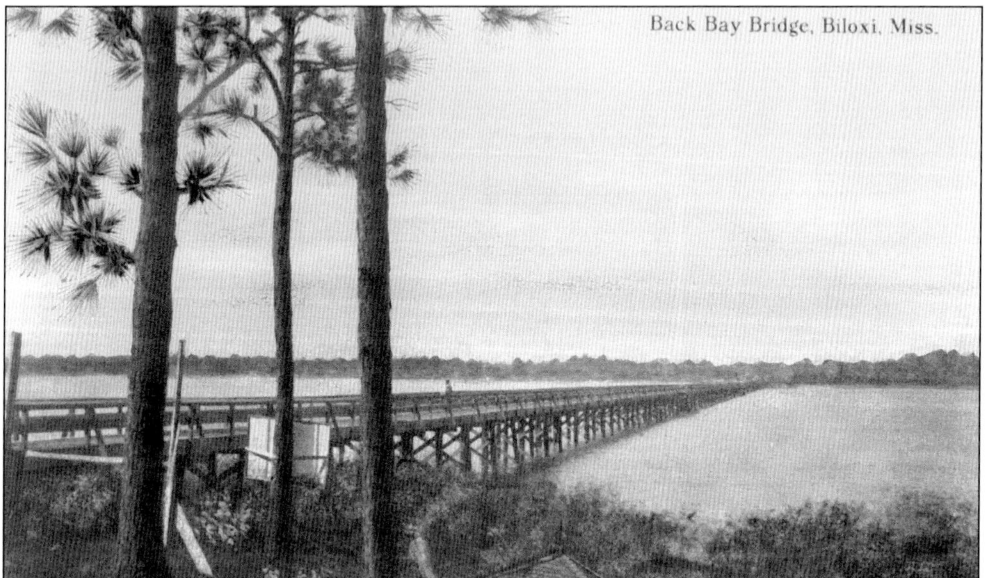

BILOXI-D'IBERVILLE BRIDGE, C. 1909. This $17,000 wooden walking bridge was opened in 1901 as a toll bridge across Biloxi Bay, stretching from Caillavet Street in Biloxi to Central Avenue in D'Iberville. Benches (love seats) were built along the sides so that walkers could stop and rest a while during their journey. It remained in operation until it was replaced by a concrete structure in 1927. (Not Mailed; SC.)

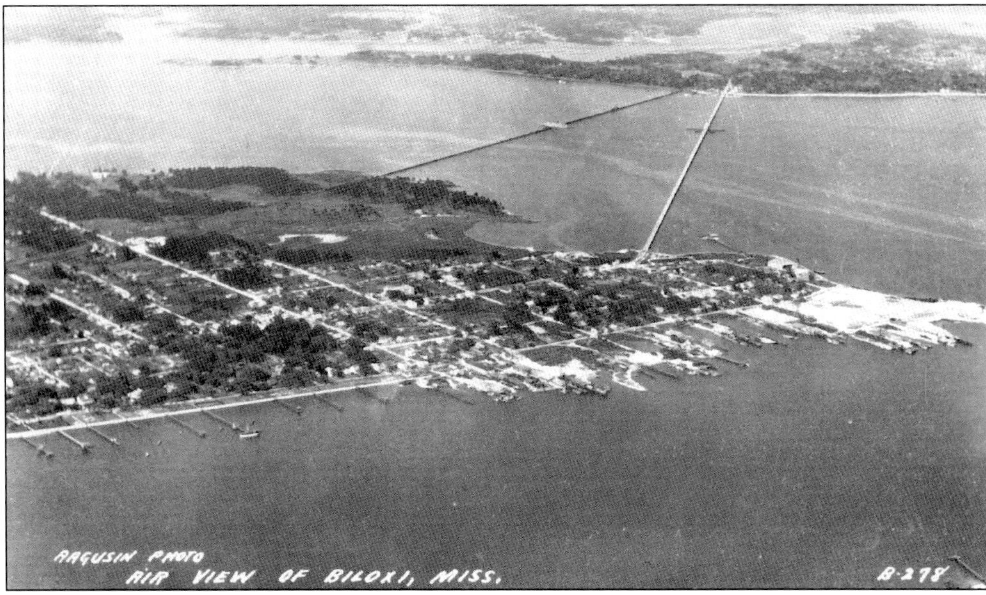

Air View, c. 1940. This real-photo postcard shows the east end of Biloxi. Great views of the railroad bridge and the Biloxi-Ocean Springs Bridge, which starts at Howard Avenue, are highlighted in the card. A two-lane Highway 90 and the absence of St. Michael's Church on the beach should also be noted. The photograph was taken by Biloxi Chamber of Commerce executive director Anthony Ragusin. (Not Mailed; SC.)

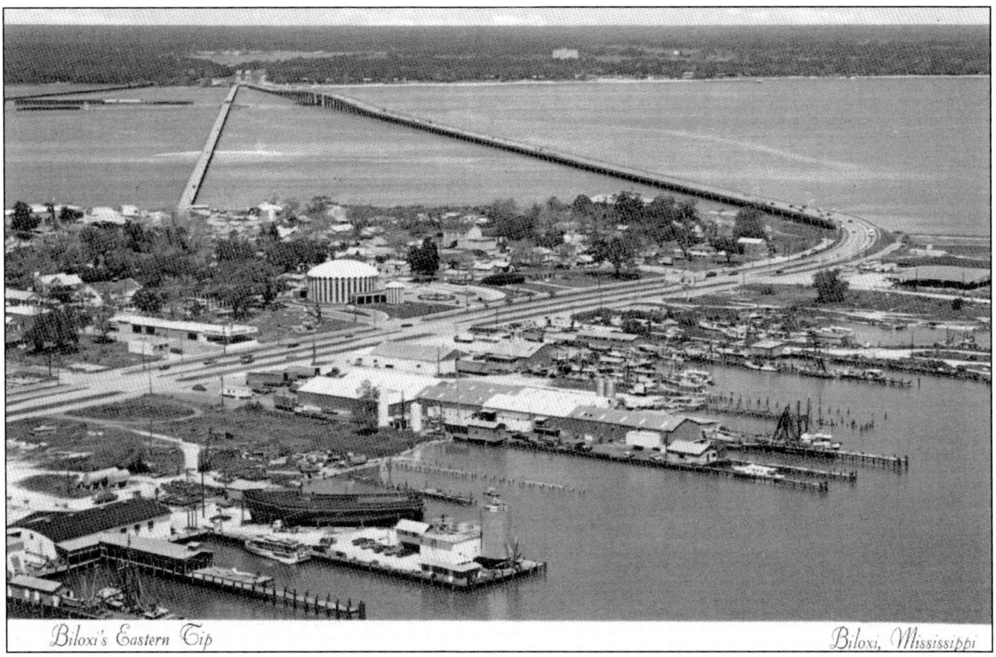

Biloxi's Eastern Tip, c. 1970. This view of Point Cadet features several items of interest. Post-Camille memories of this area include some of the seafood factories, the Fact-O-Bake, and the Point Cadet Bowling Alley. Gone are the seafood factory employee housing units, known as seafood camps, which were located east and west of Cedar Street, along the beachfront. (Not Mailed; BL.)

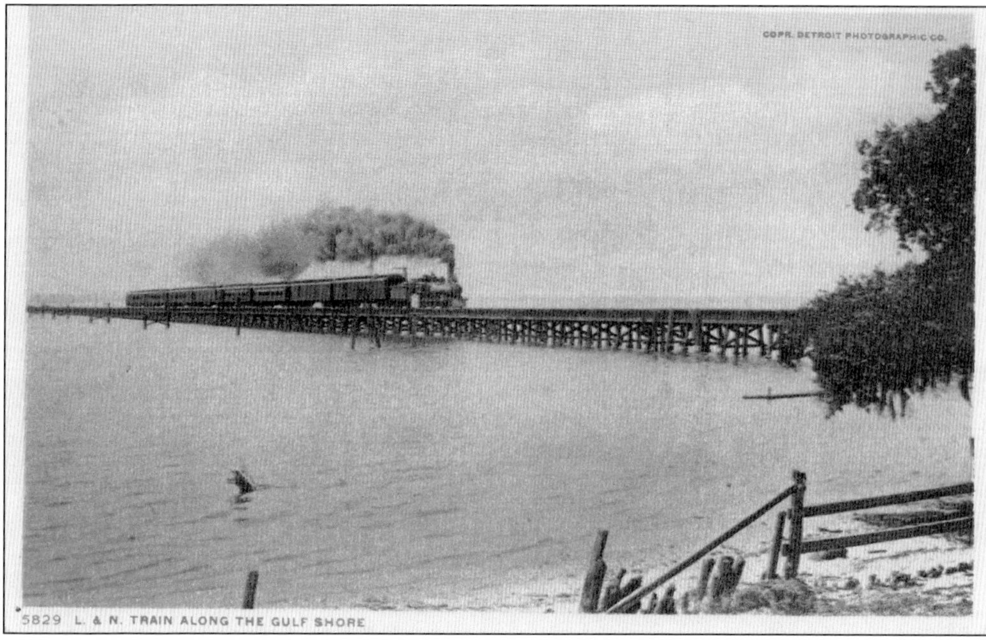

L&N Railroad Bridge, 1907. A steam locomotive crossing the one-mile stretch of Biloxi Bay is featured in this card. Rail service travel, which began in 1870 along the coastline from Mobile to New Orleans, required the construction of several bridges. Trains brought tourists into the area and took seafood and other items to their destinations, greatly enhancing the development of the Gulf Coast. (Not Mailed; SC.)

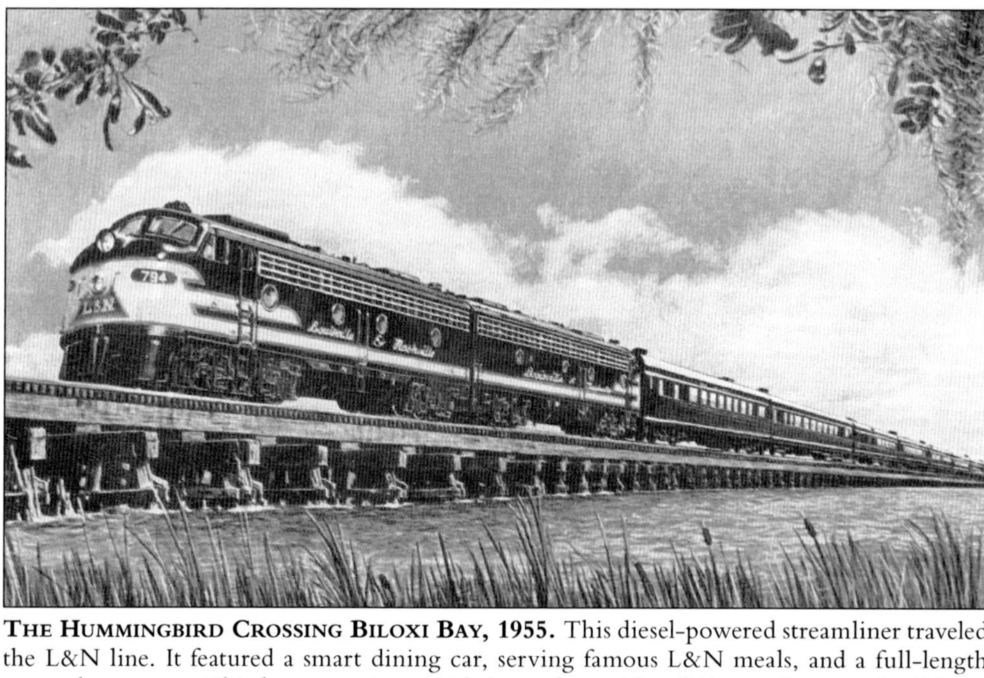

The Hummingbird Crossing Biloxi Bay, 1955. This diesel-powered streamliner traveled the L&N line. It featured a smart dining car, serving famous L&N meals, and a full-length tavern-lounge car. This luxury train provided travelers with a full complement of rail-born amenities. Coach, sleepers, and Pullman facilities were available on the luxury liner. (Not Mailed; BL.)

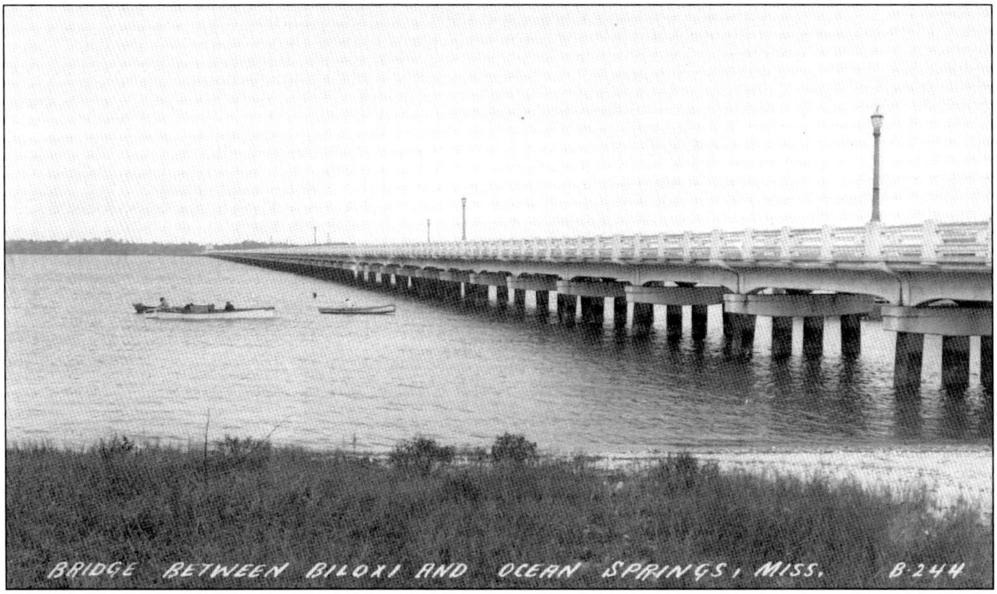

BRIDGE BETWEEN BILOXI AND OCEAN SPRINGS, C. 1950. This postcard features the two-lane bridge crossing the Biloxi Bay. This structure not only provided a means for motorized transportation between the two cities, but also provided a walkway for pedestrians. However, the majority of the users of the walkway were rod and reel fishermen, fishing the abundant waters of Biloxi Bay. (Not Mailed; SC.)

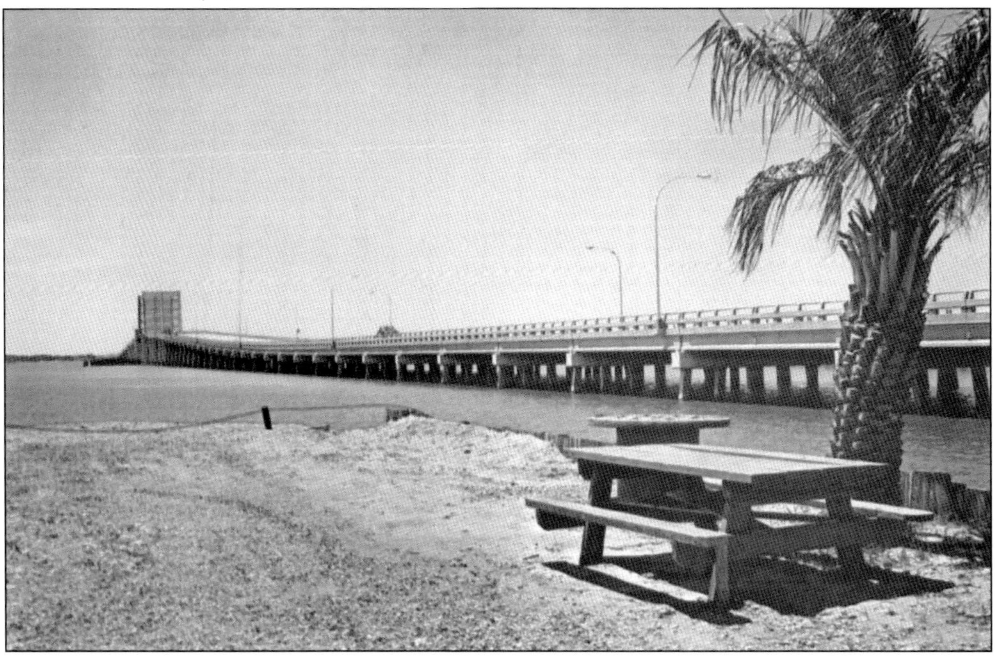

BILOXI-OCEAN SPRINGS BRIDGE, C. 1965. This four-lane, two-mile bridge was completed in 1962 and moved the Biloxi terminus to the beach instead of Howard Avenue. The bridge featured a raising draw rather than the rotating draw used on previous bridges. The structure was damaged during Hurricane Camille but was repaired and returned to use until 2005, when the bridge was destroyed in Hurricane Katrina. (Not Mailed; BL.)

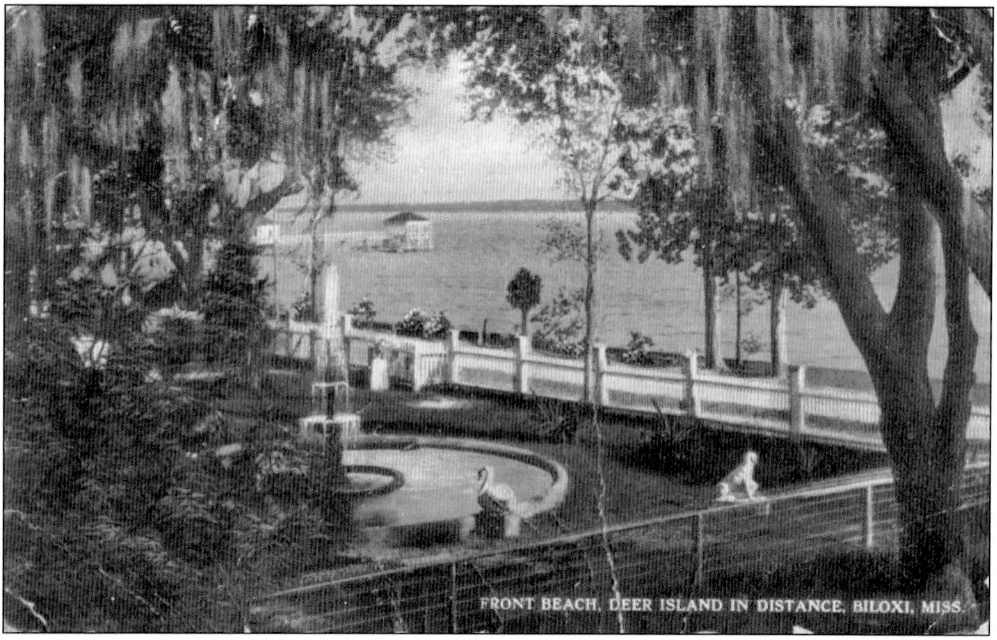

FRONT BEACH, 1913. Moss-draped oaks and an elaborate Victorian fountain are featured in this beachfront view. The east beach photograph highlights the bathing houses located at the end of the elongated piers and Deer Island in the background. By the angle of the photograph, it was probably taken from the bell tower of the Church of the Redeemer and overlooks the yard of the Howard Mansion. (Postmarked 1917; SC.)

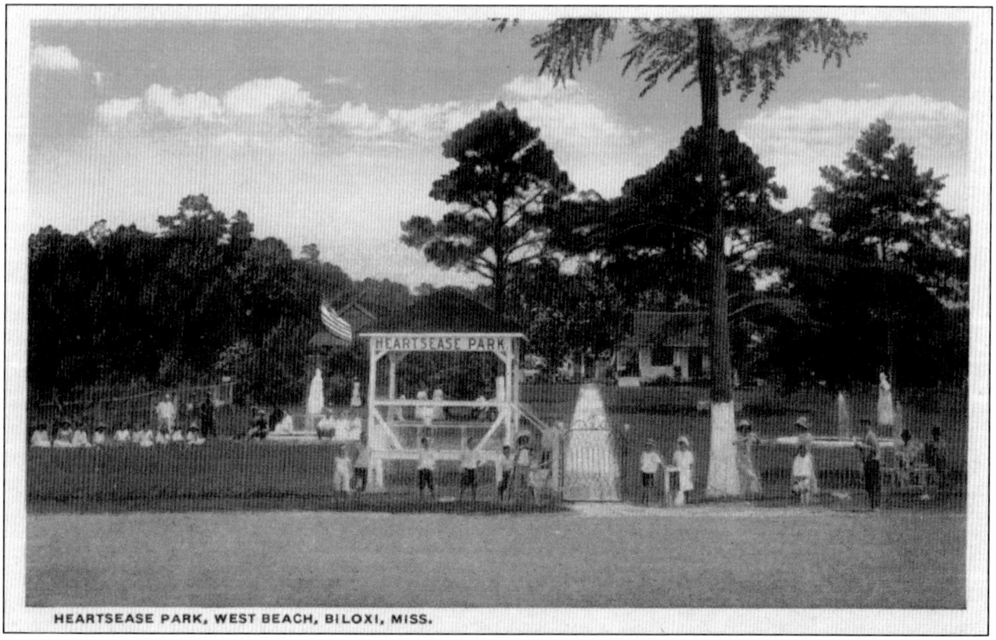

HEARTSEASE PARK, 1913. This West Biloxi neighborhood park was a popular campsite during the 1890s, and the Heartsease neighborhood developed into a small community. In 1925, the area name was changed to Mir-a-mar. The beachfront park, now known as Miramar Park, remains a popular attraction for families. (Not Mailed; SC.)

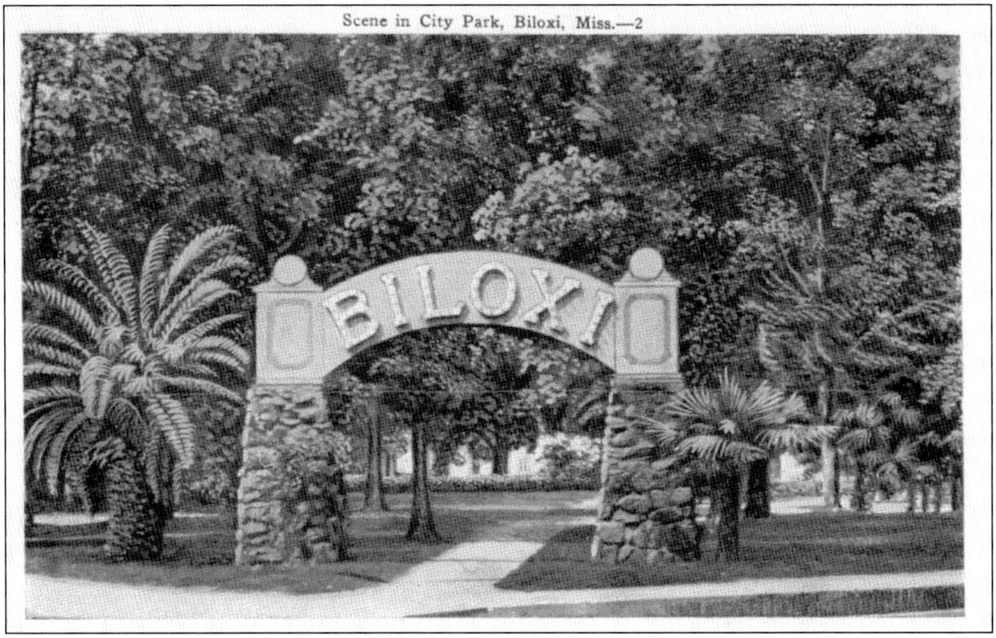

CITY PARK, 1930S. This large, electric sign was used to greet visitors arriving at the adjacent Biloxi train station. The park was located on the south side of Railroad and Reynoir Streets. A replica of the sign is now located at the Town Green, at Highway 90 and Main Street. (Postmarked 1932; BL.)

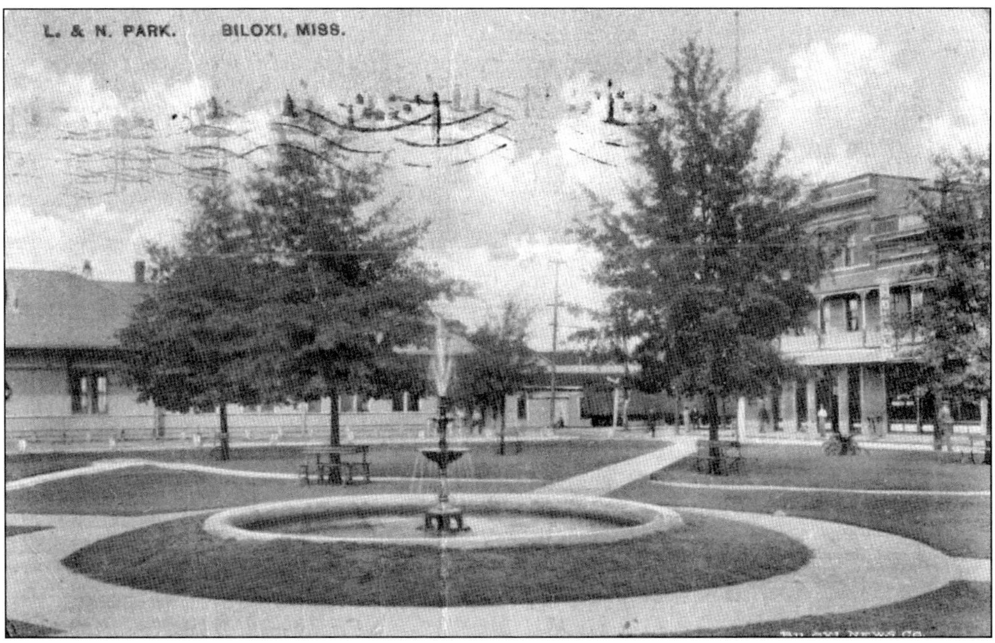

L&N PARK, 1913. Known as L&N Park, Railroad Park, or City Park, this beautifully landscaped facility featured walkways, an elaborate fountain, and bench seating around the trees. This early card highlights the train depot and the Kennedy Hotel in the background. A closer look shows pedestrians on the sidewalks, a bicycle parked near the hotel entrance, and freight cars on the tracks. (Postmarked 1913; SC.)

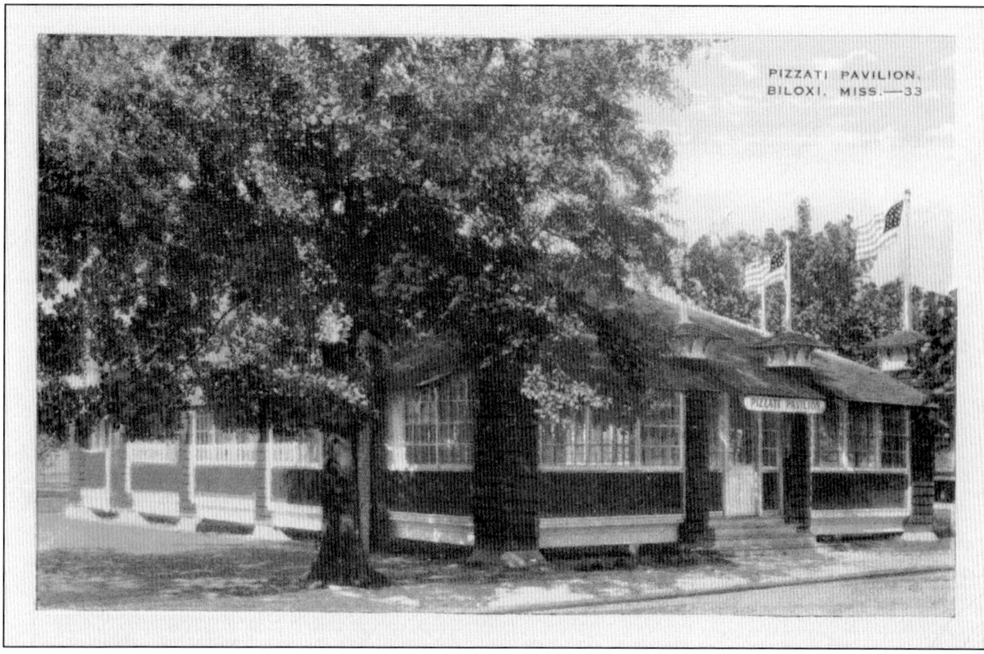

PIZZATI PAVILION, C. 1925. A $1,000 donation to the city by Col. Salvadore Pizzati resulted in the dance hall and meeting room pictured in this card. The pavilion was located on City Park property, south of the L&N passenger depot, and was dedicated in 1915. Meetings and dances were held in the building, and it later became a voting precinct. (Not Mailed; SC.)

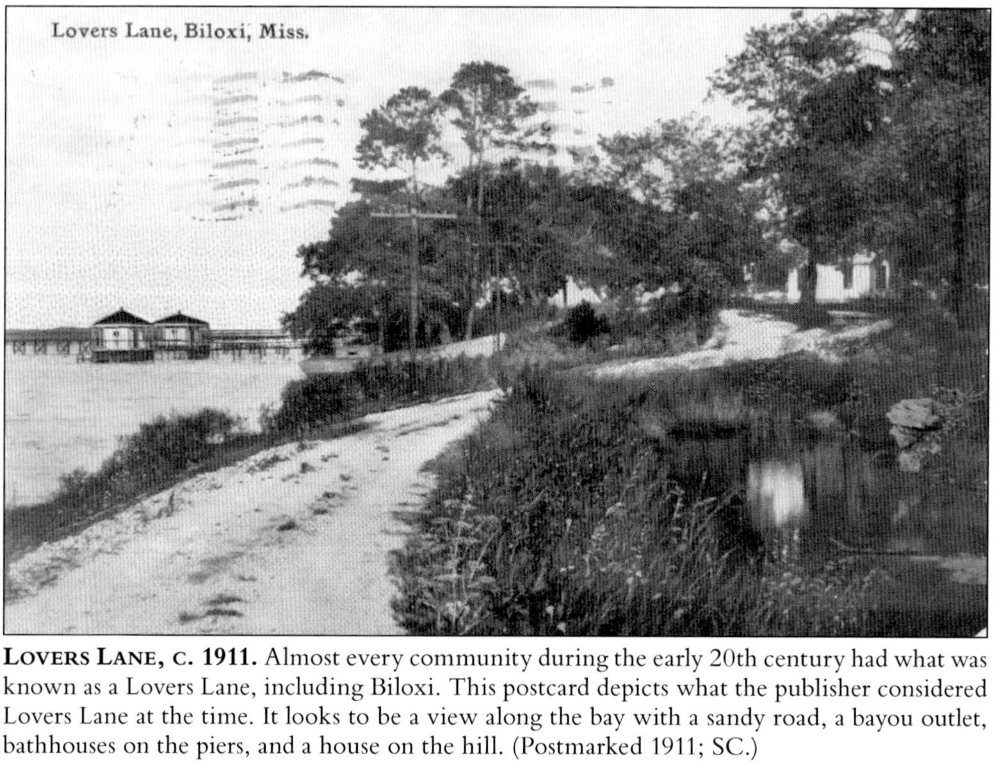

LOVERS LANE, C. 1911. Almost every community during the early 20th century had what was known as a Lovers Lane, including Biloxi. This postcard depicts what the publisher considered Lovers Lane at the time. It looks to be a view along the bay with a sandy road, a bayou outlet, bathhouses on the piers, and a house on the hill. (Postmarked 1911; SC.)

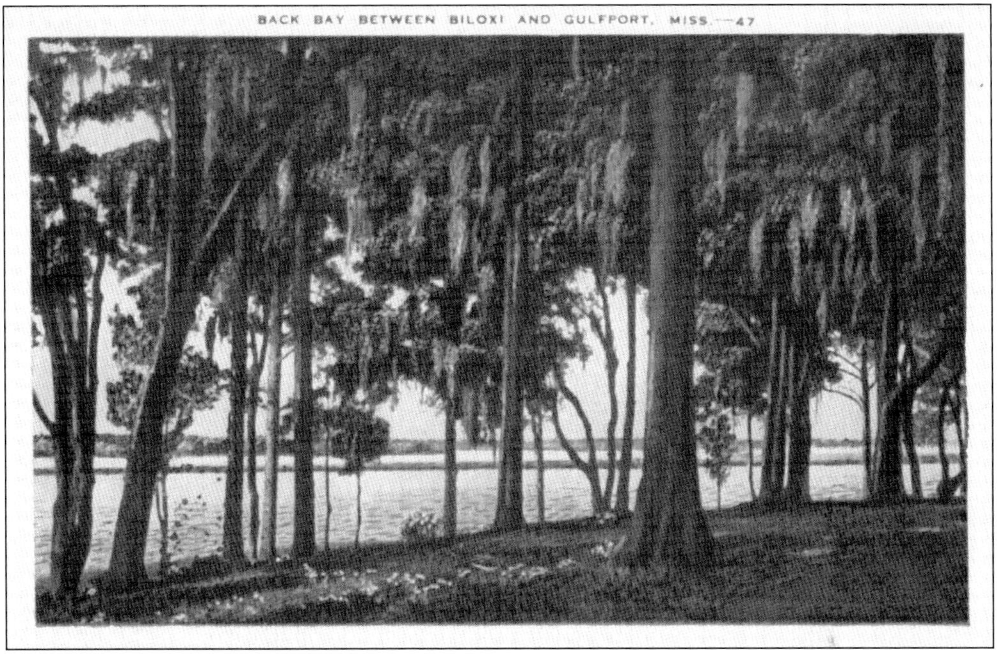

BACK BAY BETWEEN BILOXI AND GULFPORT, C. 1930. This view of the moss-draped oaks overlooking the bay is typical of much of the undeveloped land on the peninsula during the early part of the 20th century. The caption on the reverse side of the card describes the ideal picnic and fishing grounds of the area, which were available year-round. (Not Mailed; SC.)

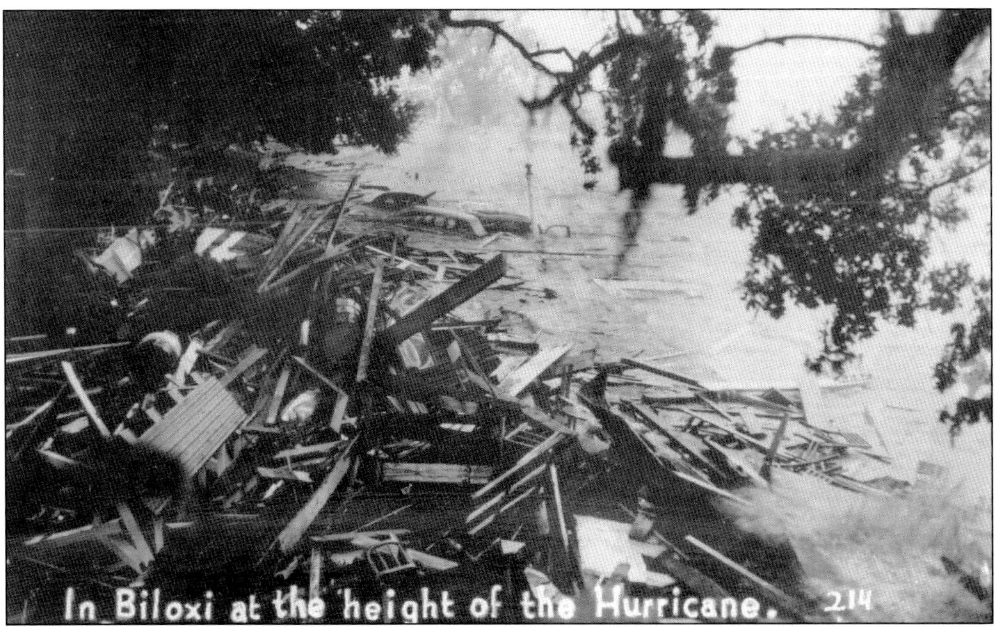

THE HEIGHT OF THE HURRICANE, 1947. At this stage, "they all look alike" with the waters up, the winds blowing, the rain coming down in sheets, and stacks of debris all over the place. However, the view of the 1947 hurricane shows some of the fury of this fierce storm, which was the local benchmark hurricane prior to Hurricane Camille. (Not Mailed; SC.)

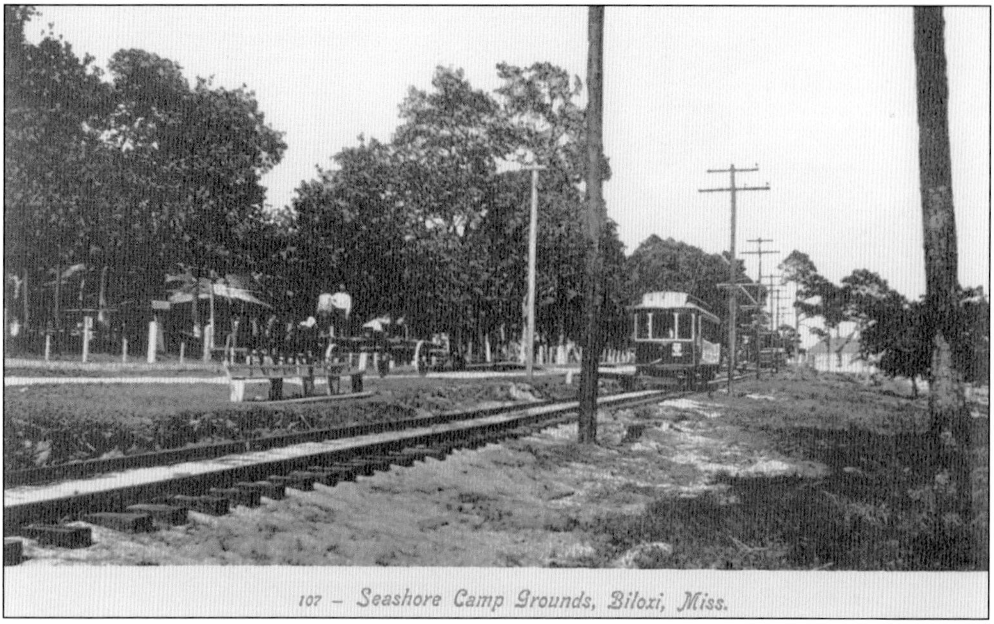

SEASHORE CAMPGROUNDS, C. 1906. From the view on this postcard and the undivided back, this photograph was taken between 1904, when the trolley line was completed, and 1907, when divided-back postcards were established. Pictured on the card are the local trolley and a horse and wagon carrying supplies. During the summers of the early 20th century, about 2,000 Methodists visited the campground. (Not Mailed; SC.)

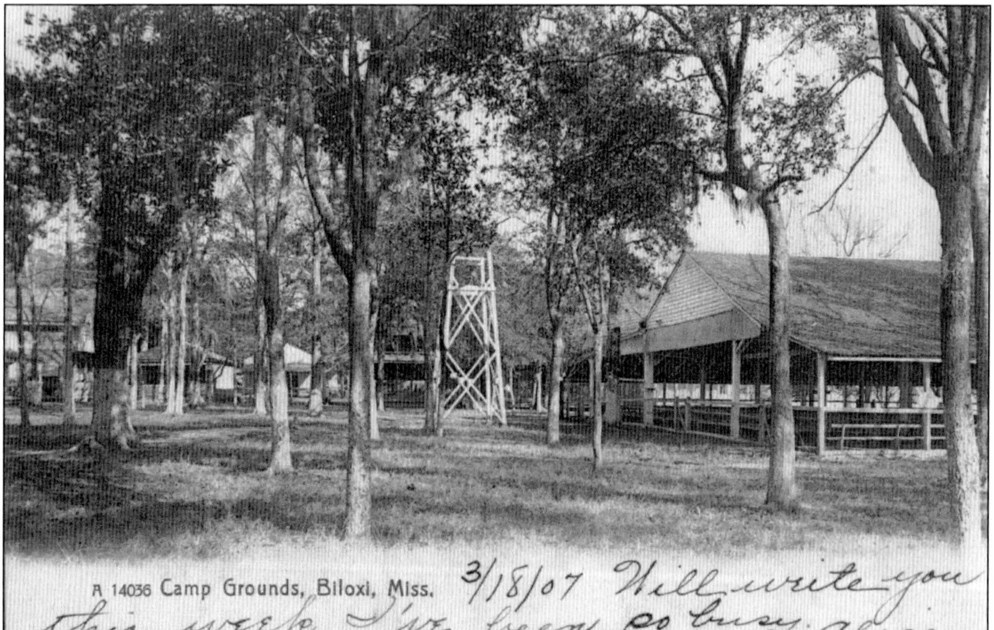

CAMPGROUNDS, 1907. The Seashore Campgrounds have been used by southern Methodists for their religious camp meetings since 1872. Tents and crude cabins were used by visitors in the early years, and meetings were held in the open tabernacle shown on this card. Light was provided at night by bonfires in sandboxes located on elevated posts. (Postmarked 1907; SC.)

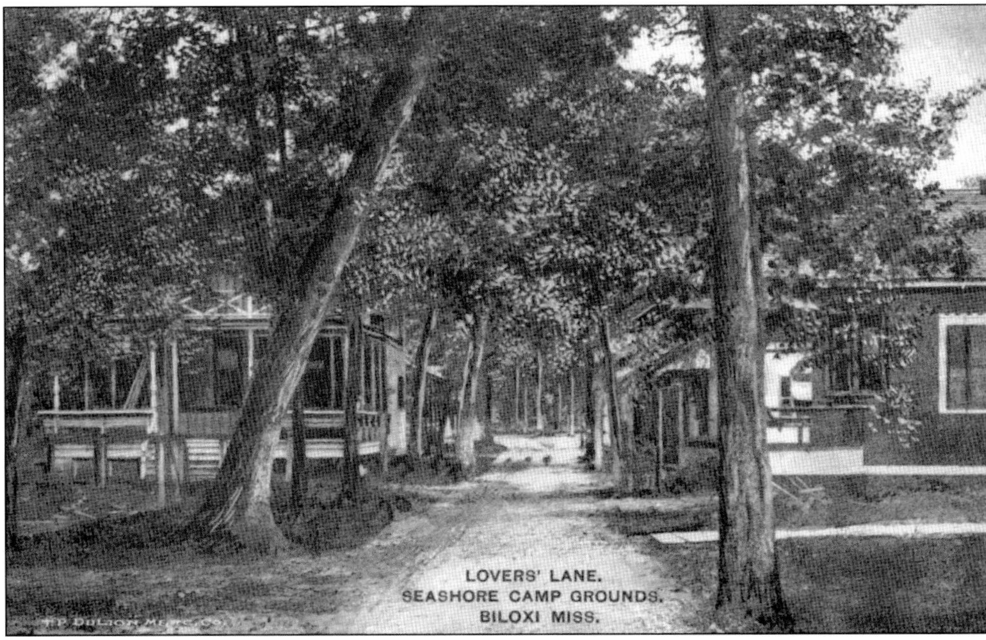

LOVERS LANE, SEASHORE CAMPGROUNDS, C. 1910. As time went on, many Methodists built summer homes, featuring functioning windows and large porches, on land rented for $10 to $15 per lot. At one time, there were over 200 buildings located on the campground property, and water was obtained for all purposes from one of the artesian (free-flowing) wells. (Not Mailed; SC.)

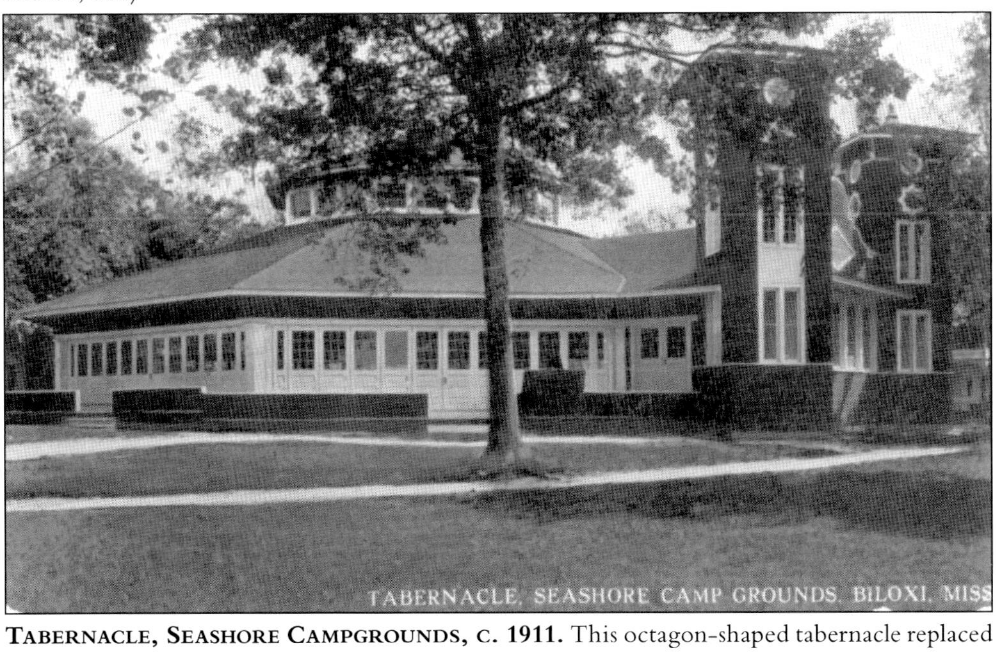

TABERNACLE, SEASHORE CAMPGROUNDS, C. 1911. This octagon-shaped tabernacle replaced the old, open-air meeting facility on the campgrounds in 1911. The building was made with folding doors on each side that could be opened to let in the summer breeze. The tabernacle stood until 1957; when it was torn down to make way for Leggett Memorial United Methodist Church. (Postmarked 1912; SC.)

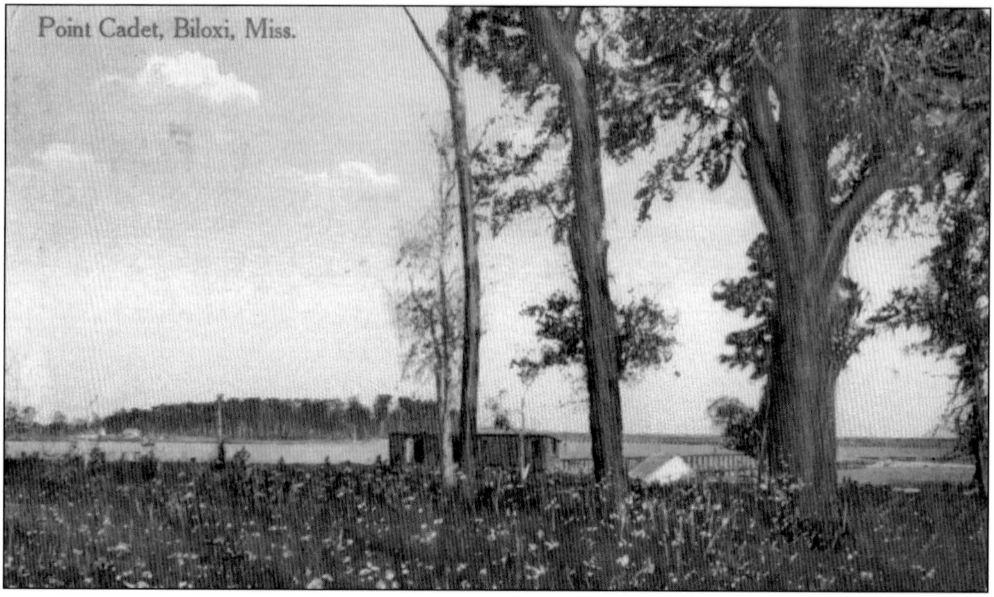

POINT CADET, C. 1910. The east end of Biloxi has been known as Point Cadet for many, many years. This picture postcard features a view of the houses and other facilities on Deer Island. Also, notice the boat in the Biloxi channel. A boathouse and long pier are seen along the Biloxi shoreline, prior to the development of the seafood industry on the point. (Postmarked 1911; SC.)

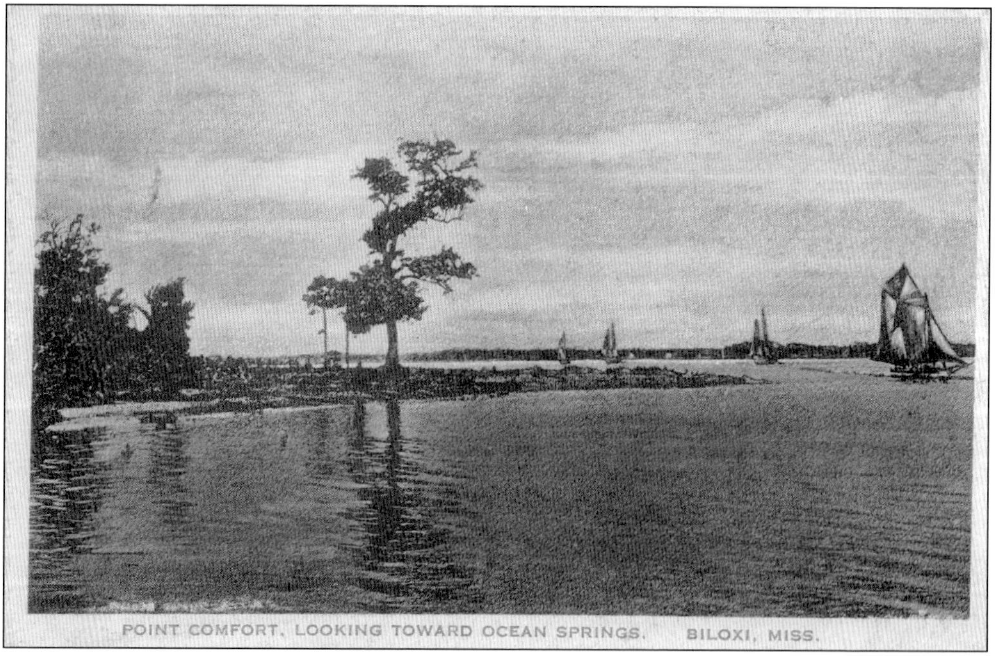

POINT COMFORT LOOKING TOWARDS OCEAN SPRINGS; C. 1915. This area of Back Bay east of Oak Street and north of the railroad tracks was known as Point Comfort around the turn of the 20th century. Sailing white-wing schooners, shown here near the resort grounds, were popular then. The area also featured summer rental cottages, picnic grounds, dance facilities, horseback riding, and open-air festivals. (Not Mailed; BL.)

Five

Where We Worshipped, Lived, and Shopped

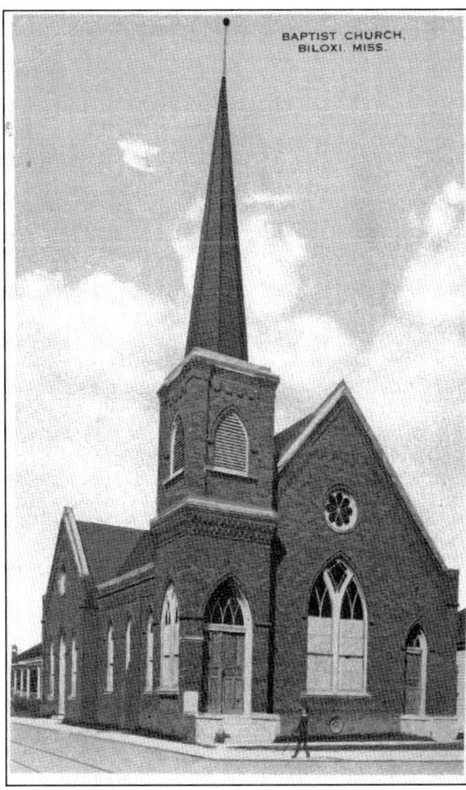

Baptist Church, c. 1920. People primarily shop and worship where they live, and Biloxi is no exception. Old Pass Christian Road, Howard Avenue, Reynoir Street, Lameuse Street, Main Street, the railroad, and the beach were, and still are, the main thoroughfares of Biloxi. This postcard shows the Baptist church, located on the corner of Washington and Lameuse Streets, which served the congregation from 1900 until 1924. (Not Mailed; SC.)

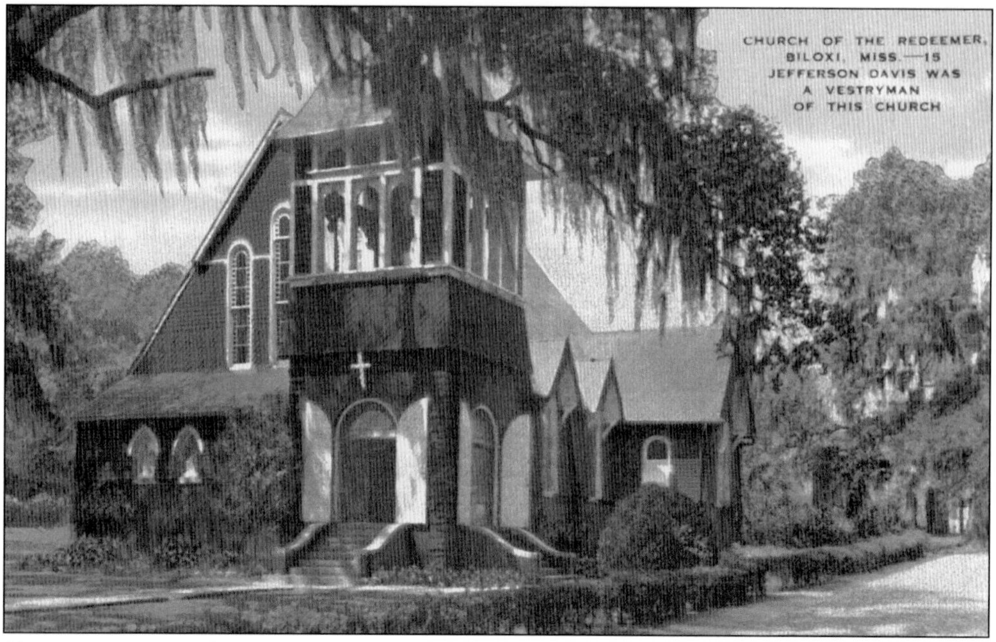

CHURCH OF THE REDEEMER, C. 1940. This Episcopal church was constructed in the early 1890s on property given to the parish by Harry T. Howard, a prominent local philanthropist (for whom Howard Avenue is named). Once construction of the church was completed, the former church was moved northward and converted into a parish hall. This church was destroyed by Hurricane Camille in 1969, and the parish hall became the church again. (Not Mailed; SC.)

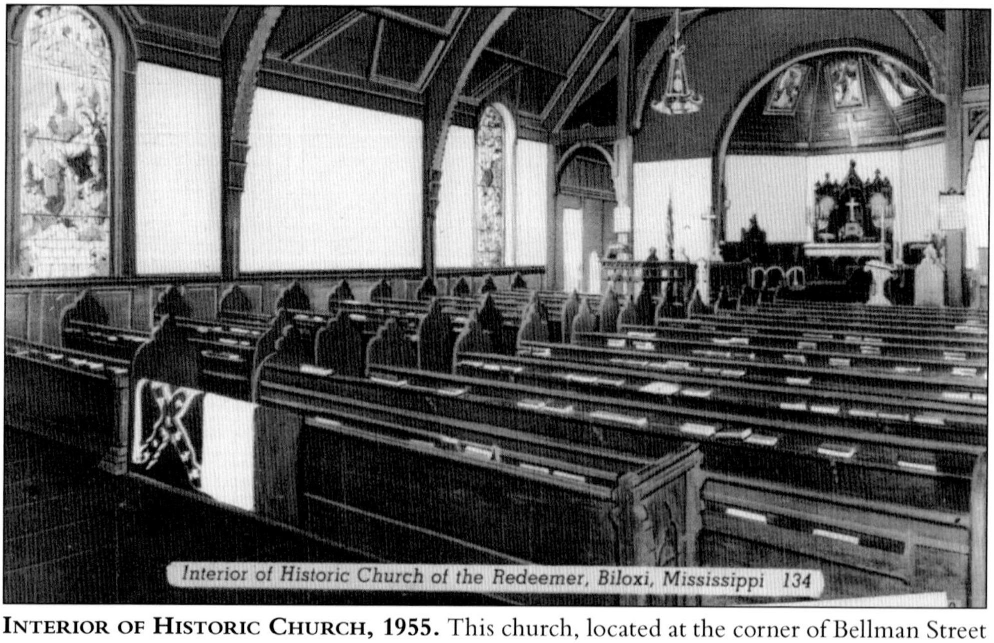

INTERIOR OF HISTORIC CHURCH, 1955. This church, located at the corner of Bellman Street and Beach Boulevard, was the home church of Jefferson Davis, president of the Confederacy. This interior view shows the flag-draped pew, one of the memorials in the church to Davis and his family. It was rebuilt after 1969, destroyed again by Hurricane Katrina in 2005, and is now located north of the bay. (Postmarked 1955; SC.)

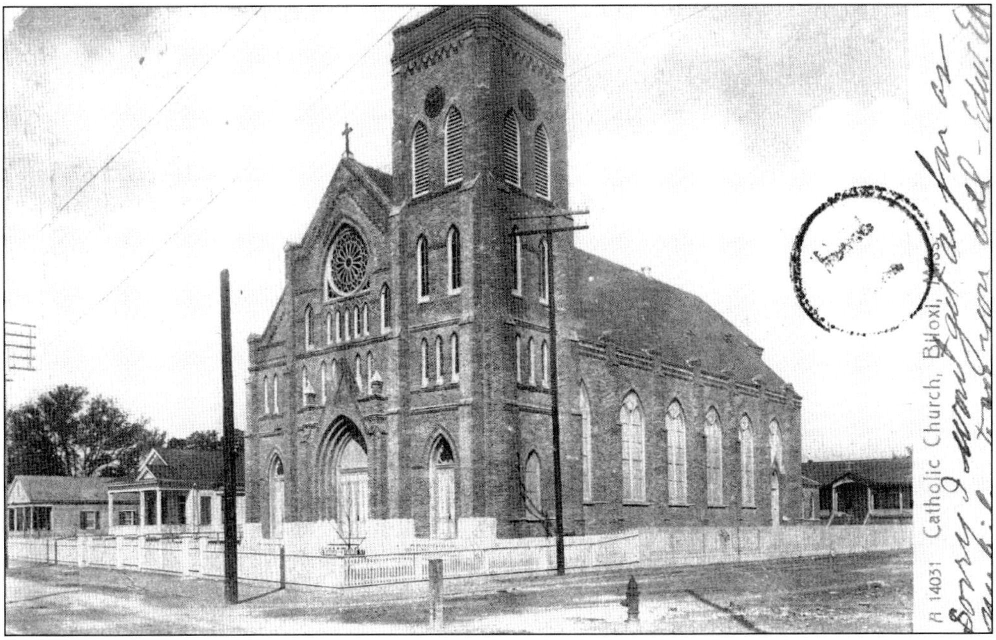

CHURCH OF THE NATIVITY, 1908. The third actual church building (shown) was constructed in 1902, after the fire of 1900 destroyed most of downtown Biloxi. The parish at Nativity was established in 1843, and the first church building was severely damaged in the hurricane of 1869. The current Cathedral of the Nativity of the Blessed Virgin Mary serves the Catholic Diocese of Biloxi as its cathedral. (Postmarked 1909; SC.)

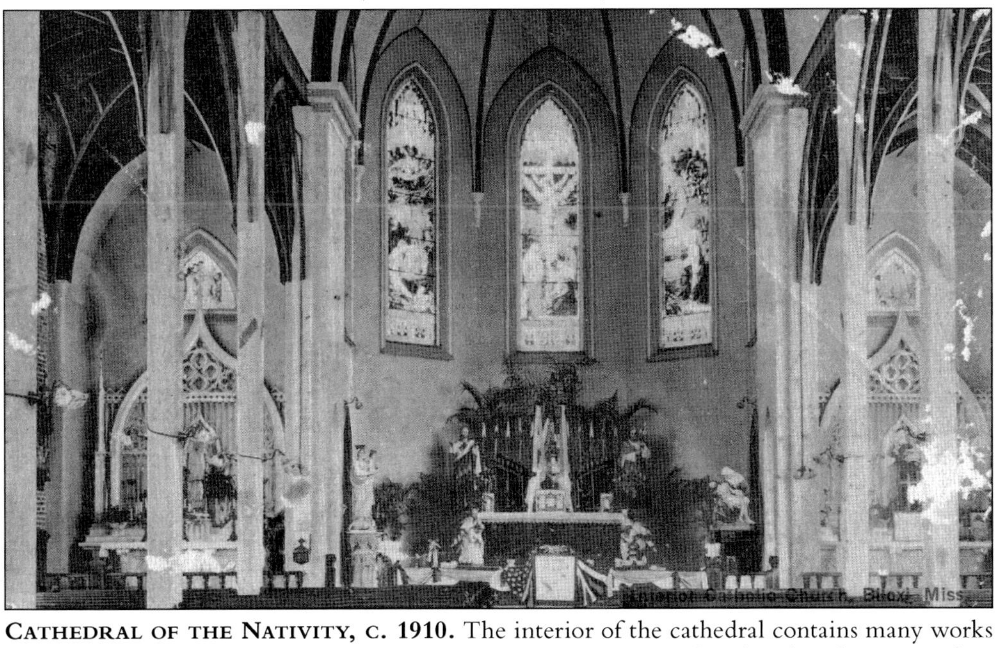

CATHEDRAL OF THE NATIVITY, C. 1910. The interior of the cathedral contains many works of art and artisans. Twenty-four stained-glass windows adorn the church. The story of 30 Keesler airmen laying a new floor in the church overnight in 1942 is one of many. The three Italian marble altars were installed in 1943, and the Seth Thomas clock in the bell tower was electrified in 1959. (Not Mailed; BL.)

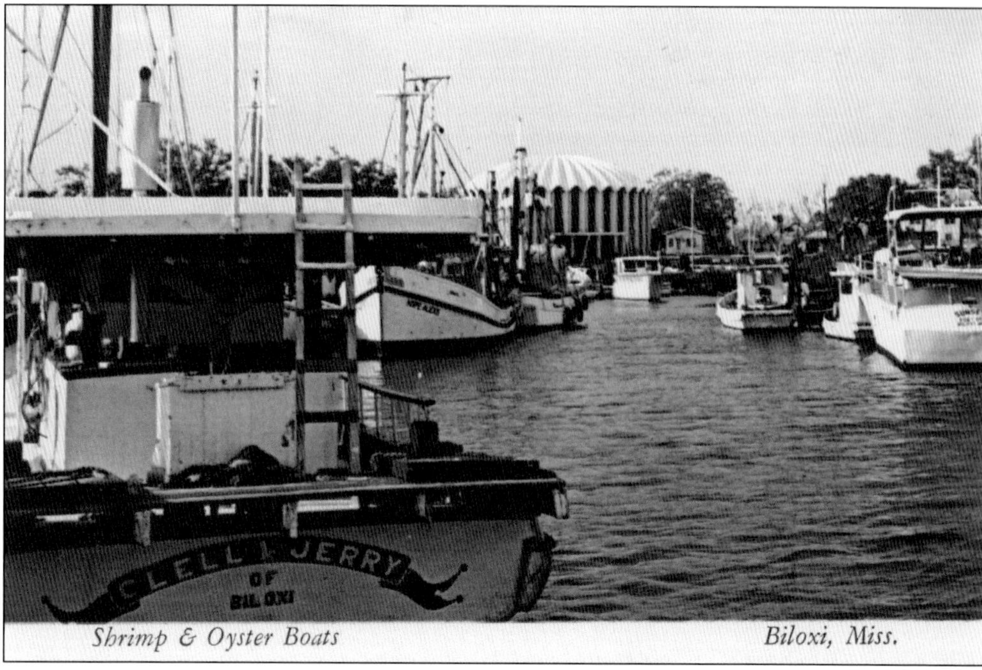

St. Michael's Church and Seafood Industry, Mid-1960s. The church, seafood factories, boats, and workers went hand-in-hand in the building of Point Cadet in the 20th century. Established in 1907 as a mission church, the parish was started in 1917. The church, rectory, nun's convent, elementary school, Holy Angels Nursery, and O'Hanlon Recreation Center were the hub of life for the multiethnic seafood capital in East Biloxi. (Not Mailed; SC.)

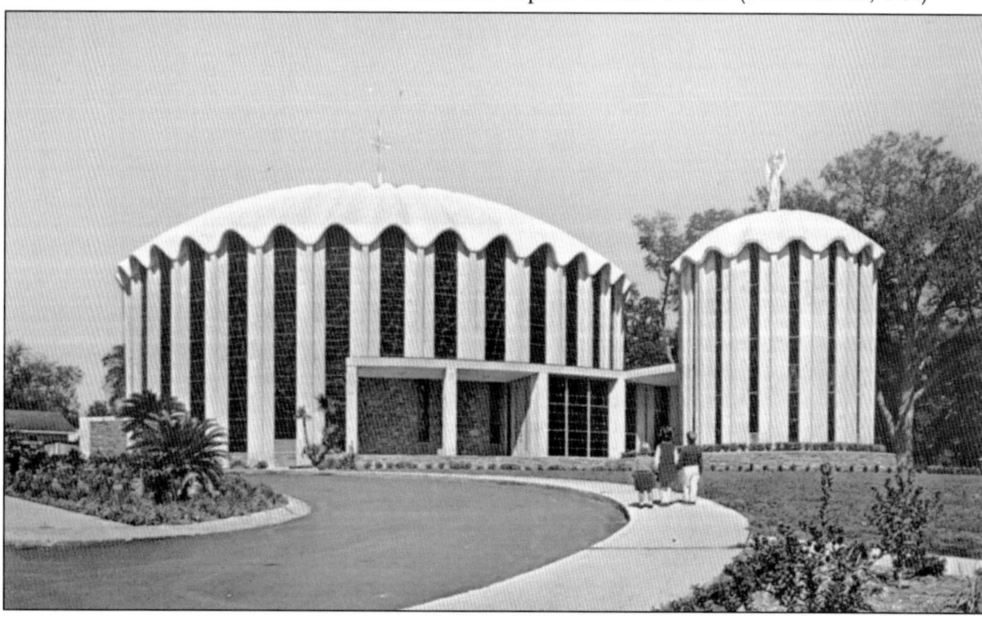

St. Michael's Church, Mid-1960s. The fisherman's church, with its scalloped shell roof, stands as a symbol of perseverance to the devout Catholic families of St. Michael's Parish. Hurricanes Camille, in 1969, and Katrina, in 2005, ravaged the church and the surrounding neighborhoods, but the church still stands, and the parishioners rebuilt. (Not Mailed; SC.)

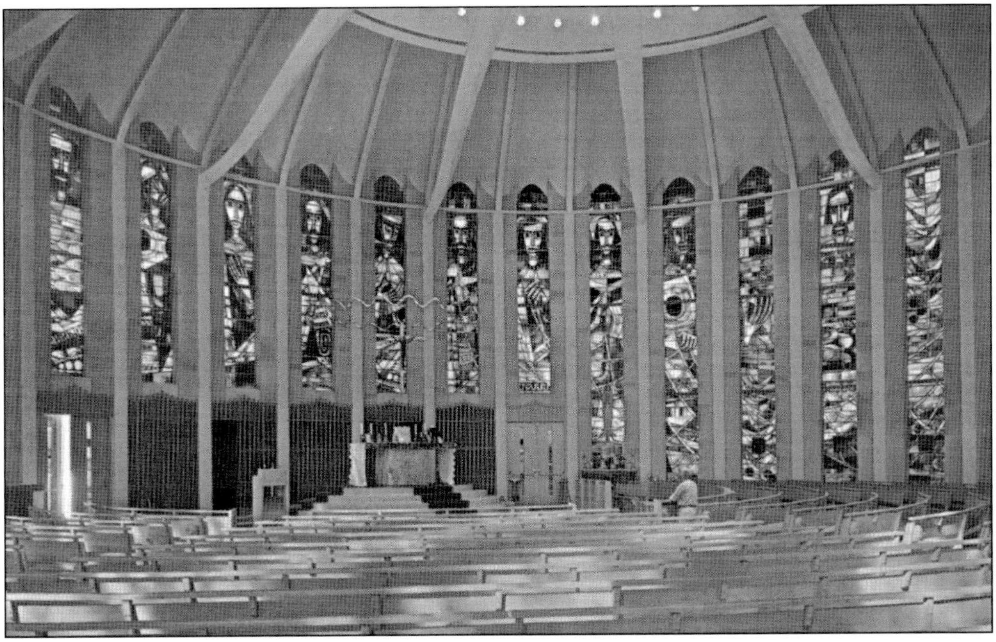

INTERIOR, ST. MICHAEL'S CHURCH, C. 1975. A bronze crucifix and halo suspended above the main altar serve as the focal point in this round church. However, the beautiful floor-to-ceiling stained-glass windows, featuring the 12 figures of the apostles gathering their nets, are awe-inspiring to parishioners and visitors alike. Catching the sunlight, the windows are truly a sight to behold. (Not Mailed; BL.)

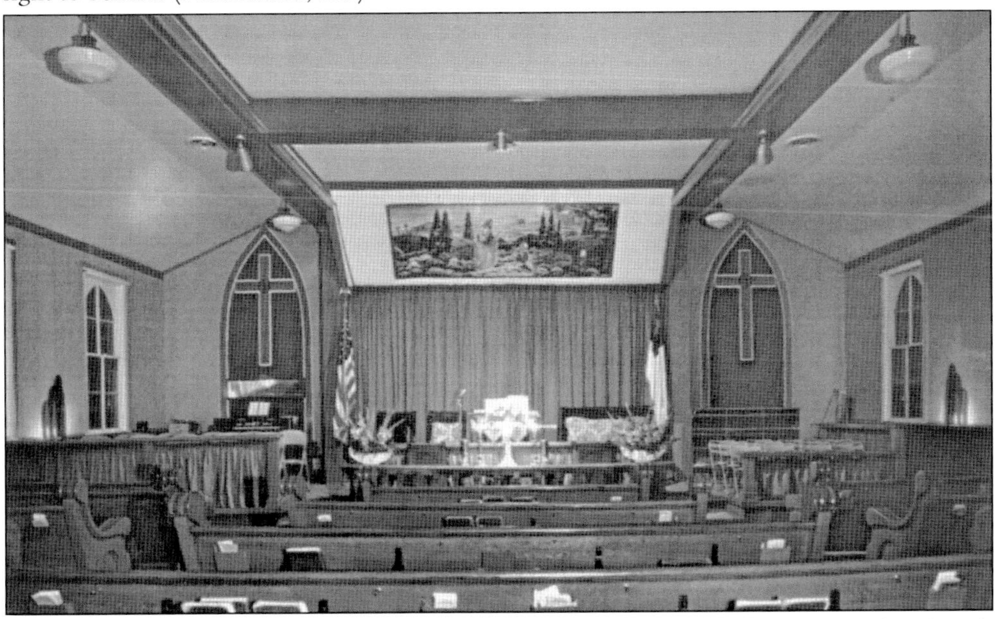

EAST END METHODIST CHURCH, C. 1975. This postcard shows the sanctuary lined with long wooden pews. The church was located at 1015 East Howard Avenue, across the street from Dukate Elementary School. A large painting of Christ was featured over the altar, and crosses adorned the large cathedral-shaped windows above the choir lofts, which included a piano and organ. (Not Mailed; SC.)

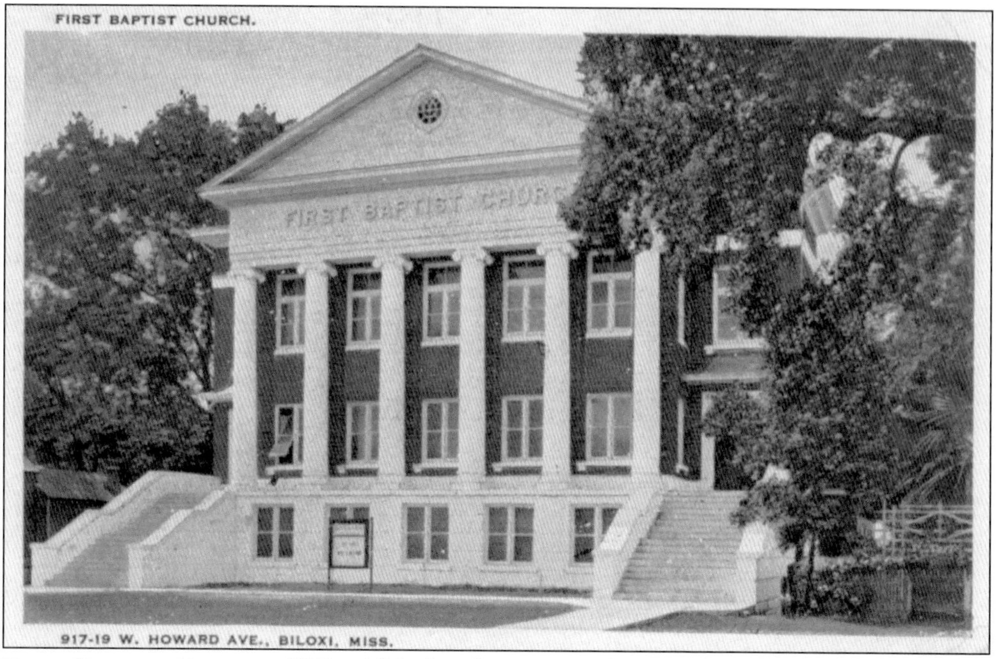

FIRST BAPTIST CHURCH, 1950S. This church was erected at 917 Howard Avenue and worship began there on August 23, 1924. It was a modern church building with 56 rooms and a seating capacity of 1,200 in the main auditorium. Worship services continued there for 76 years, when the property was sold and a much larger church was built in North Biloxi to accommodate the increased membership. (Not Mailed; SC.)

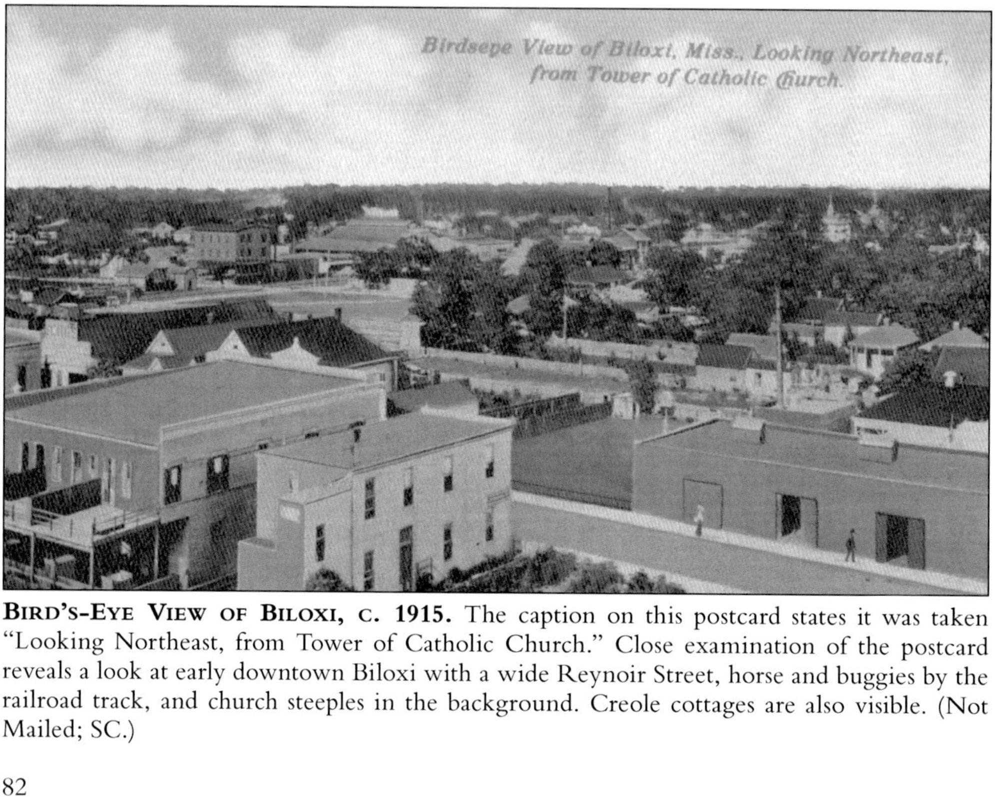

BIRD'S-EYE VIEW OF BILOXI, C. 1915. The caption on this postcard states it was taken "Looking Northeast, from Tower of Catholic Church." Close examination of the postcard reveals a look at early downtown Biloxi with a wide Reynoir Street, horse and buggies by the railroad track, and church steeples in the background. Creole cottages are also visible. (Not Mailed; SC.)

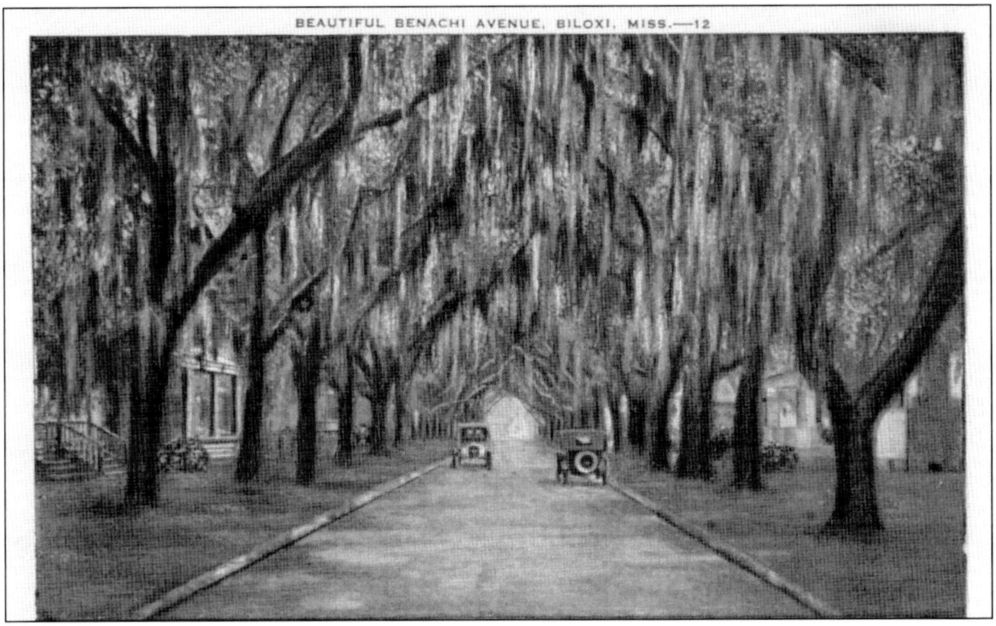

BENACHI AVENUE, 1930S. These moss-draped live oaks are believed to have originally lined a path to the summer home of N.M. Benachi, consul of Greece at New Orleans and founder of the Greek Orthodox Church in the western hemisphere in 1864. Many postcards show a white-winged schooner sailing along east of the lighthouse and framed through this cathedral-shaped archway between Howard Avenue and the beach. (Not Mailed; BL.)

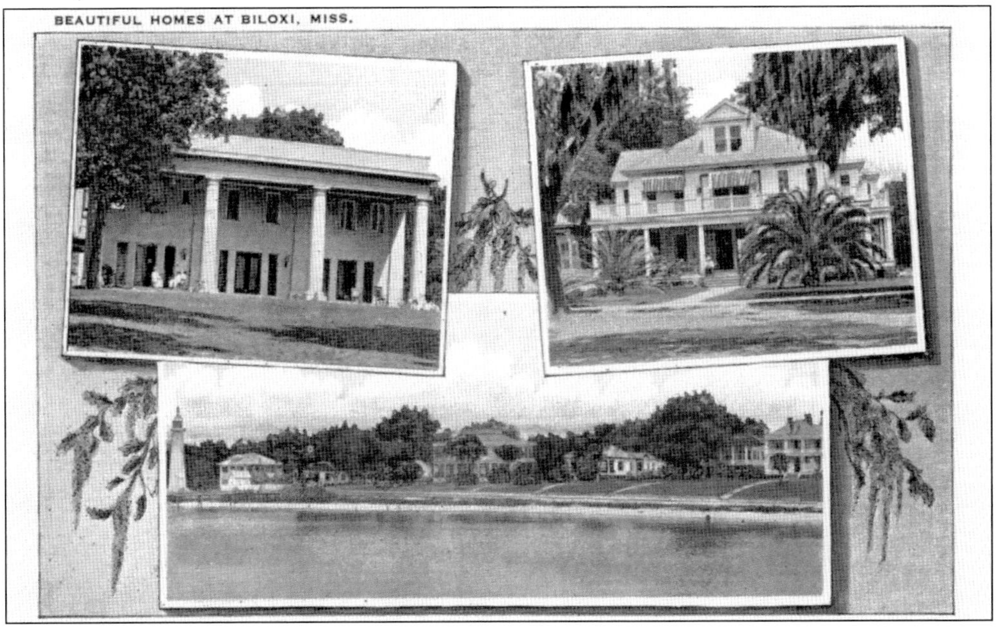

HOMES AT BILOXI, C. 1920. This multi-view postcard depicts the beautiful beach houses in historic Biloxi. The upper left view depicts a columned structure in West Biloxi, and the view to the right is of a house with palm trees and moss-covered oak on the point. The view at bottom captures the lighthouse, the beach without a seawall, and the Maloney-Dantzler House along the beach road. (Postmarked 1929; BL.)

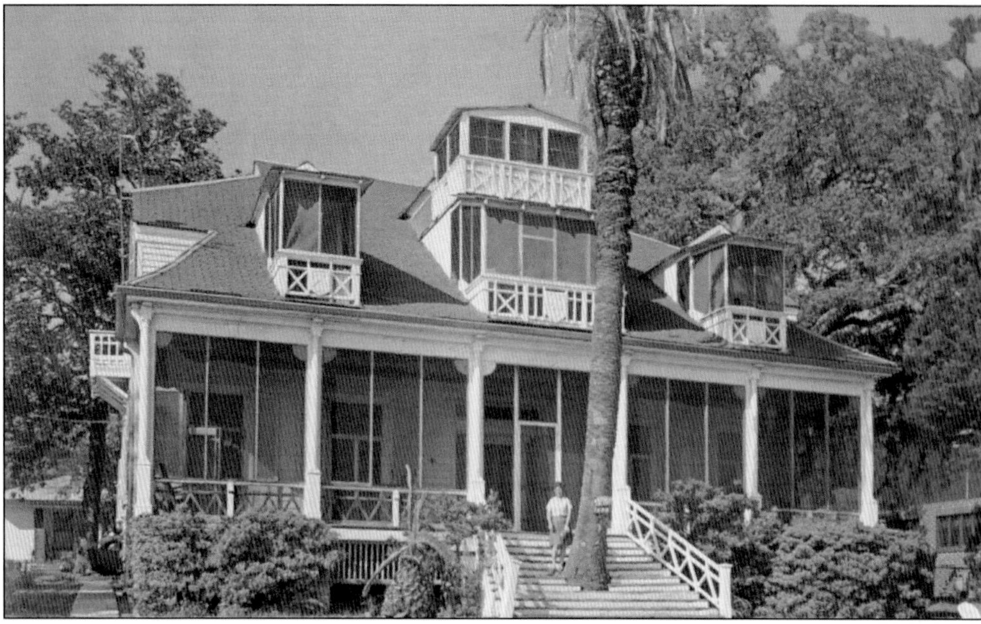

THE FATHER RYAN HOUSE, 1960S. Built in 1841, this charming former home of Fr. Abram Ryan, soldier, priest, and poet laureate of the Confederacy, was located at 1196 Beach Boulevard, where he wrote "Sea Rest" and "Sea Reverie." The National Historic Landmark, known for a palm tree growing through the front steps, was a bed-and-breakfast prior to complete destruction during Hurricane Katrina in 2005. (Hand Stamped 1968; SC.)

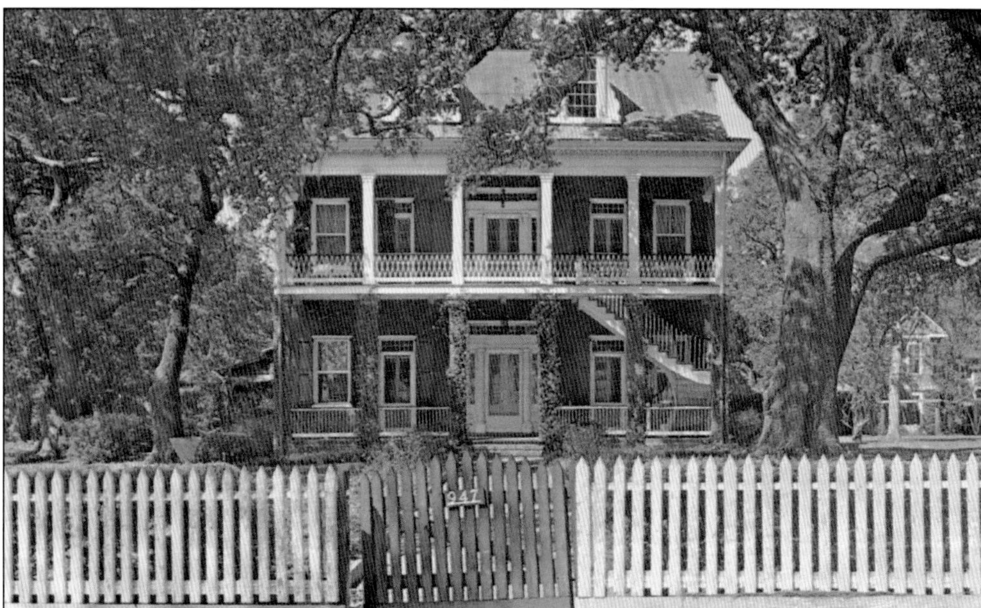

TULLIS-TOLEDANO MANOR, 1966. This charming example of antebellum French architecture was noted for its finely executed doorways and outside stairway. The bricks for the building were made using slave labor with clay ferried from Back Bay. The two-story slave quarters and outside kitchen were located behind the main building. Years later, a swimming pool was built on the eastern side of this East Beach property. (Not Mailed; BL.)

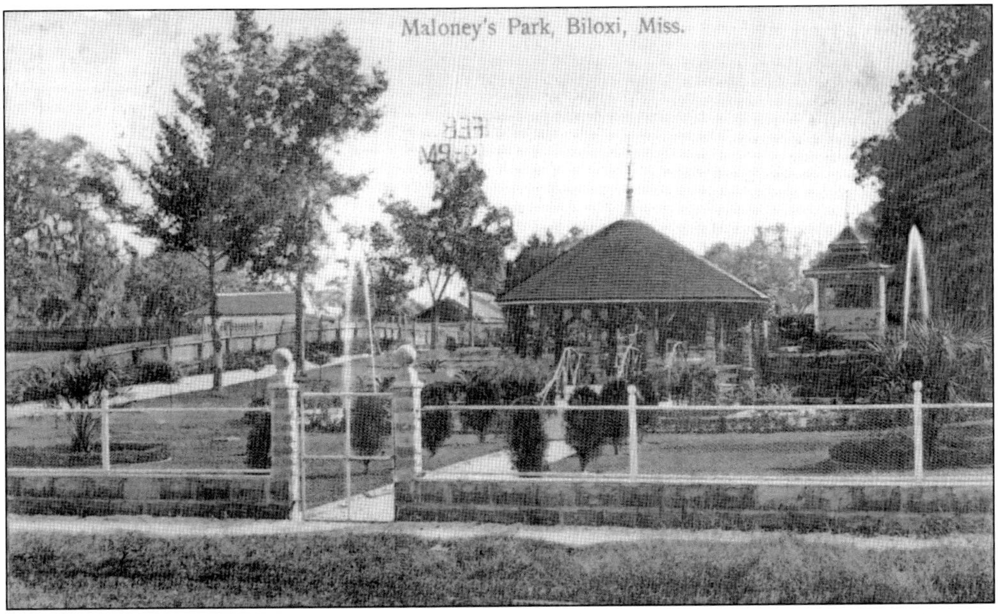

E.C. MALONEY RESIDENCE, 1909. This gazebo and pond were part of the rear yard of the Maloney family home, located on the beach east of the lighthouse. It later became known as the Dantzler House and Maloney Park. The rear yard is the current site of the Nativity BVM Elementary School. The house was built in 1849 and finally met its match with Hurricane Katrina in 2005. (Postmarked 1910; SC.)

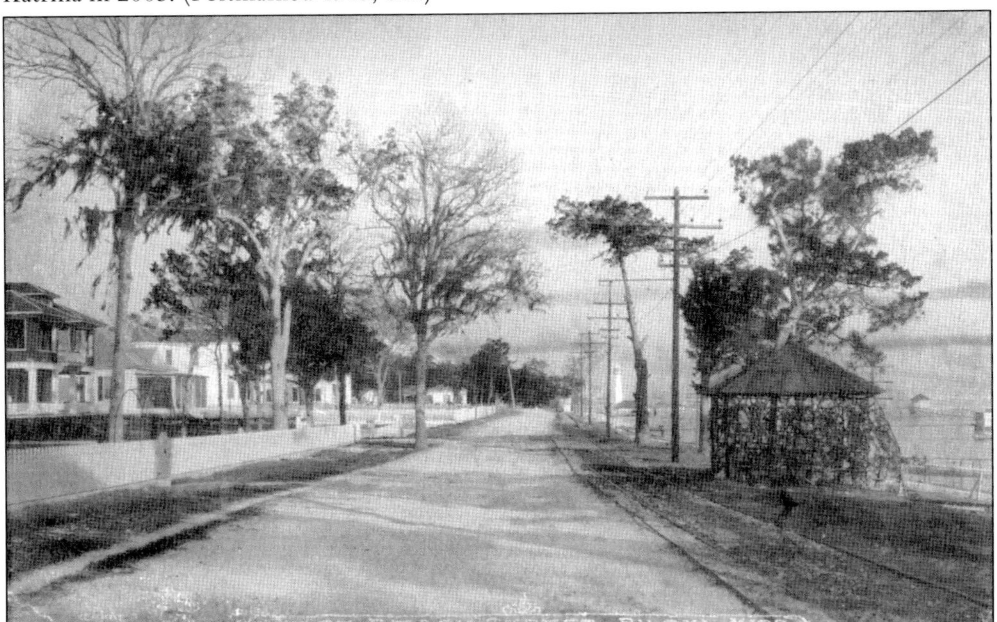

WEST BEACH BOULEVARD, C. 1908. This view of West Beach Boulevard faces the lighthouse to the east, showing beach road in the early 20th century. The photograph highlights the stately residences with their picket fences. The postcard also depicts the shell road with trolley tracks, utility lines, and a fine, covered gazebo located south of the thoroughfare. (Postmarked 1908; BL.)

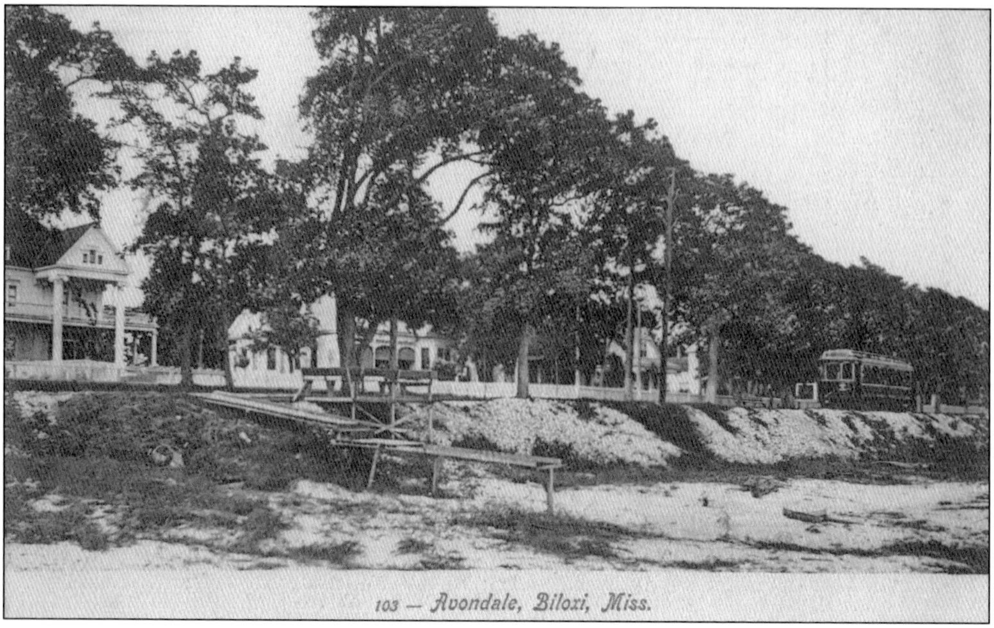

AVONDALE, C. 1906. The trolley line, short pier, beachfront seating area, and bluff without a seawall are pictured in this postcard of the fashionable beachfront subdivision in the late 19th century. Located just west of White Avenue, between the beach and the railroad, this high-fashion neighborhood continued westward to the Seashore Campgrounds. Frequent garden parties, luncheons, and dinner parties were hosted here. (Not Mailed; SC.)

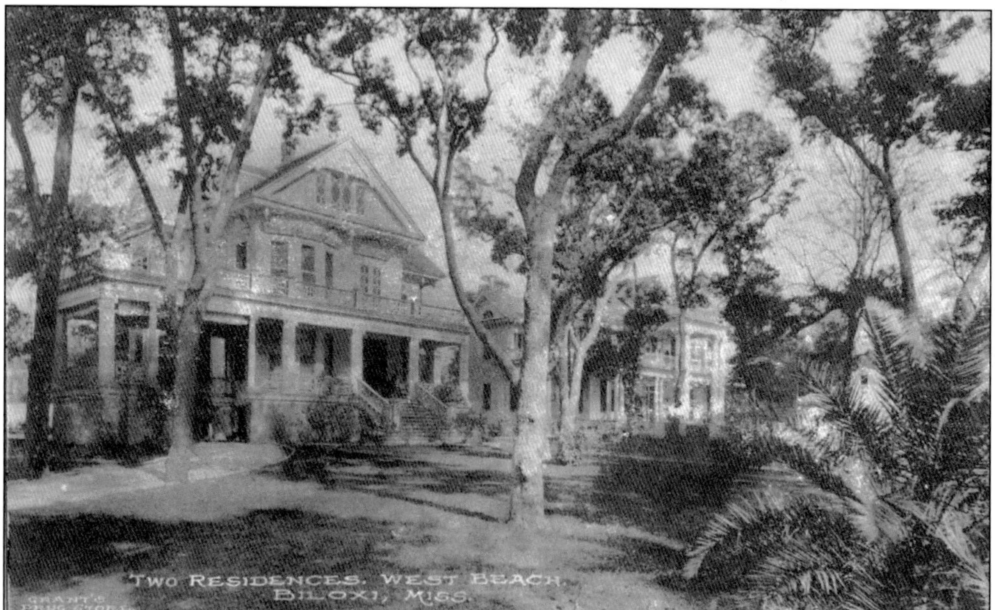

TWO WEST BEACH RESIDENCES, C. 1910. This early postcard published by Grants Drug Store shows two of the stately mansions located along West Beach Boulevard. The multistory structures featured elevated first floors, grand porches, and massive columns. Palm trees, flowering plants, and shrubs were features on these Victorian-era lawns. The postcard also depicts towering live oak trees early in their development. (Illegible Postmark; SC.)

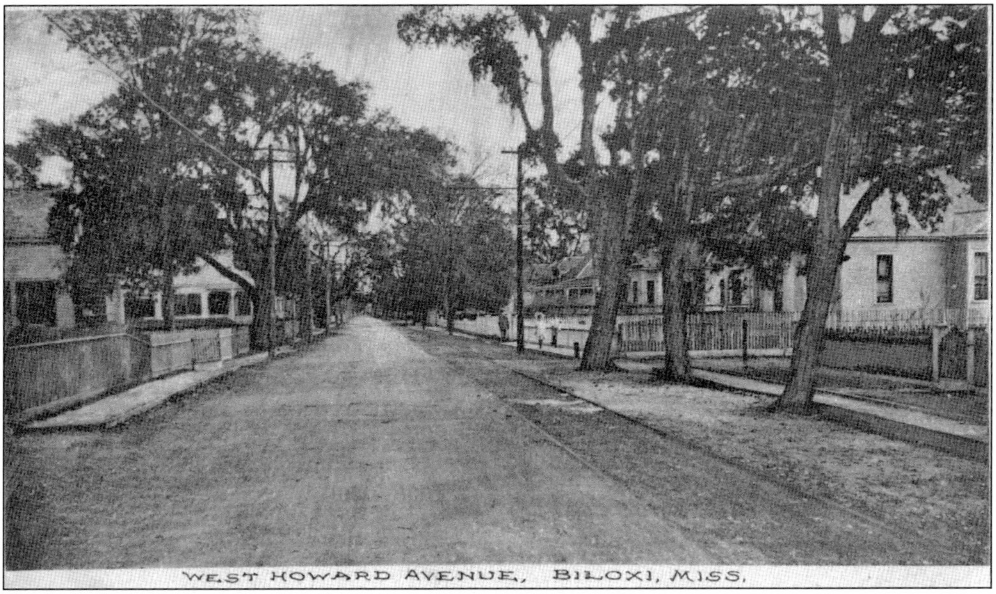

West Howard Avenue, c. 1908. The view of this street, formerly known as the Old Pass Christian Road, features a neatly lined shell thoroughfare with pedestrians strolling along the sidewalk. The trolley tracks, located near the roadway, are very apparent in this photograph. Numerous Biloxi Creole cottages are shown on the picture postcard with their fenced-in and well-manicured lawns. (Postmarked 1908; SC.)

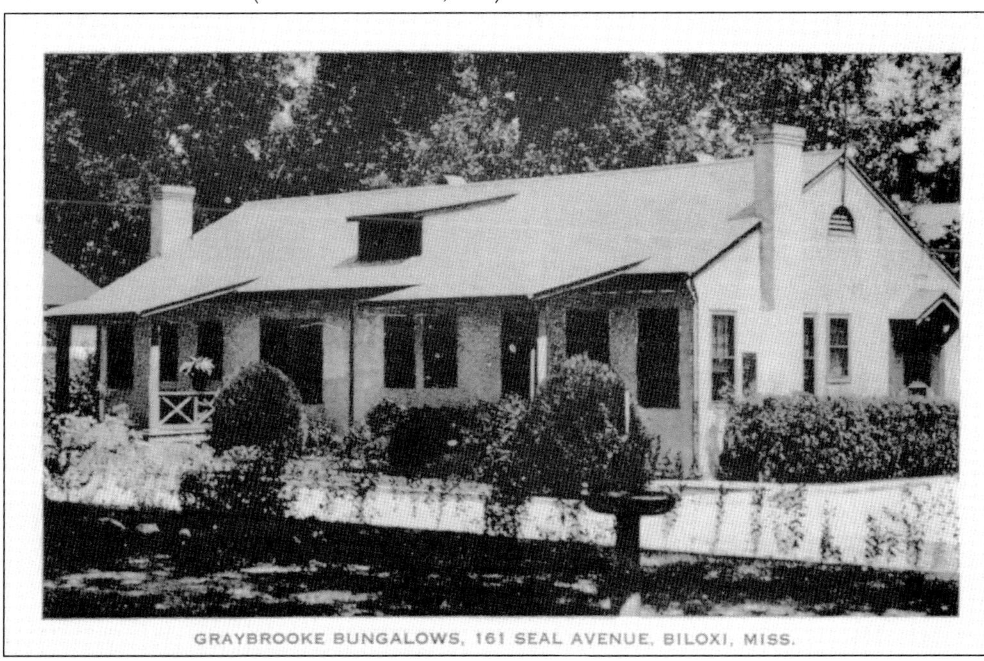

Graybrooke Bungalows, c. 1935. The rental cottages located on the W.G. Grayson property at 161 Seal Avenue offered their residents "every comfort you could wish for." The bungalows were furnished with furniture of charm and distinction, innerspring mattresses, steam heat, deep carpet, and fans in every room. The property, located a half block from the beach, had a Biloxi phone number of 256. (Not Mailed; SC.)

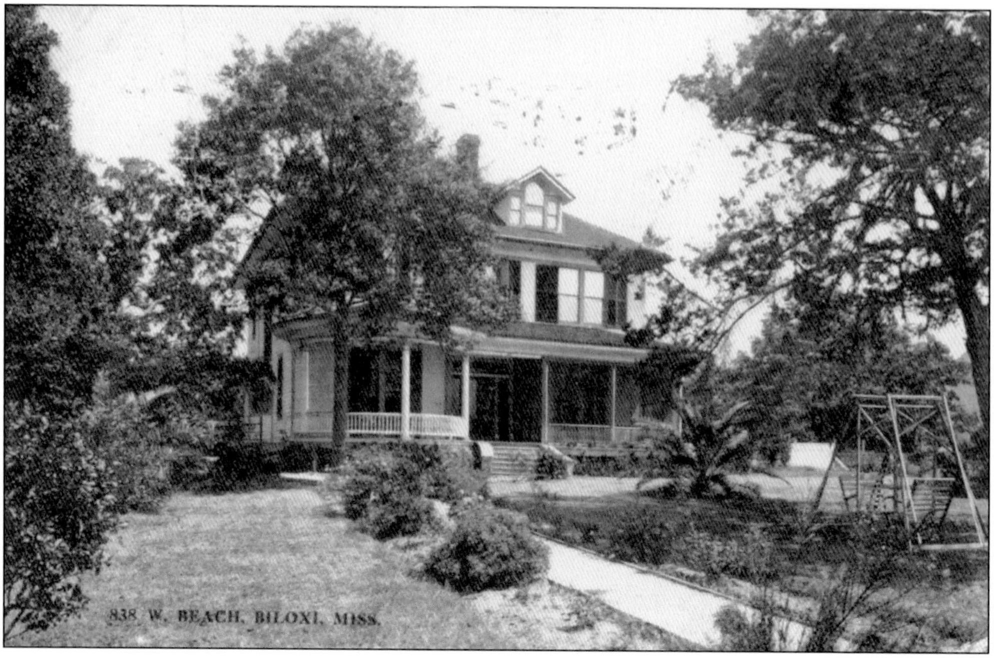

West Beach Residence, c. 1909. This beachfront home, located in the Hopkins Boulevard/ Seal Avenue area of the thoroughfare, features a raised, multistory dwelling with a massive front porch. Note the vegetation and palm trees of the era and the swing glider in the front yard. A concrete walkway leads from the house to the beach road. (Postmarked 1909; SC.)

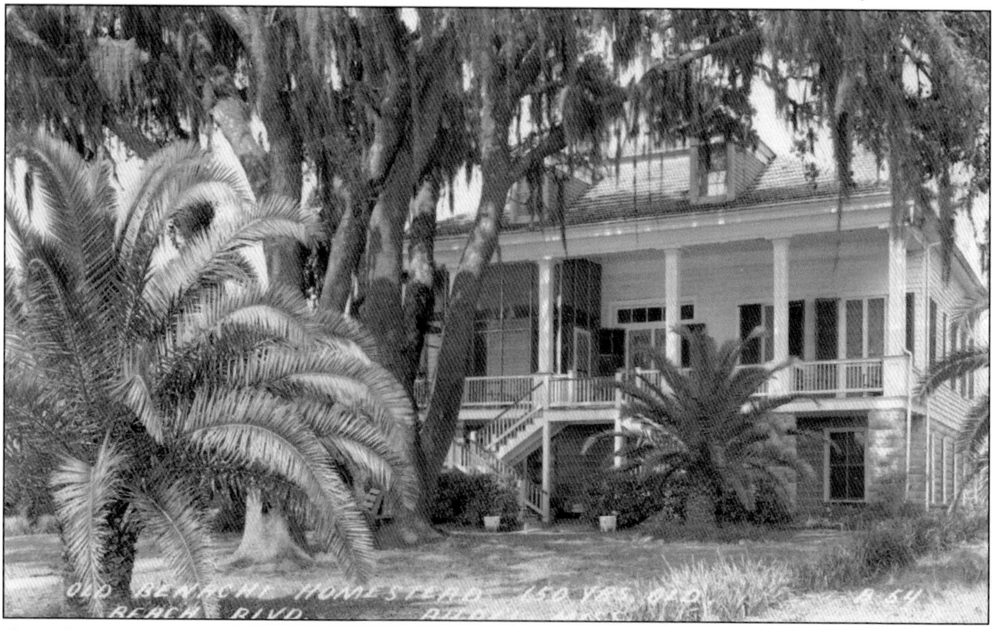

Old Benachi Homestead, c. 1940. The Benachi Homestead was located on a strip of land roughly 230 feet wide that stretched from the beach to the bay. At the time of this postcard, the house was located west of the present-day Benachi Avenue and east of the lighthouse. Many postcards have depicted Benachi Avenue as the avenue of the oaks because many live oaks lined the street. (Not Mailed; SC.)

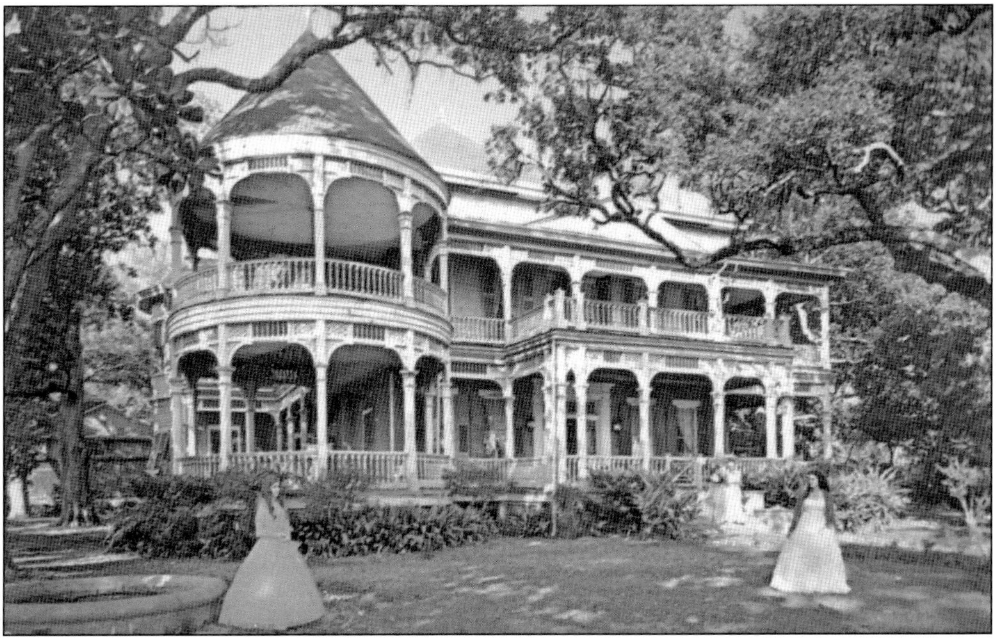

HOUSE OF TREASURE, C. 1960S. Located on the southeast corner of Bellman Street and the beach, this spacious, Victorian-style home was the residence of one of Biloxi's greatest benefactors, Charles T. Howard (Howard Avenue). He was one of the founders of the Louisiana Lottery, and his family contributed much to the city of Biloxi for construction and improvements around the turn of the 20th century. (Not Mailed; SC.)

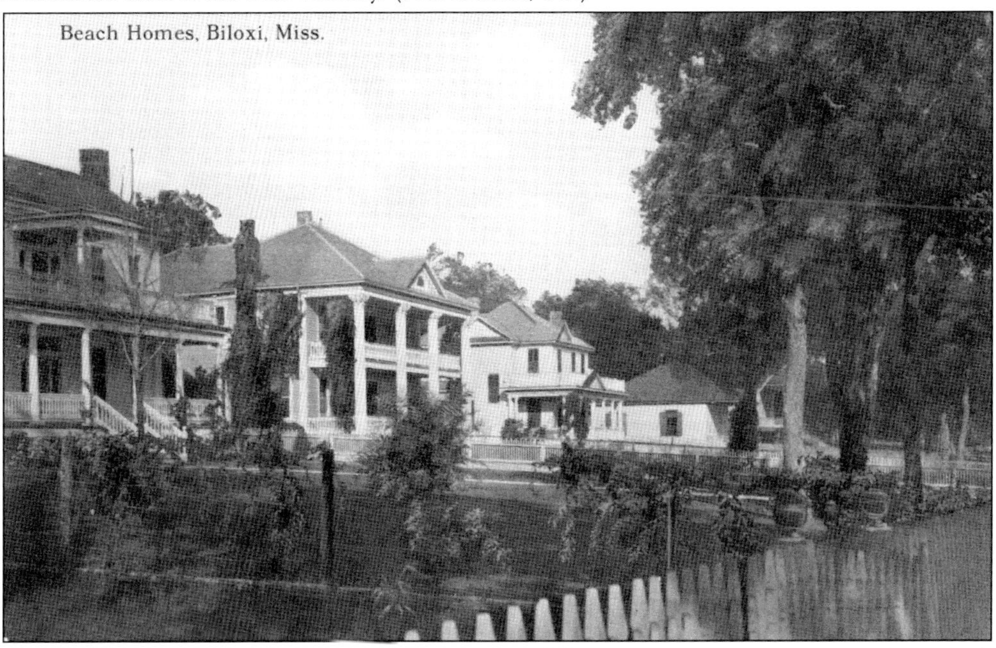

BEACH HOMES, C. 1912. This typical view of beachfront homes in the early 1900s features all of the normal amenities of shorefront properties during that era. On this particular postcard, the author noted on February 20, "It has rained all the afternoon and spoiled the Mardi Gras." She also said that she "had hoped it would clear up for the night parade." (Postmarked 1912; SC.)

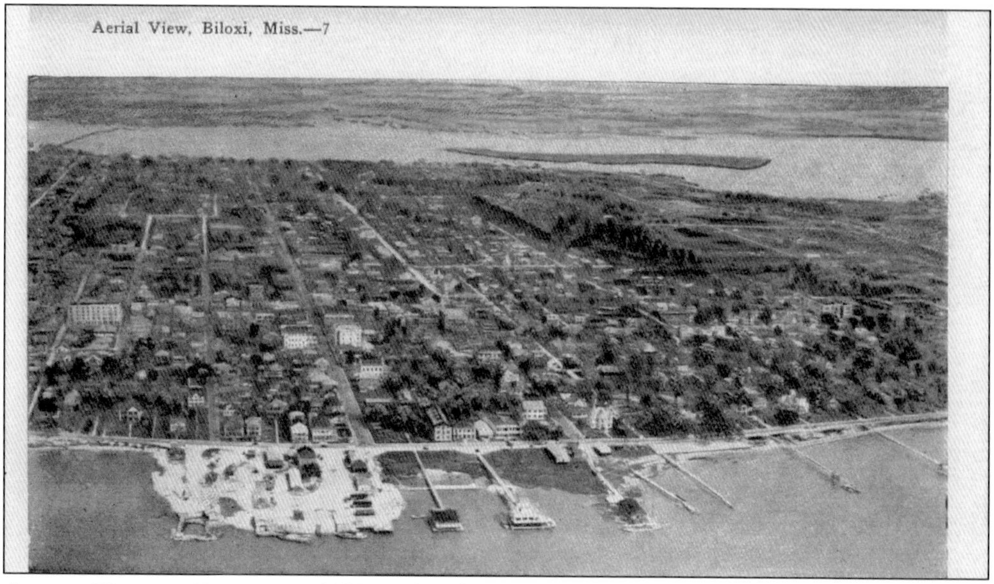

Aerial View of Biloxi, c. 1930. A close look at this postcard reveals several historical Biloxi landmarks. The shell pile was located west of Lameuse Street. The Government Building, library, and the Elks Lodge were all located on Lameuse Street. The Avelez Hotel, located on Howard Avenue, and the old city hall building, located at Main Street and Howard Avenue, are also featured on the postcard. (Not Mailed; SC.)

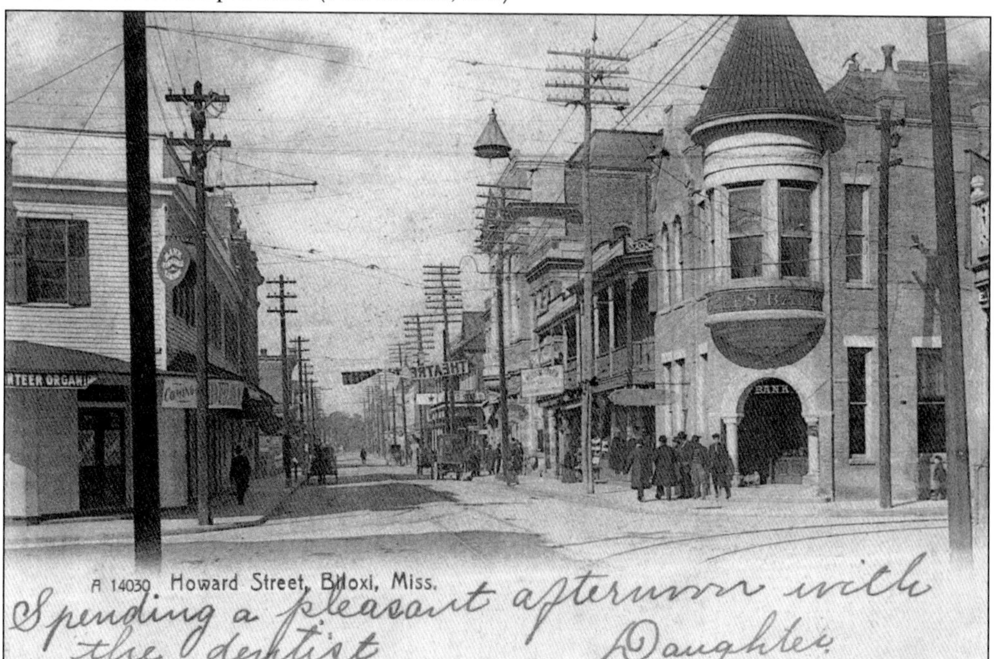

Howard Avenue, 1907. This vintage postcard shows Howard Avenue from the southeast corner of Lameuse Street, looking west. A closer look reveals a bank (People Bank), trolley tracks from Lameuse Street turning eastward on Howard Avenue, and a banner in front of the Dukate Theater that reads, "Theater Tonight." The hustle and bustle of pedestrians and horse-drawn carriages in the background complete the scene. (Postmarked 1907; SC.)

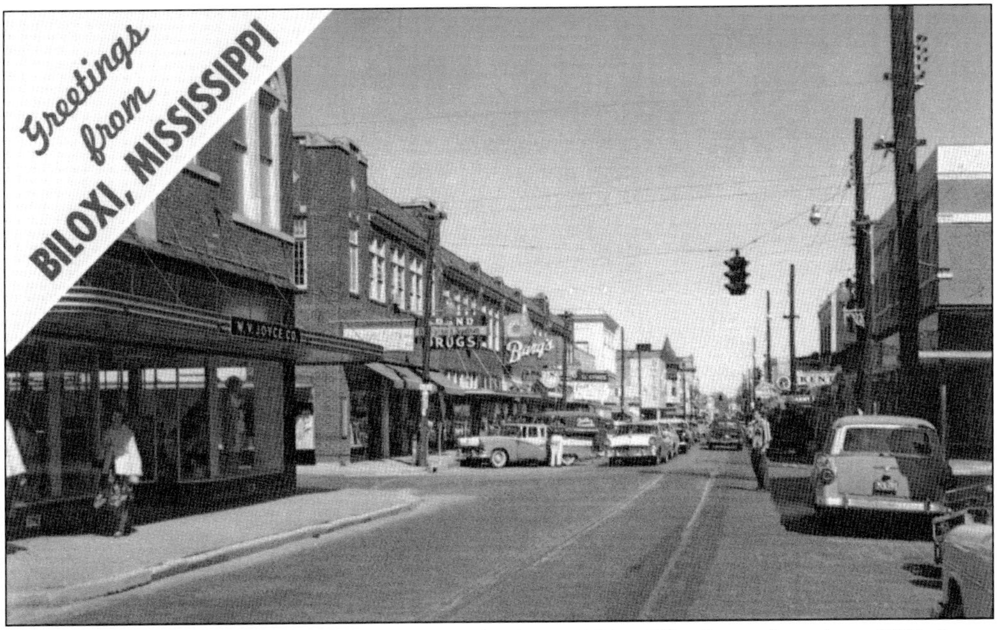

Greetings From Biloxi, c. 1956. In the late 1950s, Biloxi was hopping. W.V. Joyce Department Store anchored the corner of Howard Avenue and Reynoir Street. The Grand Drug Store and the Barq's were located on the north side, and Howard and Kent's (the Shop for Smart Gent's) was located on the south side. Traffic, parking, and pedestrians were all common problems of the day. (Not Mailed; BL.)

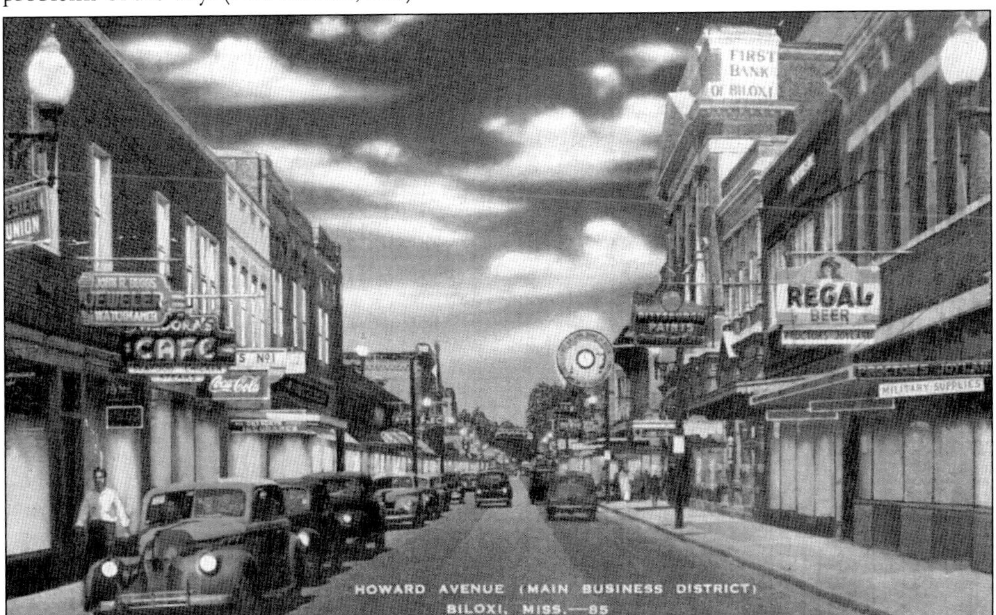

Main Business District, Early 1940s. Downtown Biloxi in the mid-20th century looked much different than it does today. Traffic, shops, bars, cafés, and businesses dotted every spot on the avenue. Street lighting allowed pedestrians and shoppers to stroll the thoroughfare from morning until early evening except on Thursday afternoon, when most all of the stores were closed. (Not Mailed; BL.)

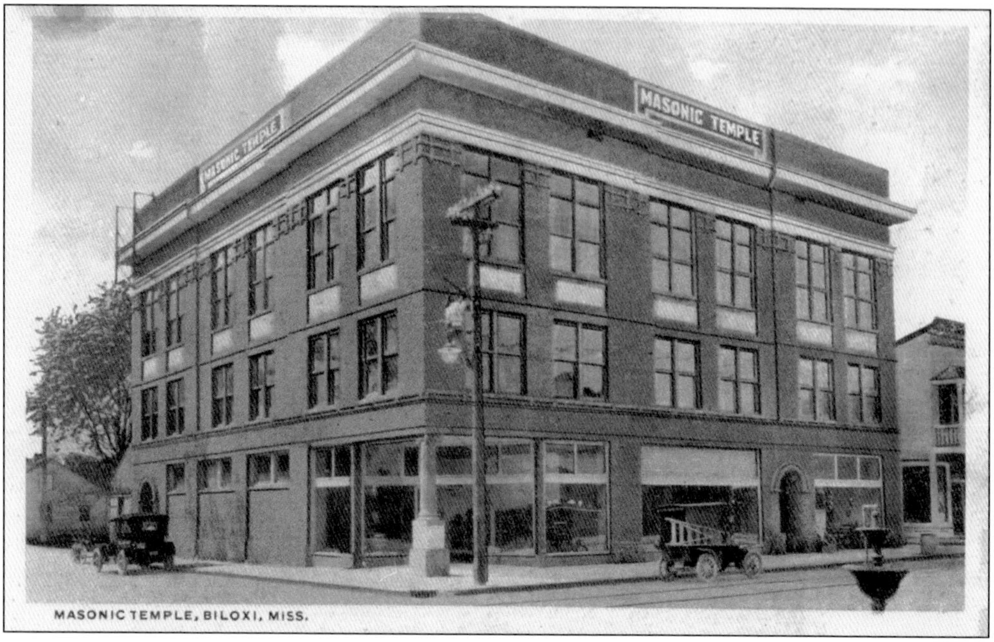

MASONIC TEMPLE MAGNOLIA LODGE NO. 120, 1913. On June 24, 1911, the cornerstone of the new temple was laid on Main Street and Howard Avenue. This structure, which was constructed by the labor of many of the lodge members, took two years to complete and all of the money they could raise. Most officers' stations and the other furniture were built by the local membership. (Not Mailed; SC.)

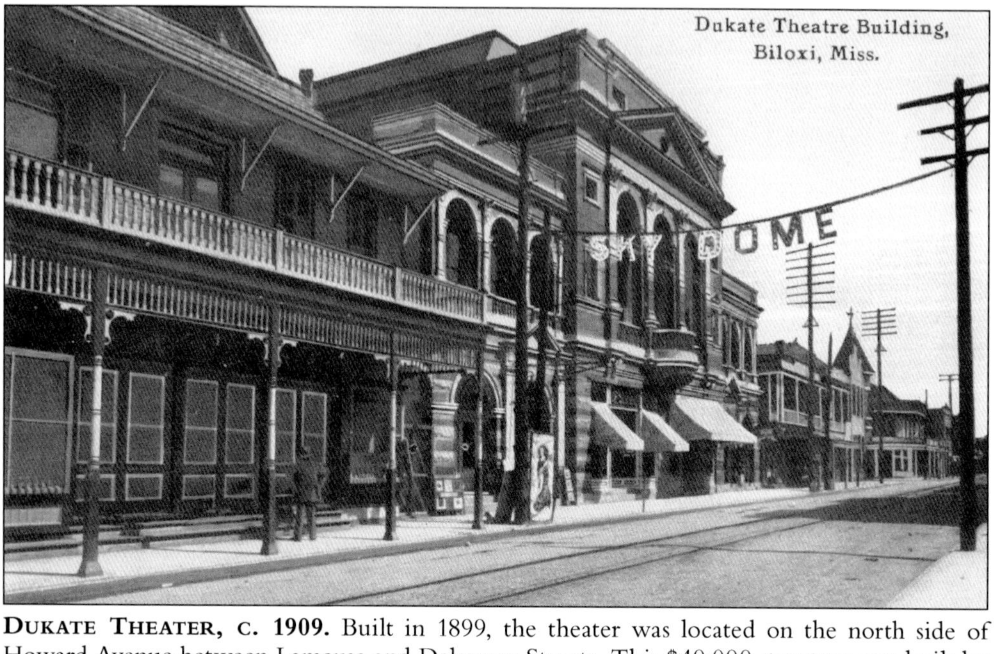

DUKATE THEATER, c. 1909. Built in 1899, the theater was located on the north side of Howard Avenue between Lameuse and Delauney Streets. This $40,000 structure was built by W.K.M. Dukate, one of the pioneers of the Biloxi seafood industry. This grand and elaborately decorated theater was home to many traveling theatrical troops until about 1916. The structure presently houses Bancorp South in Vieux Marche. (Not Mailed; SC.)

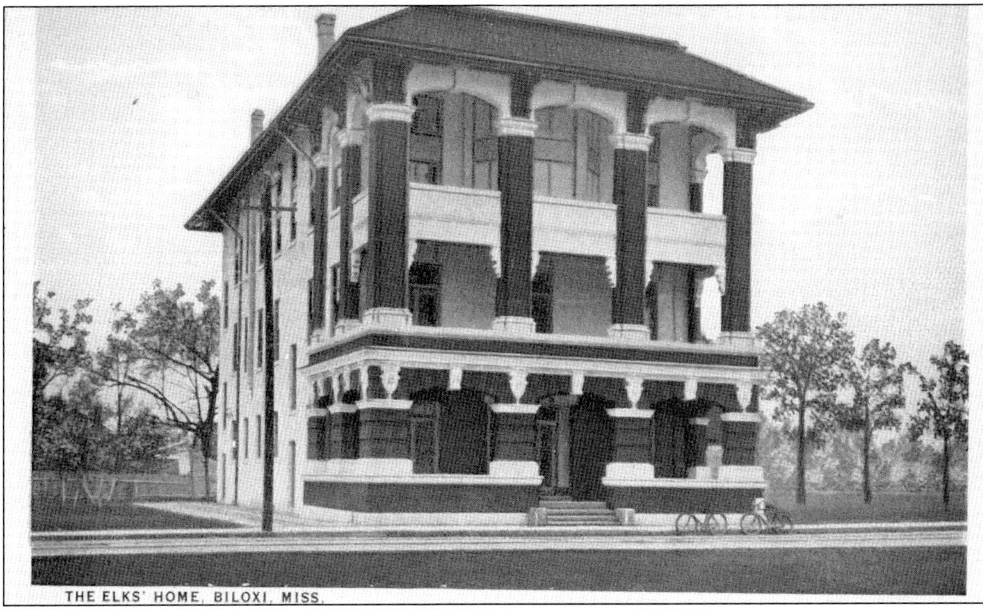

ELKS LODGE NO. 606, 1913. The Biloxi Elks home was built on the west side of Lameuse Street across from the Government Building (now Biloxi City Hall). The imposing structure also served other community organizations, and the massive third-floor ballroom was the setting for many carnival balls in the 1930s. The site was home to the Biloxi Library from the mid-1970s until Hurricane Katrina in 2005. (Not Mailed; SC.)

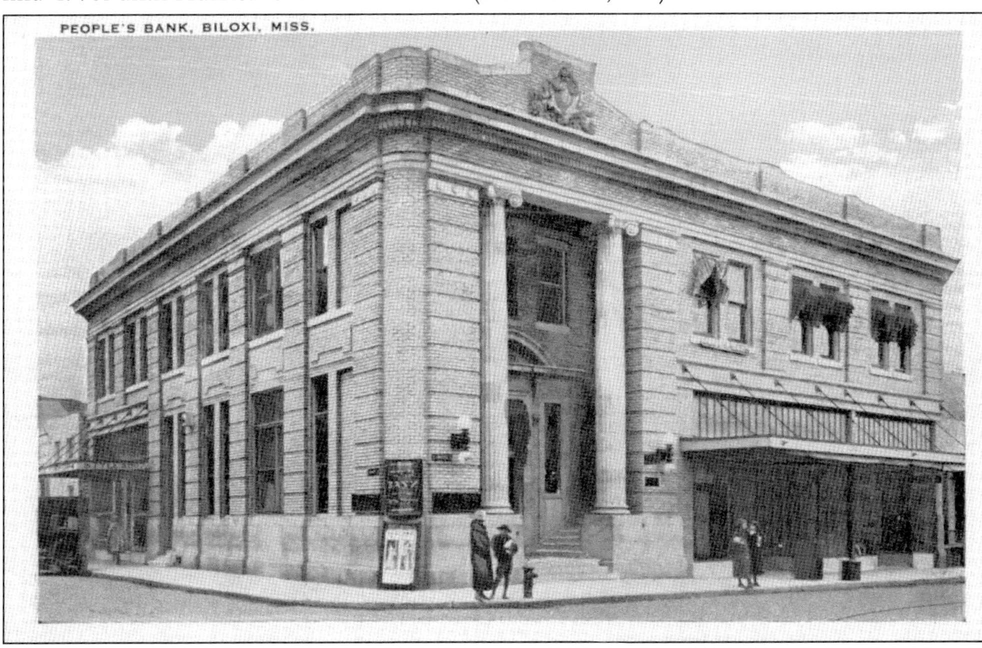

PEOPLE'S BANK, 1928. In the mid-1920s, People's Bank, having outgrown its facilities on the northwest corner of Howard Avenue and Lameuse Street, moved to a new building on the southeast corner of the same intersection. The bank's former location was occupied by Ellzey's Hardware. Both businesses serve as well-known landmarks to downtown Biloxi and remain in these locations today. (Not Mailed; SC.)

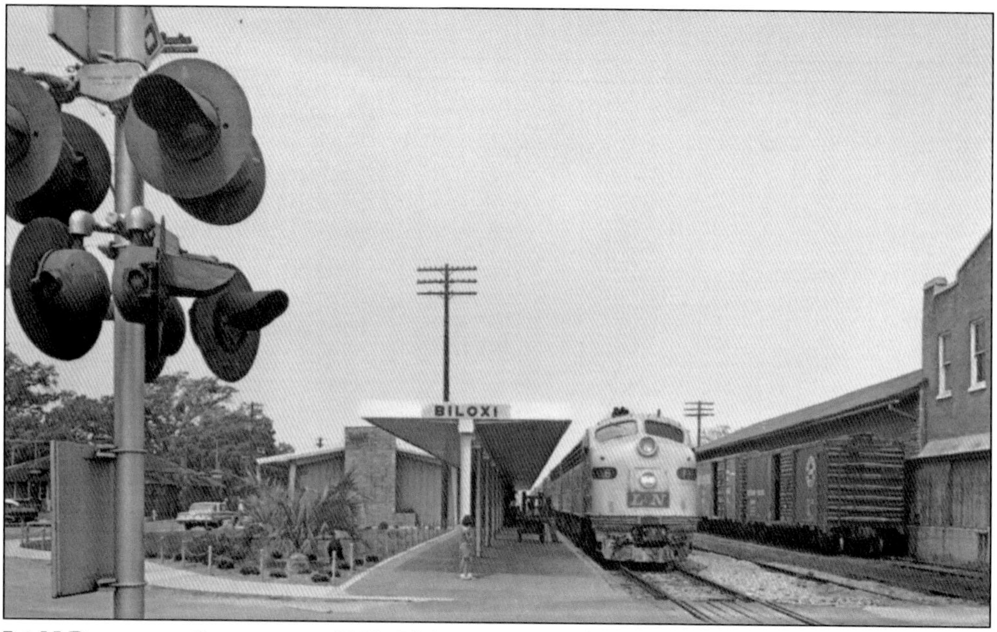

L&N Railroad Station, c. 1960. This great view of the Biloxi passenger and freight depots highlights the facilities located between Reynoir and Caillavet Streets. Established in the 1870s, these railways moved locals, tourists, military personnel, and seafood and other freight to and from the Gulf Coast. The train shown at the station was the Hummingbird, one of the fastest L&N passenger trains. (Not Mailed; SC.)

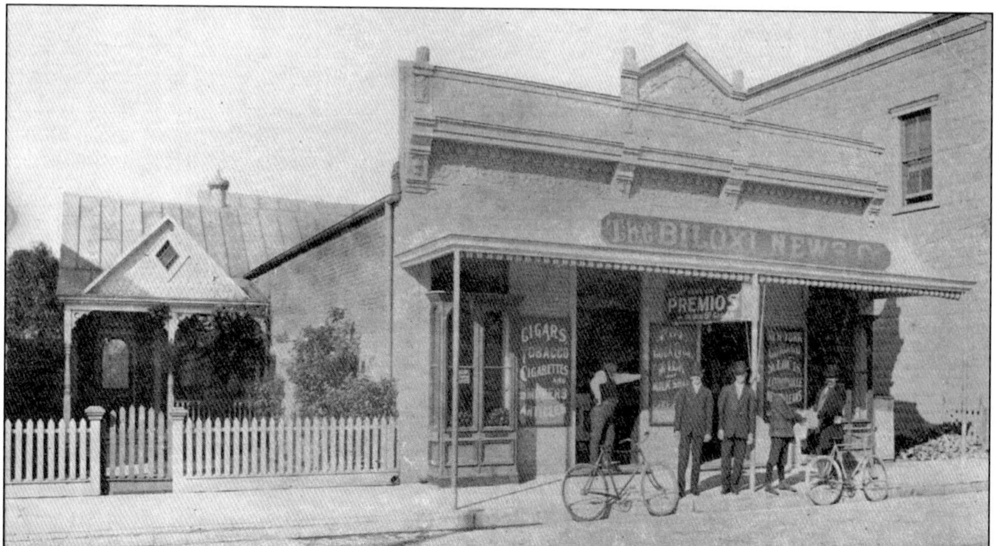

Biloxi News Company, 1906. Locals and visitors alike frequented this store to catch up on the latest news from major cities of the United States and around the world. The store, located on Reynoir Street between Howard Avenue and the railroad, featured pop, Coca-Cola, milk shakes, and tobacco products. The Biloxi News Company was also the publisher of many local postcards. (Not Mailed; SC.)

Six

The Public Sector

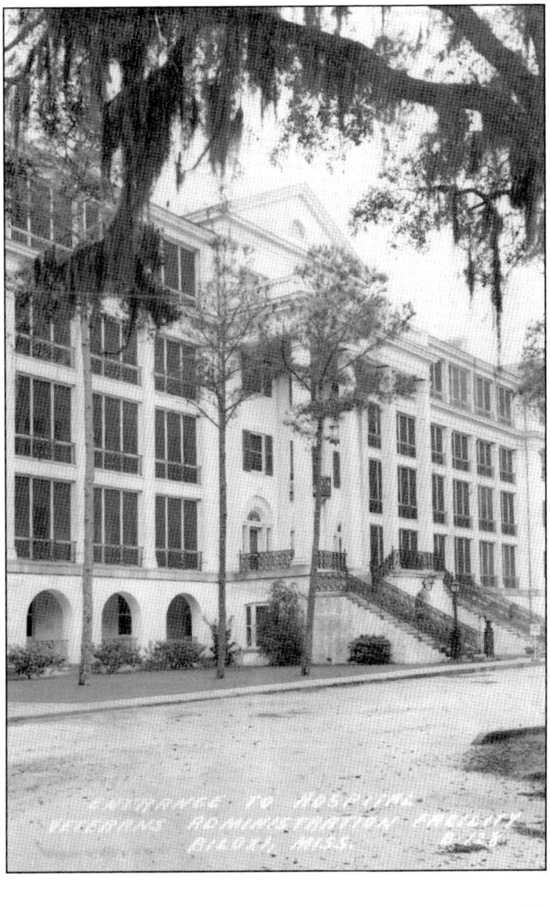

Veterans Administration Hospital Entrance, 1941. Various levels of government have influenced the lives of the people of Biloxi and the Gulf Coast. The eight flags, naval reserve timbers, schools, hospitals, and cemeteries all had an effect while doing "The People's Business." This real-photo postcard shows the US Veterans Hospital, which opened in 1933, overlooking the Bay of Biloxi. (Postmarked 1941; SC.)

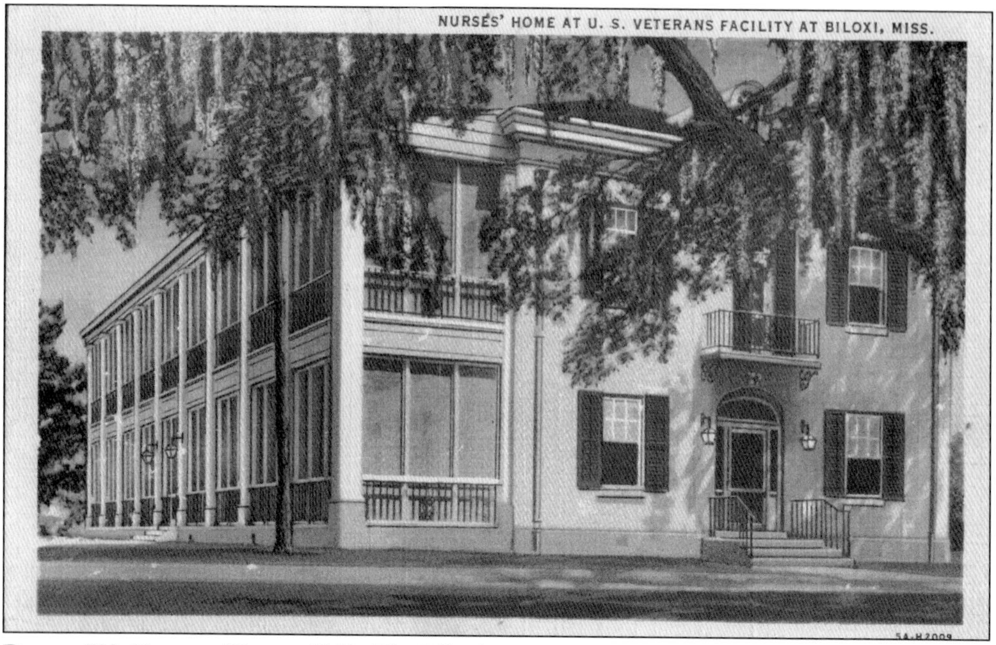

Biloxi VA Nurses Home, 1938. The Biloxi Veteran Administration Medical Center campus was designed by VA architects in the late Southern Colonial Revival style and was laid out to compliment the natural forested setting of the Back Bay. The hospital, nurses' quarters, dormitories, and other facilities were constructed to be an all-inclusive campus for the nation's war veterans. (Not Mailed; SC.)

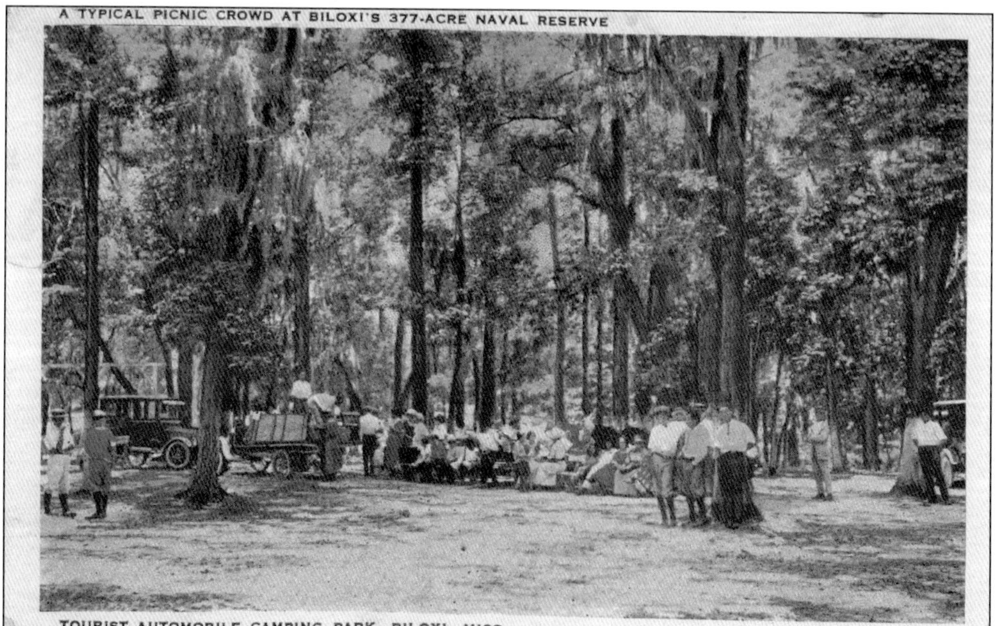

Tourist Camping Park, c. 1930. There were many outdoor amenities in the 377-acre Naval Reserve Park. The park got its name, not because of the Navy Reserve sailors stationed there, but because the giant oak trees on the parkland provided the US Navy with wooden warship building and repair materials. (Not Mailed; SC.)

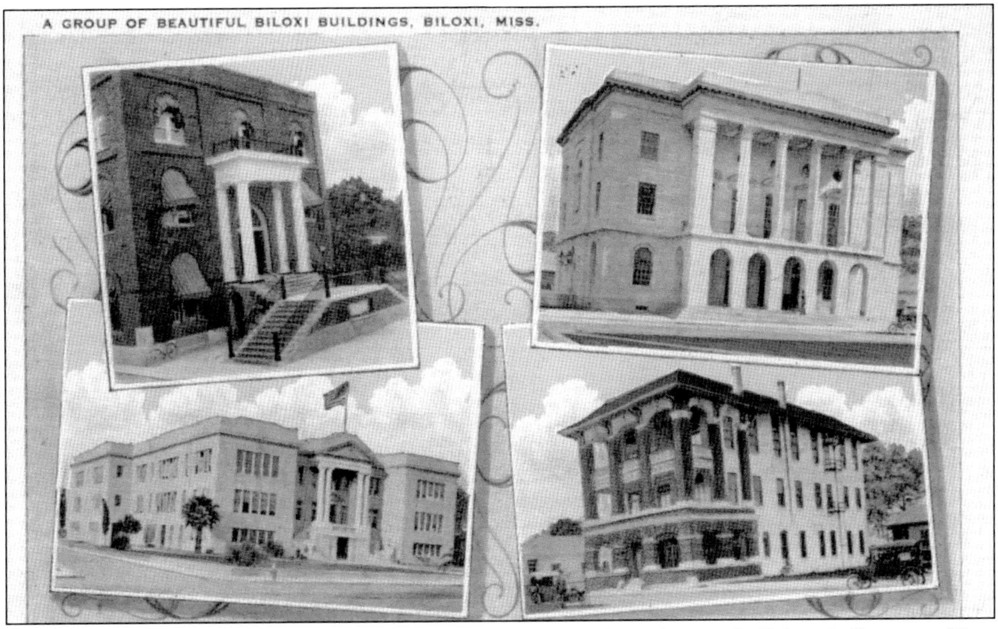

Beautiful Biloxi Buildings, 1924. Citizens took pride in the city hall (top left), post office, Government Building (top right), Central High School (lower left), and Elks' Temple (lower right). Each had outstanding features. City hall featured a mineral water drinking fountain, the post office was of marble, the new high school was the largest in Mississippi, and the Elks' building was the most beautiful in Mississippi. (Postmarked 1924; BL.)

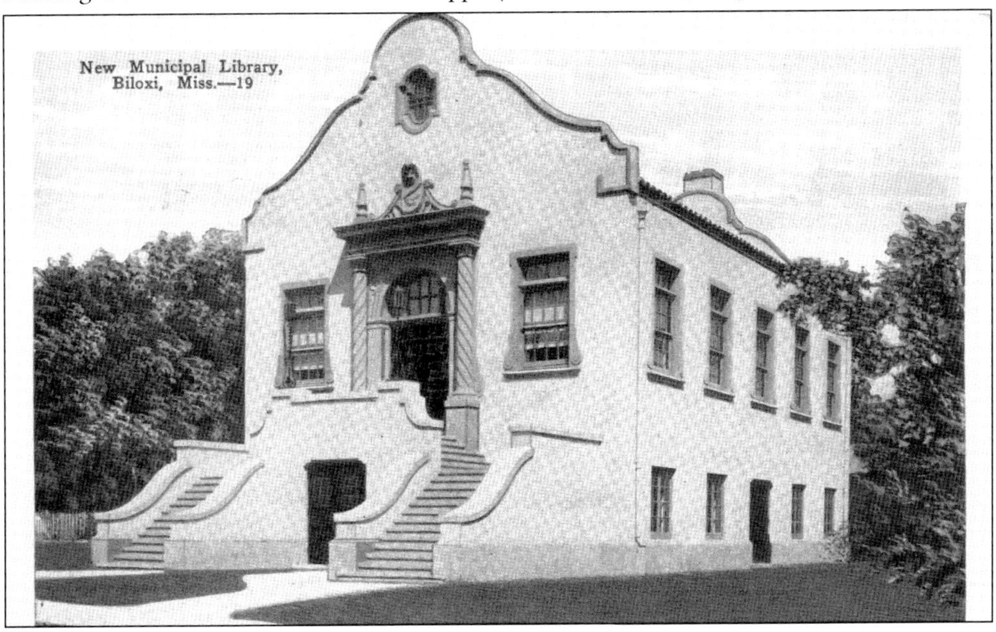

New Municipal Library, 1925. The Biloxi building boom of the 1920s brought many new buildings to the city. One of these was the Biloxi Library, designed by Carl Matthes, who also designed the Buena Vista and Tivoli Hotels. The new Spanish Mission–style structure replaced a small, wooden Creole cottage, which had been used as the library since 1900. The structure still stands at 124 Lameuse Street. (Postmarked 1927; BL.)

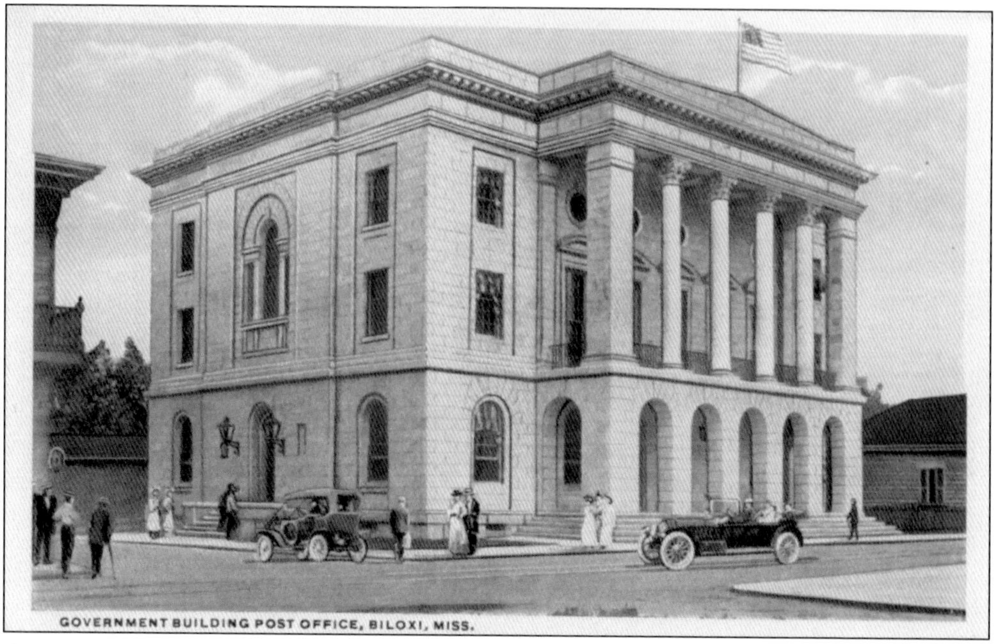

GOVERNMENT BUILDING POST OFFICE, 1920S. This marble, stone, and iron structure, located at 140 Lameuse Street, was completed in 1908. The building has served the city of Biloxi for over 100 years. Initially designated as the post office, courthouse, and customhouse, the building served in that capacity through the 1950s. In 1960, it was officially dedicated as Biloxi's city hall, which it remains today. (Not Mailed; SC.)

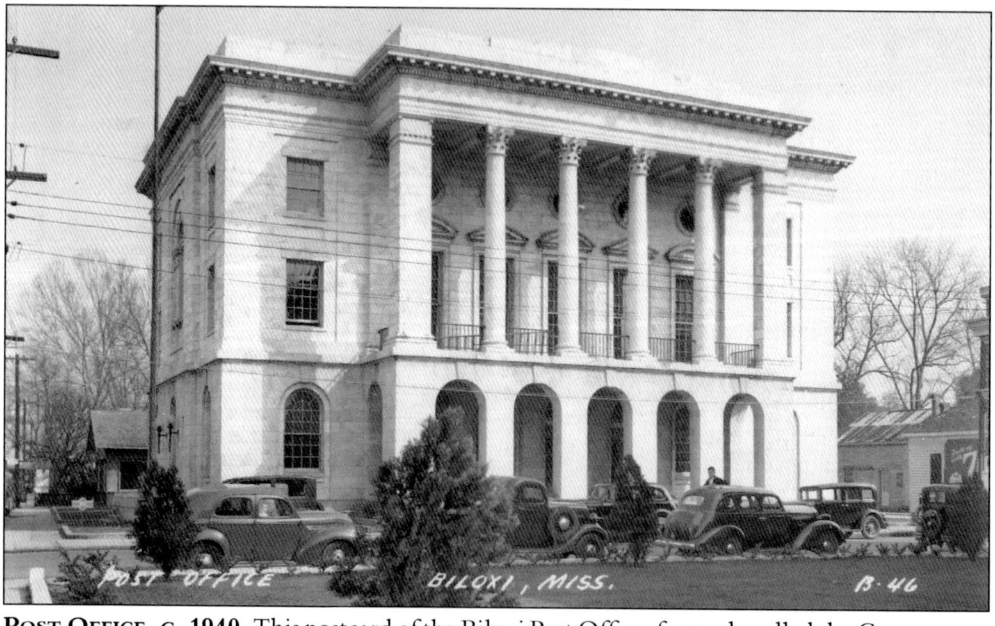

POST OFFICE, C. 1940. This postcard of the Biloxi Post Office, formerly called the Government Building, shows automobiles of the day, a glimpse of the neighborhood, and the park across the street. The original building's exterior was made in the early 1900s with over 1,200 tons of marble, costing $125,000. This was one of the last government buildings made of marble, as the cost was becoming prohibitive. (Not Mailed; BL.)

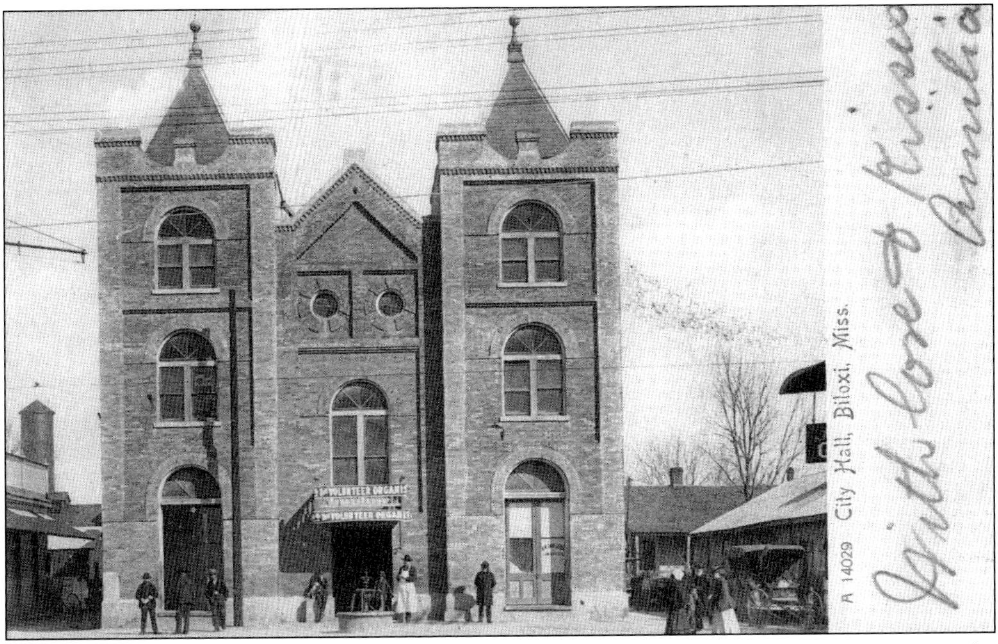

City Hall, 1906. Built in 1895 as a market place and city hall, this building stood in the center of Main Street (with one-way traffic on each side) and faced Howard Avenue. The public market was on the ground level, and city business was handled on the second and third floors. Steeples topped each corner tower, and a decorative fountain was located on the south side. (Postmarked 1906; SC.)

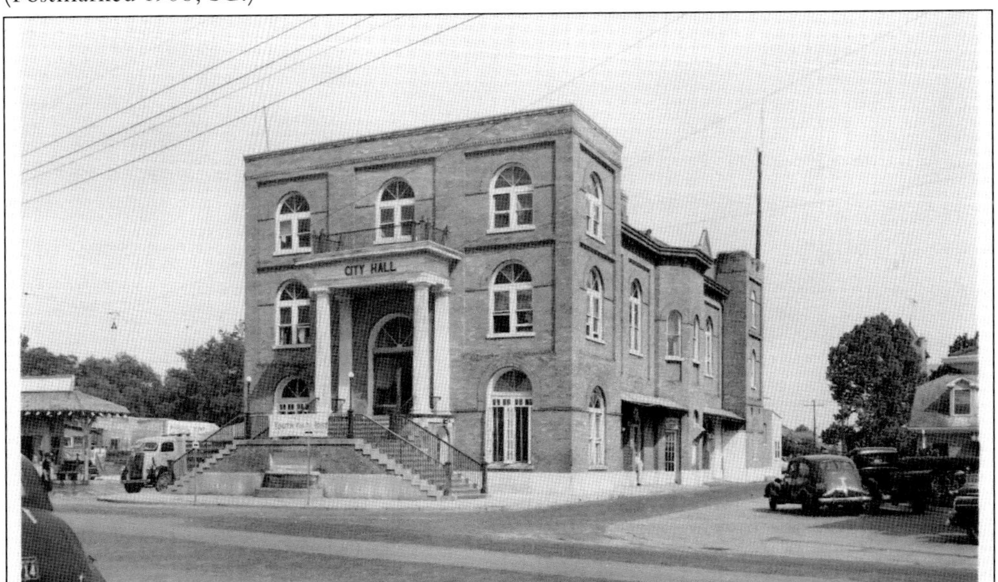

Biloxi City Hall, c. 1935. In 1922, the steeples were removed and the fountain was flanked by a dual stairway during renovation. City offices replaced the marketplace on the ground floor. The jail and police station relocated to the rear of that space, while the second floor held the courtroom. It was torn down in 1960, and bricks were salvaged for a fence around the Biloxi Cemetery. (Not Mailed; SC.)

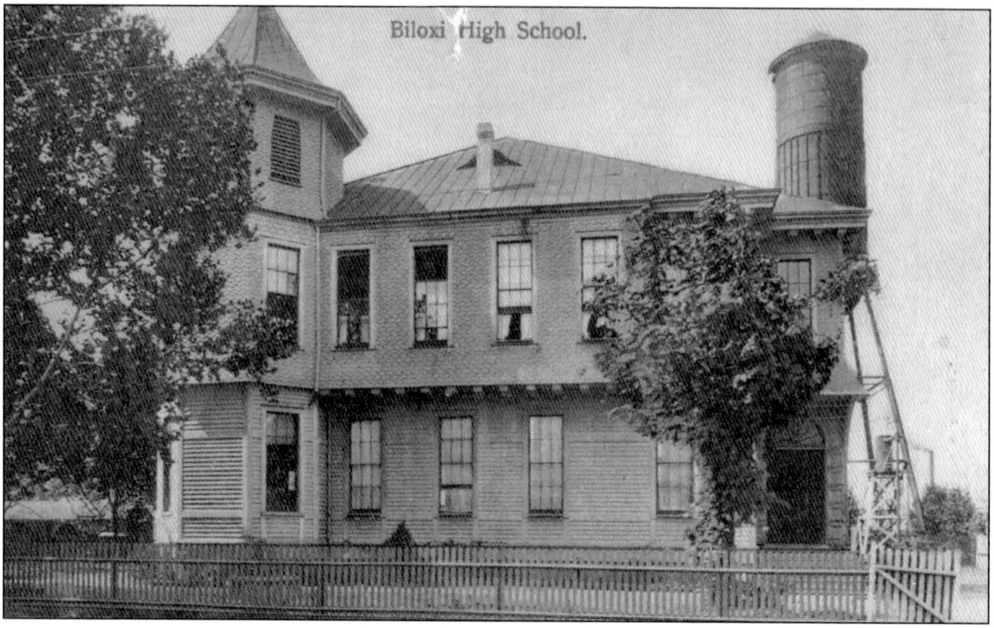

BILOXI HIGH SCHOOL, C. 1910. Located at the corner of Main Street and the railroad, this school was the primary educational facility in the city until other schools were constructed around the turn of the 20th century. The structure served as the high school until 1912, when it was replaced by Central High School, located on the corner of Howard Avenue and Bellman Street. (Not Mailed; BL.)

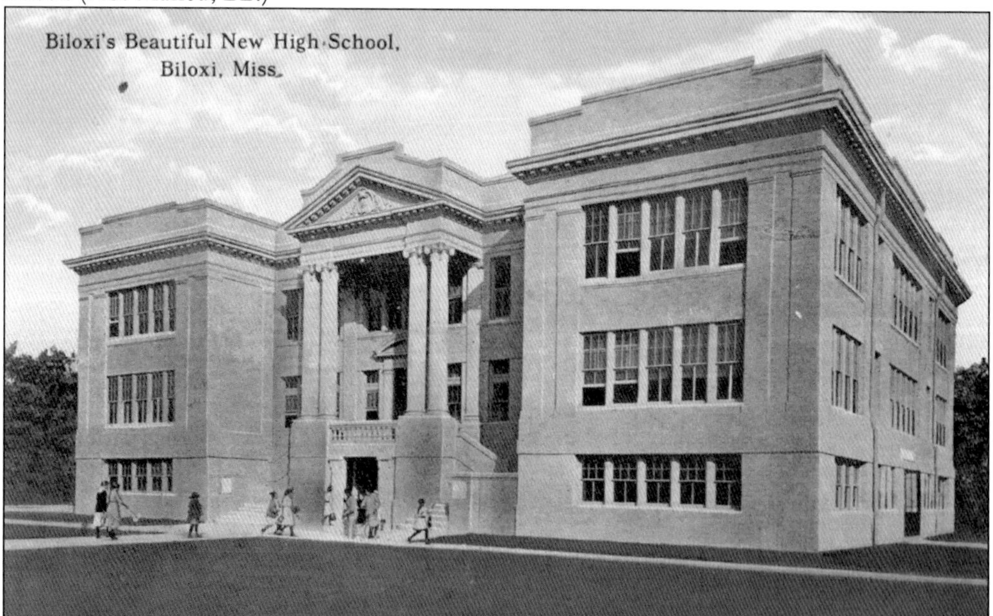

NEW BILOXI HIGH SCHOOL, 1930S. Opening in 1913, it was declared one of the most beautiful buildings in the city and one of the largest and most up-to-date schools in the state. In 1961, it became Central Junior High and the older students were moved to the high school located on Father Ryan Avenue. In 2011, the Biloxi Library and Civic Center was built on the property. (Not Mailed; SC.)

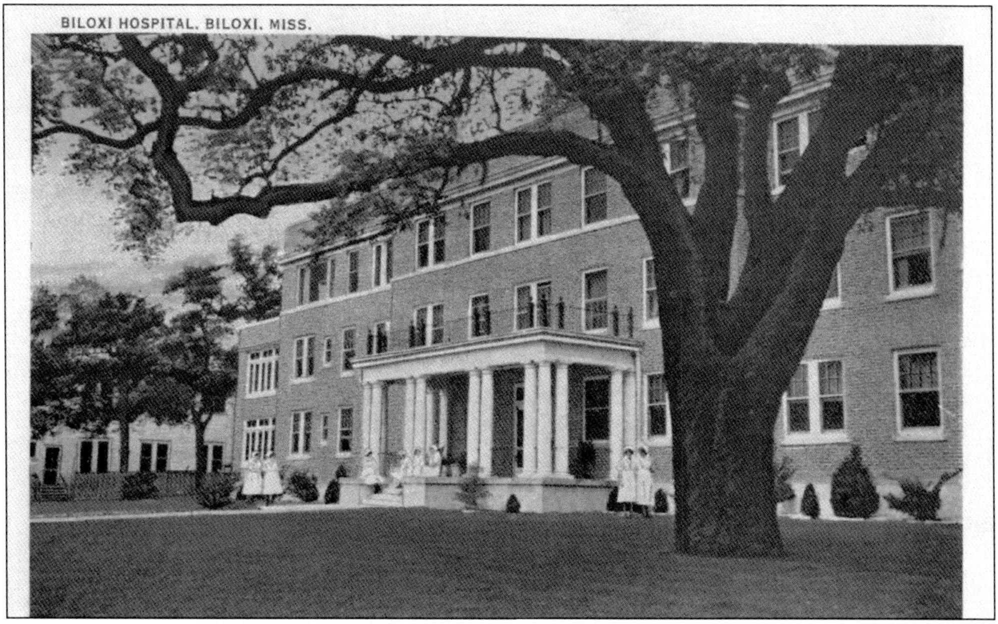

Biloxi Hospital, 1944. Harry T. Howard was a true benefactor to the city of Biloxi. He donated property and money to the city for schools, parks, churches, and this hospital. The property, located on Beach Boulevard and now Dukate Street, was the home of the hospital and nursing facility from the late 1920s until the building was destroyed in 2005. (Postmarked 1944; SC.)

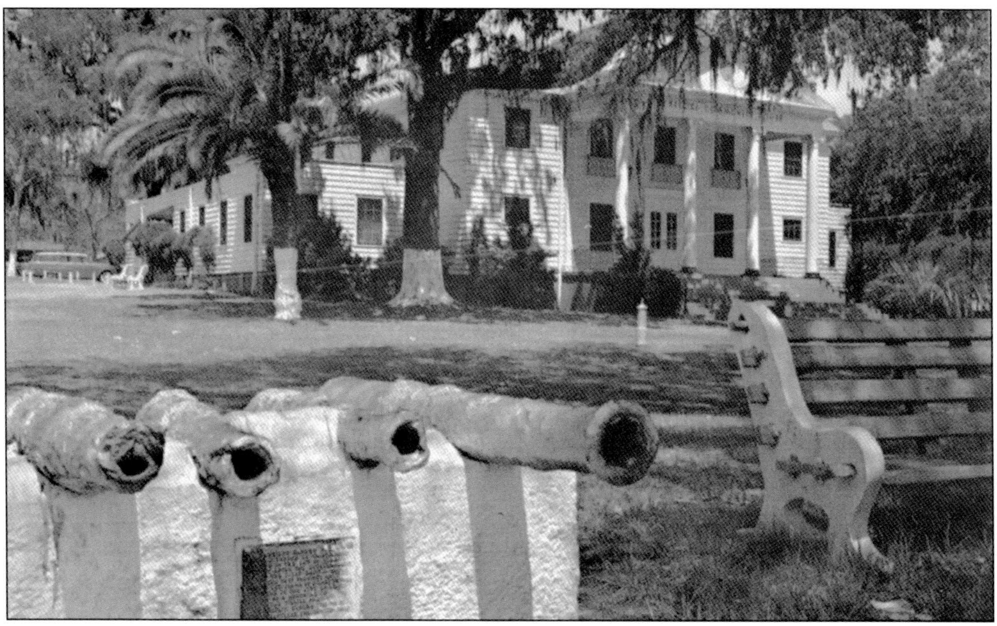

Biloxi Community Center, 1931. The cannons, shown on the front lawn, were found in Biloxi Back Bay during the 1890s. The building on East Beach hosted plays, minstrel shows, Mardi Gras balls, and many other public events. It was used as the USO during early World War II, and Elvis Presley preformed there during a benefit for the Biloxi Doll and Toy Fund in 1955. (Postmarked 1958; SC.)

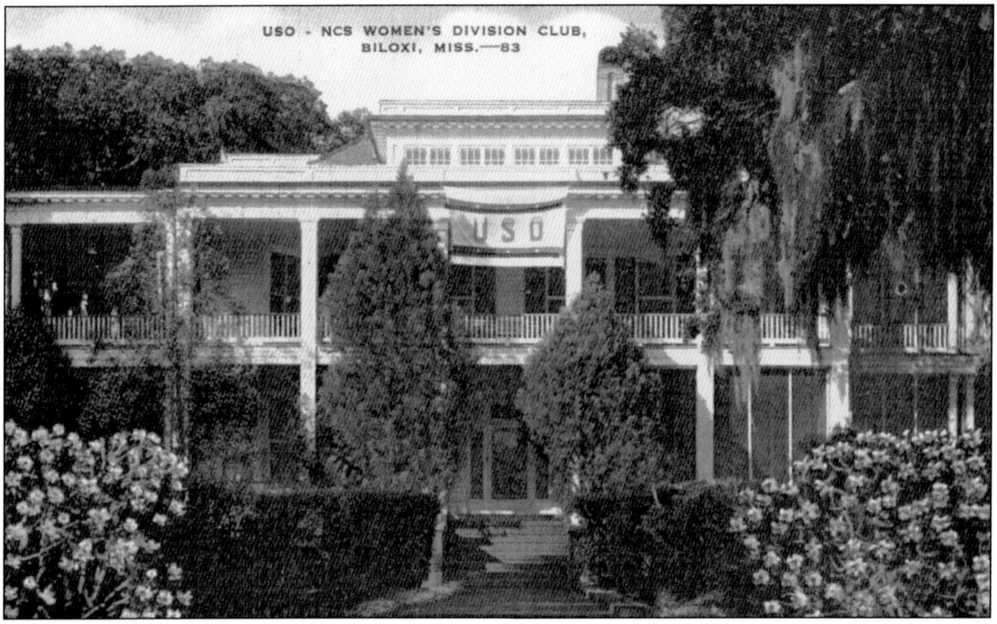

USO-NCS WOMEN'S DIVISION CLUB, 1940S. This beautiful southern estate, overlooking the Gulf, was converted into a USO for women during World War II. The facility provided "A Home Away From Home" for women in service, women workers, and relatives of service men and women stationed at Keesler Field. The building provided a dormitory, nursery, kitchen, laundry, swimming, checkers, badminton courts, reading-writing rooms, and a snack bar. (Not Mailed; BL.)

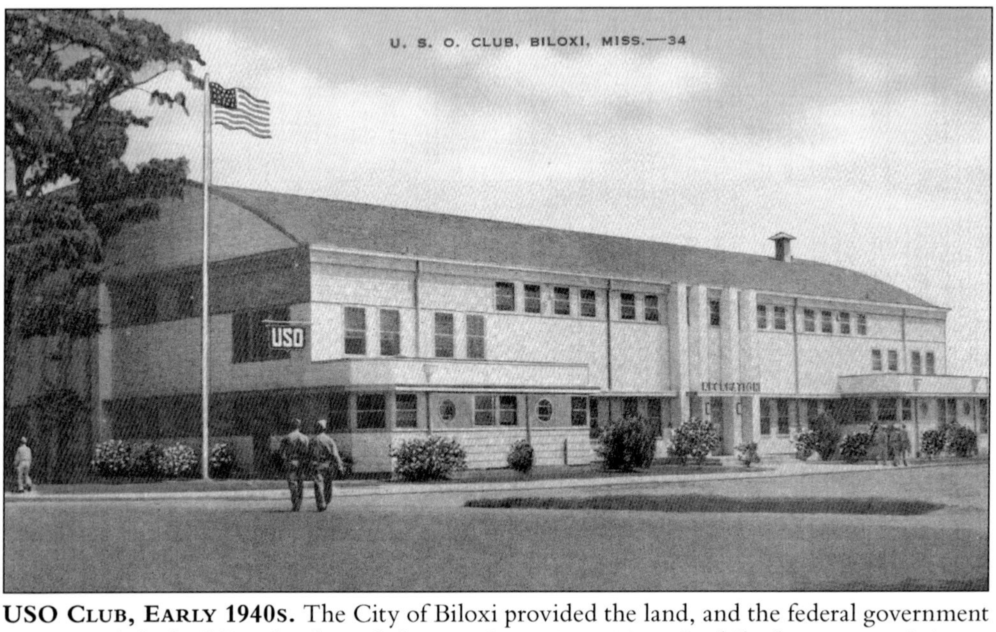

USO CLUB, EARLY 1940S. The City of Biloxi provided the land, and the federal government constructed the building for the GI's "Home Away From Home" while they were training at Keesler Field. It featured a 3,000-seat auditorium and dance floor that accommodated 1,500 dancers. The center provided facilities for the civilian community and military personnel prior to its destruction by fire in 1965. (Not Mailed; SC.)

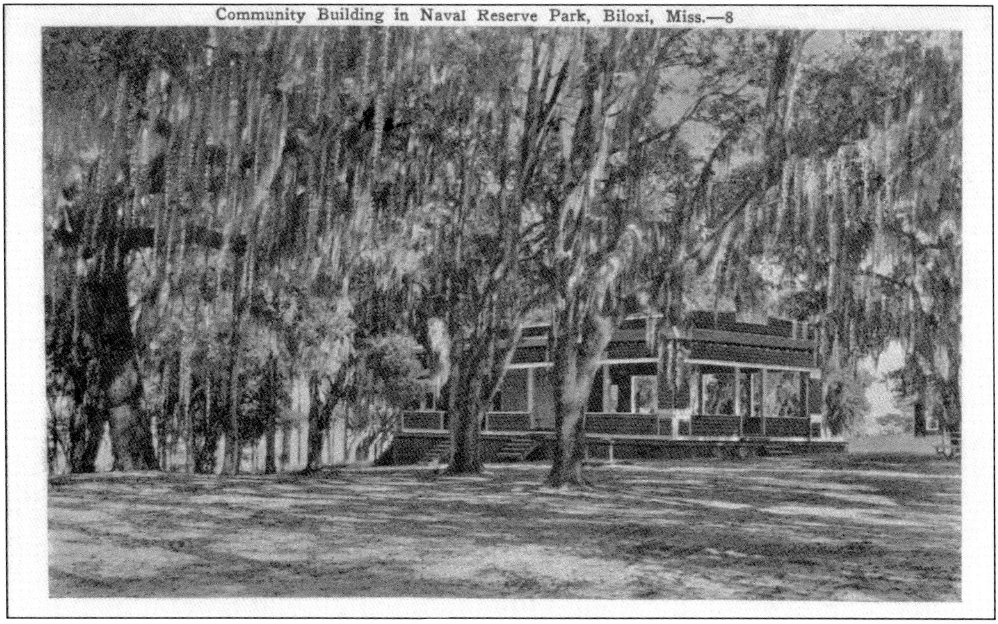

NAVAL RESERVE PARK, PRE-1940S. Once steel warships were built, wooden warships were no longer in use, and the Naval Reserve Park land was given to the City of Biloxi. The park contained a community center (shown here), piers, picnic grounds, and a baseball field. The park eventually became part of the 800 plus acres used in the late 1930s to create Keesler Field. (Not Mailed; SC.)

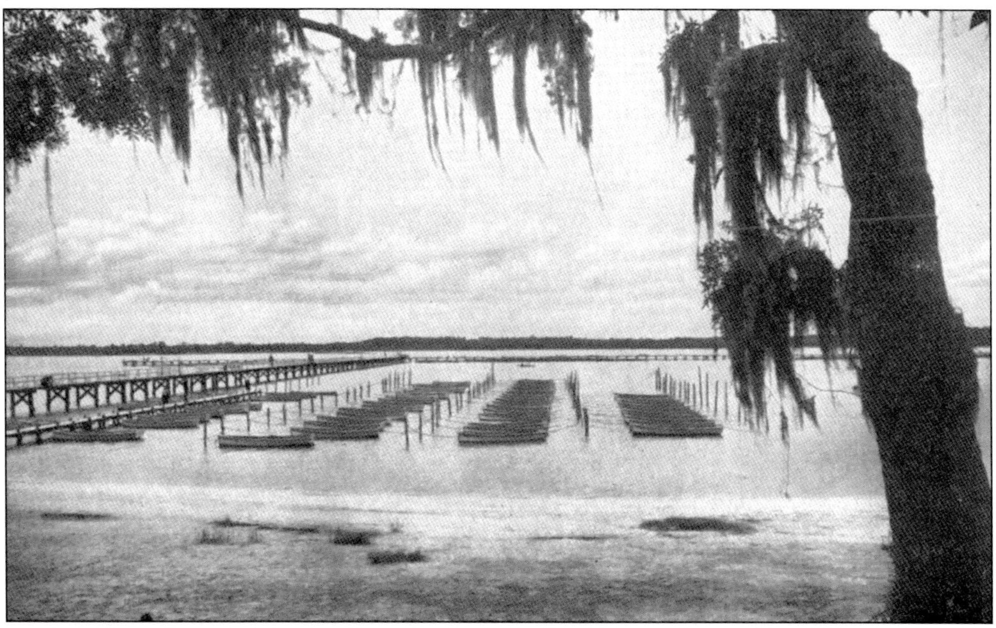

NAVAL RESERVE PARK, C. 1945. After the establishment of Keesler Field, the military continued to use the former Naval Reserve piers as a recreational area for the men stationed at Keesler. Having scant leisure time, this boating and swimming area was a popular summertime spot for off duty personnel. The Back Bay piers eventually became the Keesler Marina. (Not Mailed; SC.)

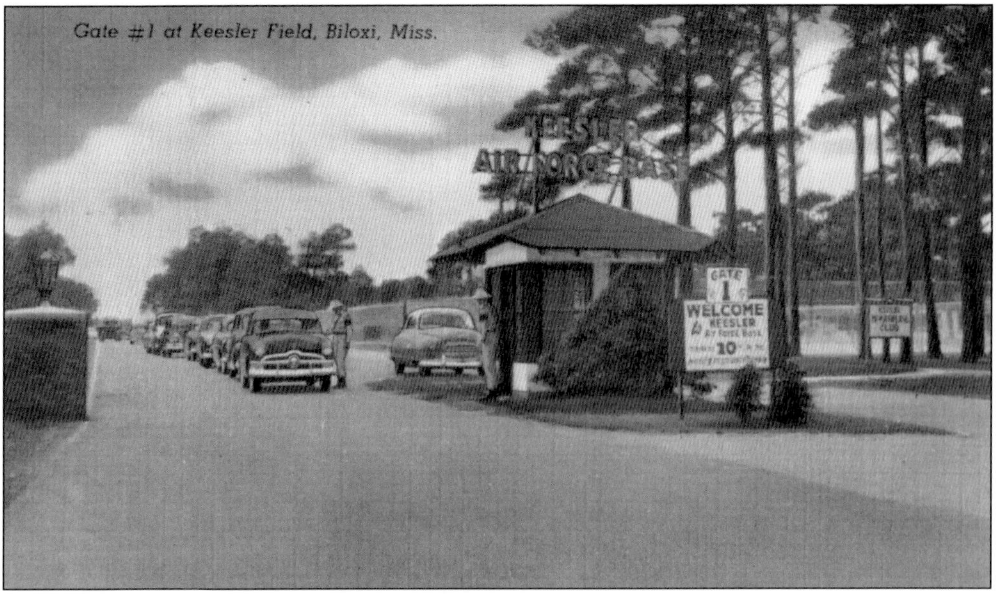

GATE NO. 1, KEESLER FIELD, EARLY 1950S. Just prior to World War II, an idea was hatched, and some good old southern politics took place. Once the deal was arranged and the land assembled, the Air Corps Station No. 8 Aviation Mechanics School (Keesler Air Force Base) was born. From 1941 until today, Keesler has been a vital part of Biloxi and the Mississippi Gulf Coast. (Not Mailed; SC.)

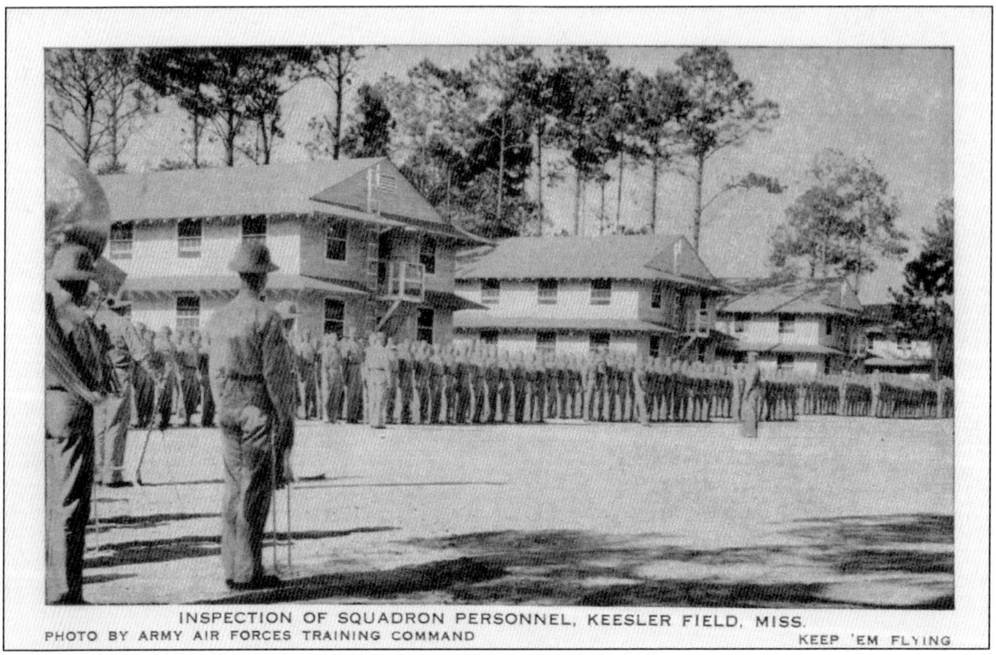

SQUADRON INSPECTION, WORLD WAR II. This Army Air Force training command photograph shows the barracks on Keesler Field as daily inspections were taking place. Training aircraft mechanics was Keesler's first job. Basic training was added later. During World War II, Keesler trained 142,000 aircraft mechanics and over 330,000 raw recruits. Many of the famed Tuskegee Airmen received their preflight and technical training at Keesler. (Not Mailed; SC.)

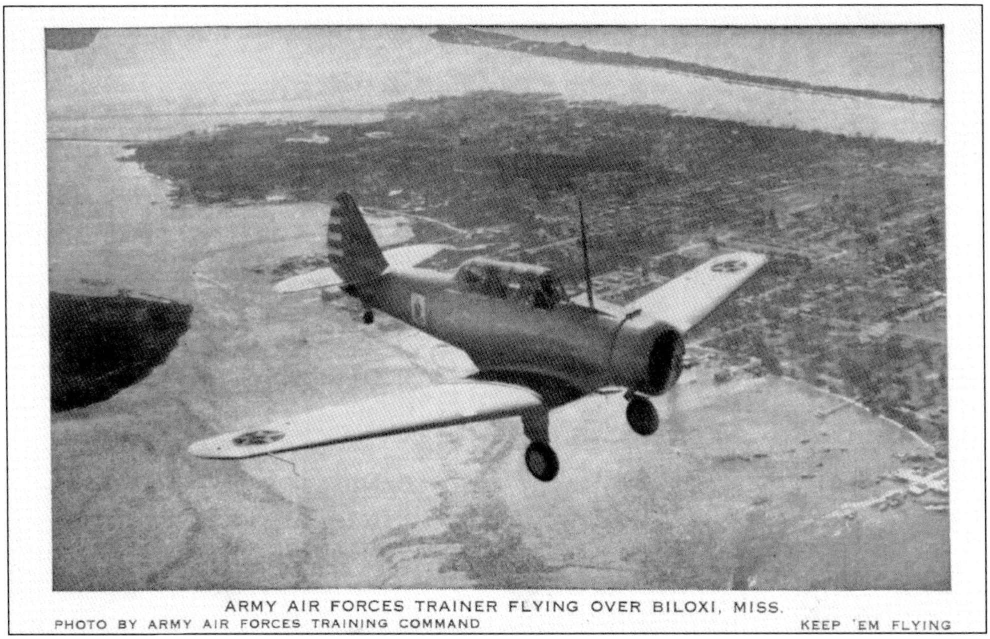

ARMY AIR FORCES TRAINER, 1940S. The motto of the Aviation Mechanics Training School was "Keep 'em Flying," and that they did. This image shows a training flight over the Back Bay of Biloxi. Students and recruits were being trained, and Keesler was becoming part of Biloxi. Trains even stopped on base, dropping off new arrivals and taking graduates to other destinations. (Not Mailed; SC.)

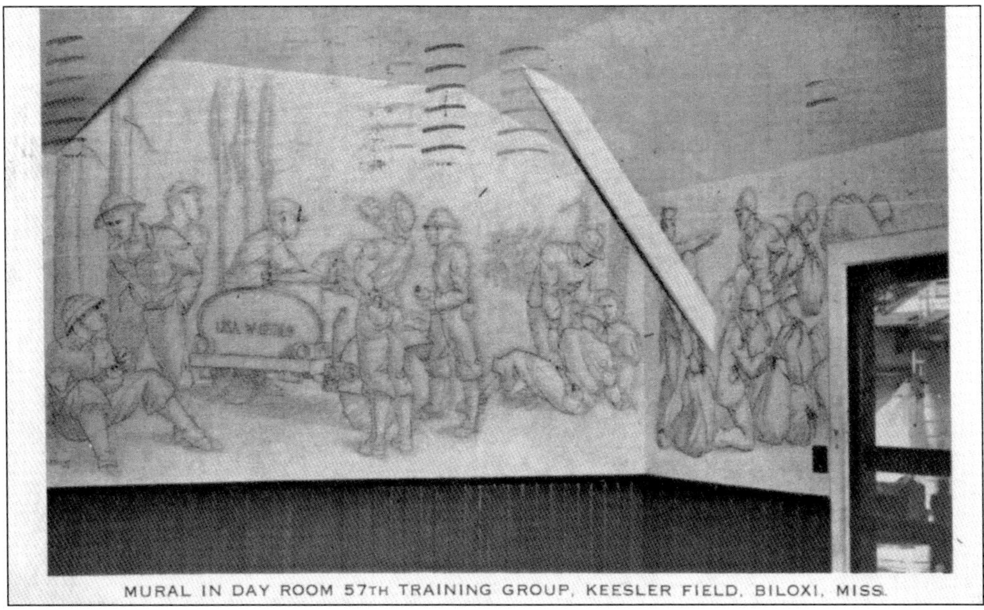

DAY ROOM 57TH TRAINING GROUP, 1943. The actual mural, shown here, was in one of the non-barracks, off-duty recreational areas provided at Keesler Field. The writer of this postcard noted that he was going to be a "Radio Operator and Mechanic" after his basic training. Also, no postage was necessary, as it was marked free and had a return address of the active-duty sender. (Postmarked 1943; BL.)

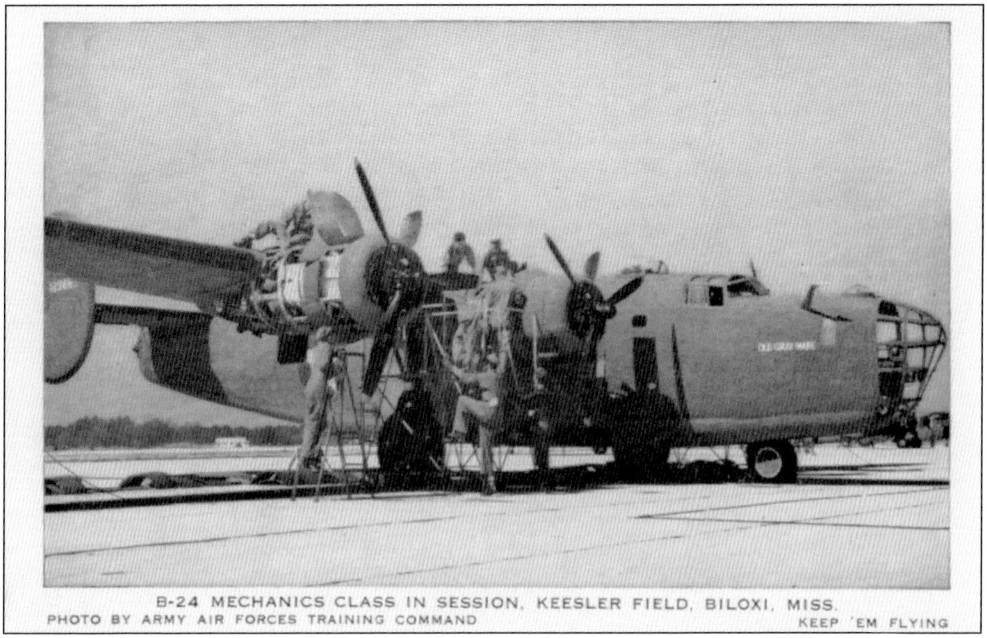

Keesler Field Mechanic Class, 1940s. From mid-1942 until mid-1944, a great part of mechanics training was on the B-24 Liberator Heavy Bomber, shown here. Training took place 24 hours a day, seven days a week, 365 days a year, preparing students for duty in others parts of the war. Many of the instructors were civilians, including many females. Women and student allies began training at Keesler in 1943. (Not Mailed; BL.)

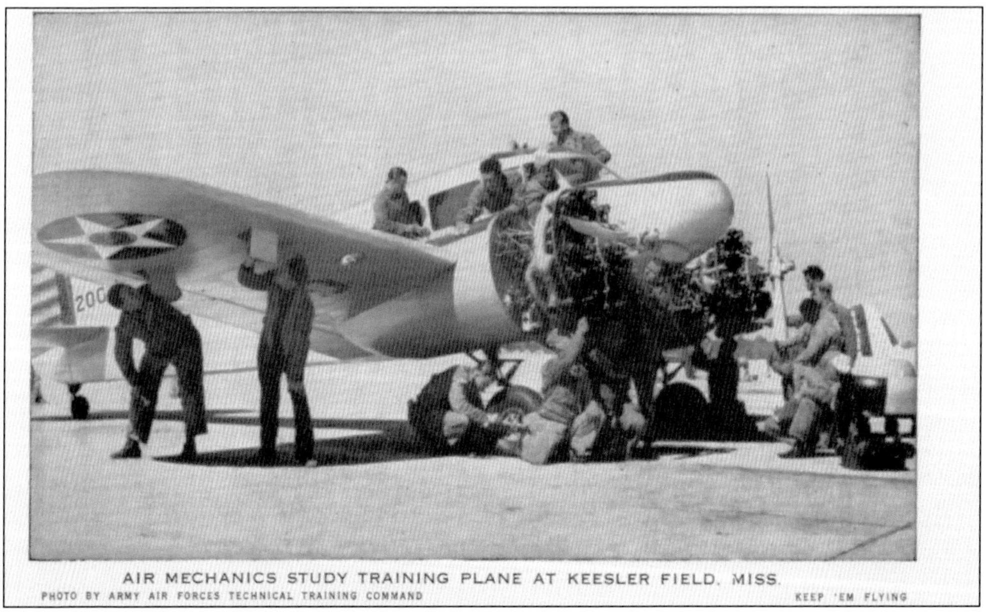

Air Mechanics Training Plane, 1940s. Study of this Cessna AT-17 at Keesler Field gave knowledge-hungry air mechanics an opportunity to learn its every part as they prepared for "on the line" service in World War II, upon graduation. As the war progressed, other specialized training was performed at Keesler, such as B-24 copilot training and emergency rescue. (Not Mailed; BL.)

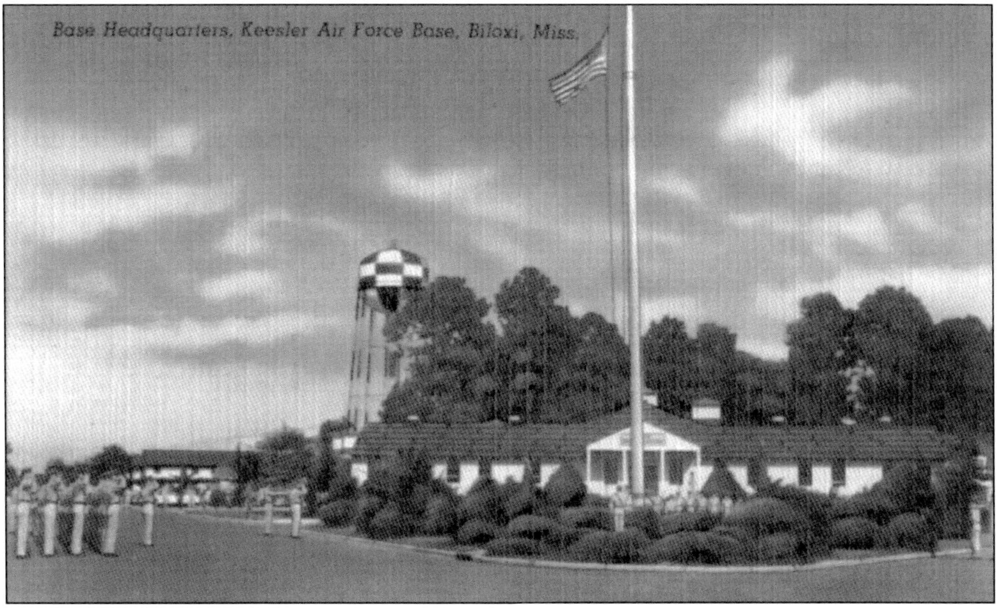

KEESLER BASE HEADQUARTERS, C. 1948. As the war ended, Keesler Field received a new mission, becoming Keesler Air Force Base, the radar training school for the newly created US Air Force. Between the end of World War II and 1950, additional technical missions were added. By 1950, Keesler was known as the "Electronics Training Center of the Air Force." (Not Mailed; SC.)

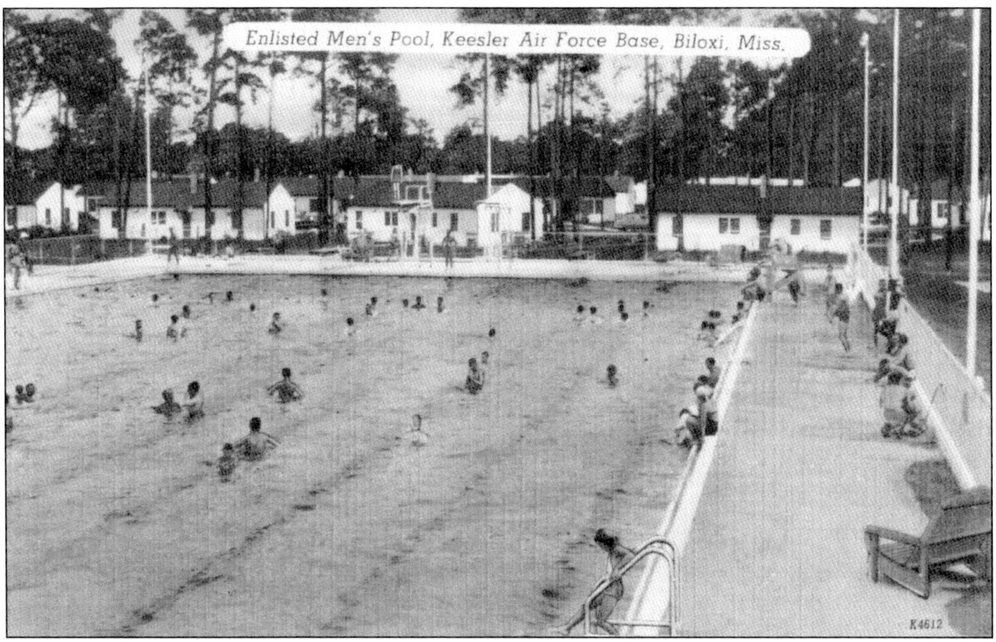

ENLISTED MEN'S POOL, C. 1950. During the postwar 1950s, Keesler Air Force Base became a large part of Biloxi and Biloxi became a large part of Keesler. Building booms took place on and off base, as more permanent-party personnel were added to serve the growing number of students. In 1950, Keesler offered only 14 courses, but by the end of the decade, that number grew to 116. (Not Mailed; SC.)

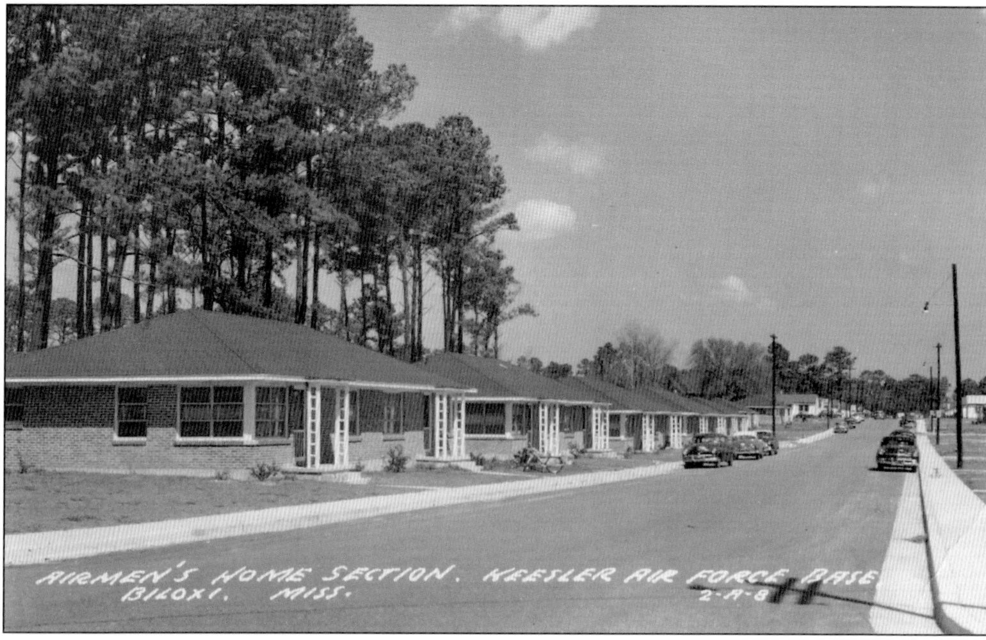

Airmen's Home Section, 1952. As the role of the technical trainer for the US Air Force increased, so did the need for housing. Airmen, noncommissioned officer, and officer housing was built on the Air Force base. The dormitory complex for student trainees, known as the Triangle, was also constructed during the early 1950s. The need for more technical personnel increased as the Air Force's mission increased. (Not Mailed; SC.)

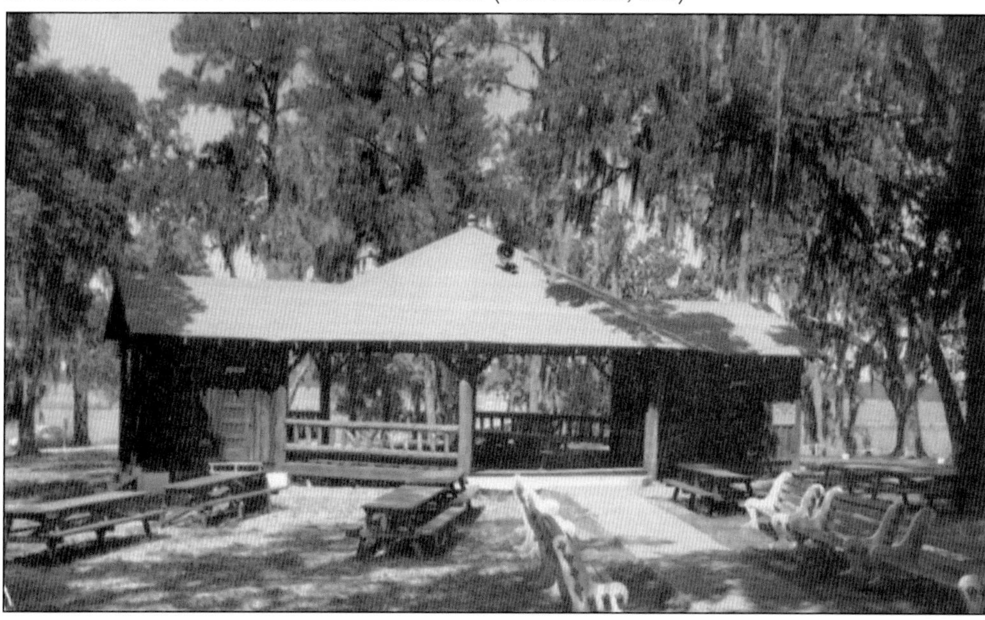

Keesler Recreational Area, c. 1960. Long after talk of the Naval Reserve Park, the park facilities along the bay were being refurbished and used by active-duty personnel. Instructors and others enjoyed the area so much that they would request repeat assignments to Keesler. Many purchased houses in the area and homesteaded here, in hopes if retiring as Biloxians. (Not Mailed; SC.)

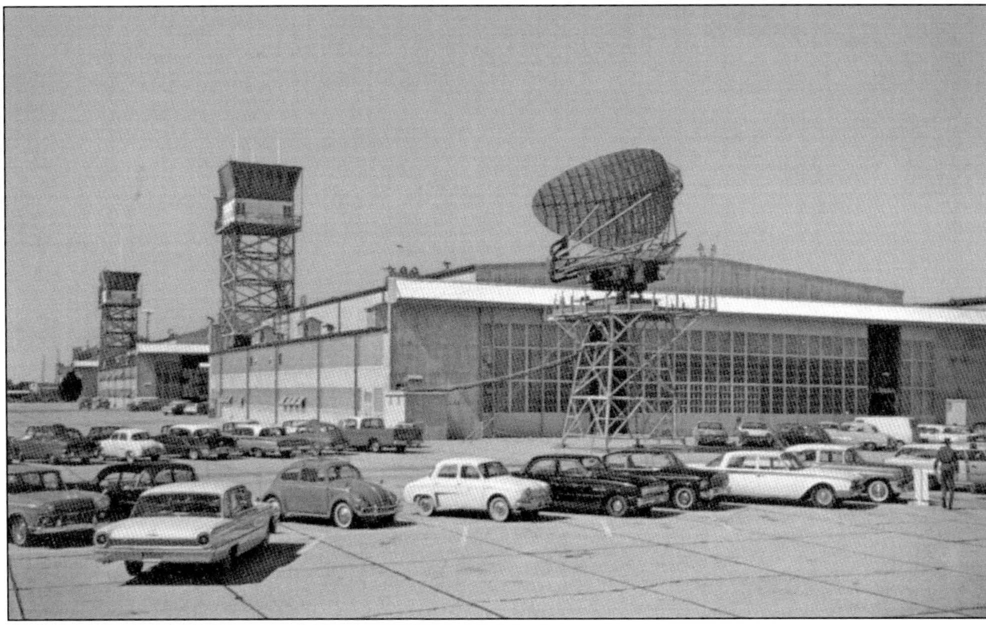

Electronics Training Center, c. 1965. The Air Force means airplane hangars, and Keesler means electronics training. Radar and control towers are highlighted on this postcard, depicting some of the specialized training taking place at Keesler. Air Force personnel and their families became a large part of the community, involved in school, churches, and civic activities in the area. (Not Mailed; SC.)

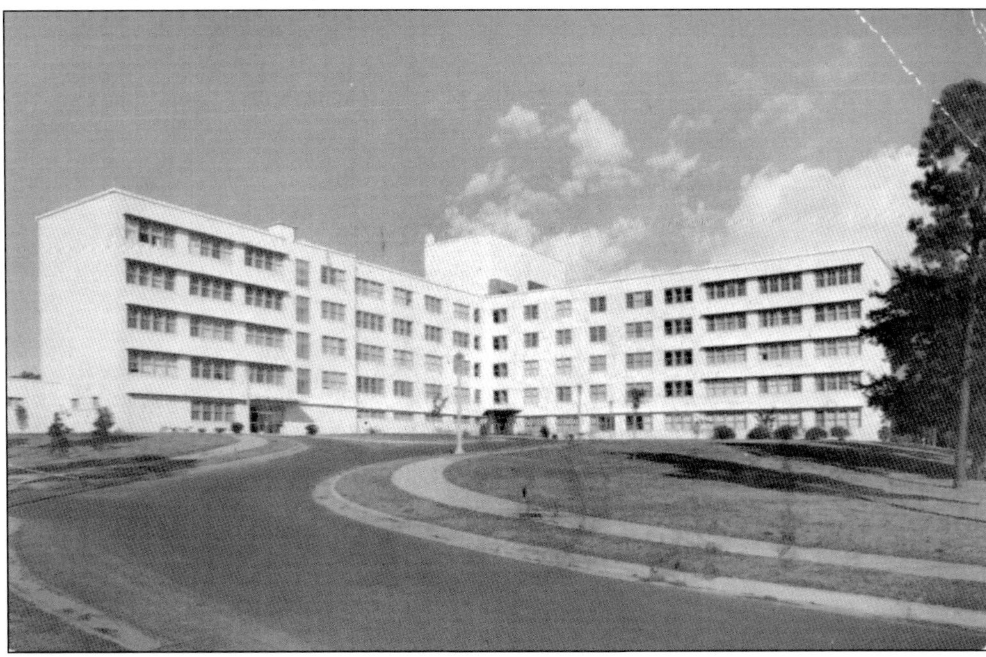

Keesler Hospital, 1960. Extensive healthcare was necessary for the large number of active duty and retired military personnel and their dependents, on and nearby Keesler. The Keesler Medical Center continues to provide some of the best medical care in the Air Force. Along with local patients, many are flown in for care unavailable at other bases. (Postmarked 1961; SC.)

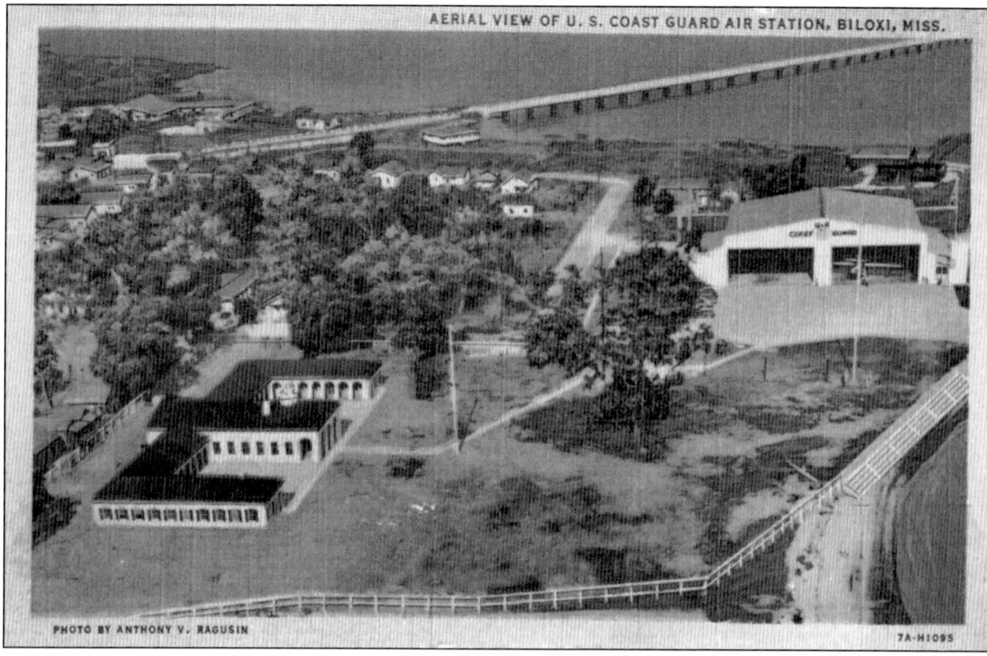

US Coast Guard Air Station, 1938. In 1924, the US Coast Guard established a revenue cutter substation in Biloxi to enforce the Prohibition laws. Located on the bay at Peters Avenue, the Naval Reserve (now Keesler Air Force Base) was home to four patrol boats that were used to catch rumrunners ferrying illegal booze from mother ships anchored in offshore, international waters. (Postmarked 1938; SC.)

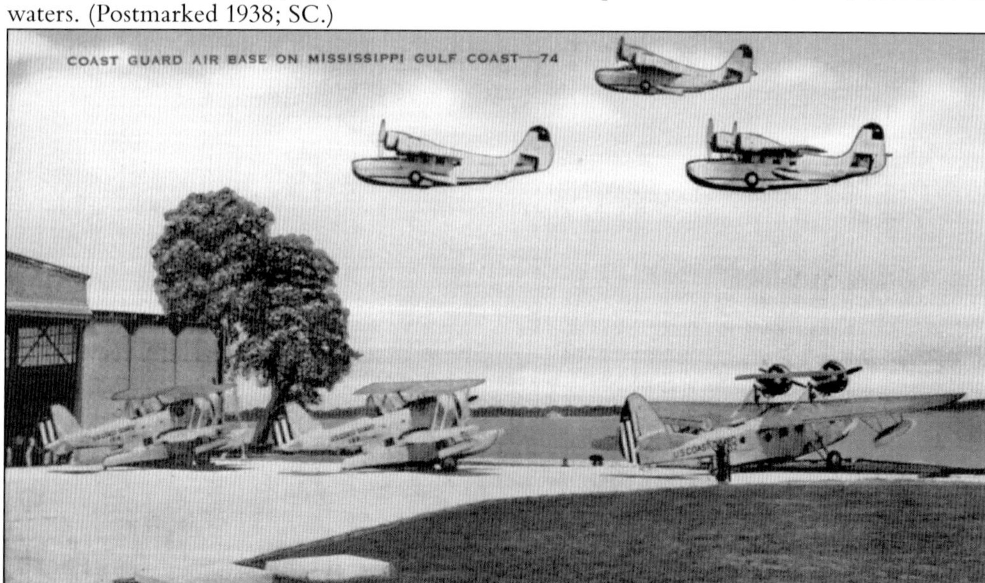

Coast Guard Air Base, c. 1940. Six seaplanes, assigned to the Coast Guard base, patrolled the Gulf of Mexico from the Florida panhandle to the Mexican border, providing search-and-rescue missions. During World War II, the station's mission was expanded to include extensive anti-submarine patrols. Thirty-five ships were lost in the Gulf of Mexico in 1942, but after a Coast Guard plane bombed a German sub, submarine activity practically came to a halt. (Not Mailed; SC.)

Seven

Extra, Extra, Read All About It

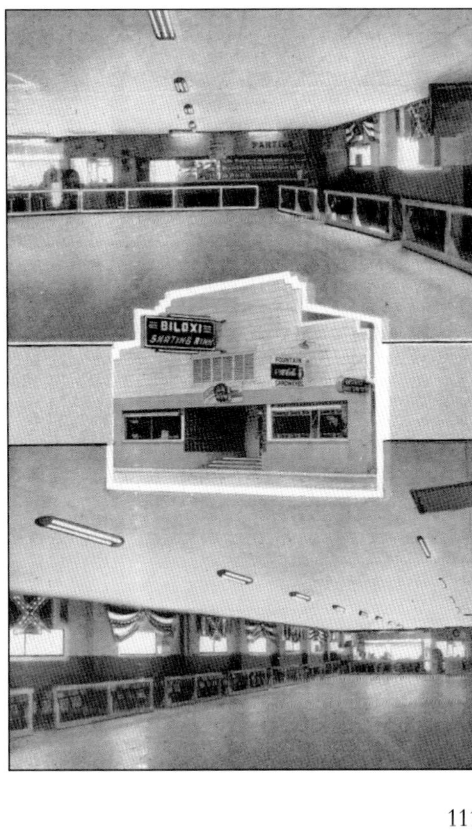

Skating Rink, 1952. Young and old skated for fun and health to electric Hammond Organ music at this rink, located at 125 West Beach Boulevard. They offered theater seating, boot skate rentals, and a Coca-Cola fountain, where sandwiches were also served. It was located on Highway 90, south of the Sun Tan Motel, which was one lot east of Mary Mahoney's Restaurant parking lot. (Not mailed; SC.)

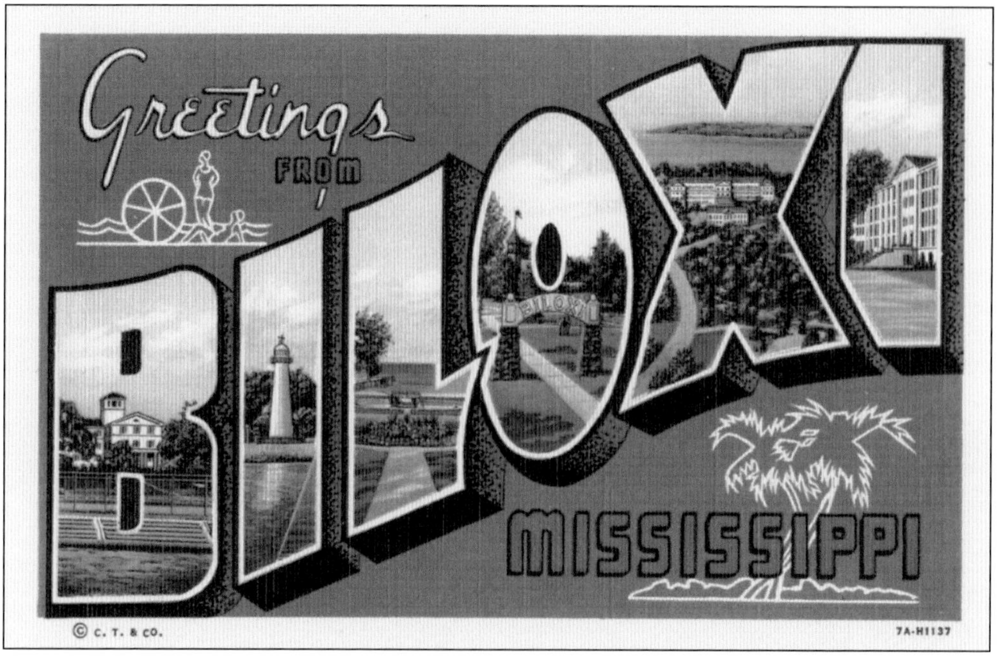

GREETINGS FROM BILOXI, 1937. This large-letter postcard shows scenes of the city of Biloxi in each of its six letters. Pictured are the following: B–White House Hotel, I–Biloxi Lighthouse, L–White House Fountain, O–Biloxi City Park sign, X–the Veterans Administration main building, and I–the Veterans Administration Hospital. (Not Mailed; SC.)

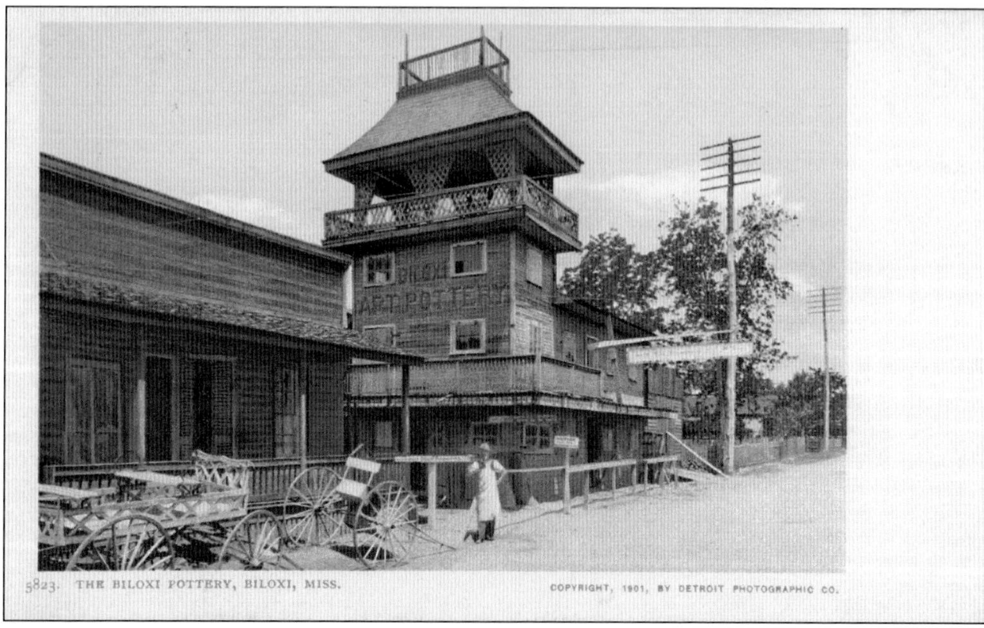

ART POTTERY, 1901. The now-famous Mad Potter of Biloxi, George Edgar Ohr (1857–1918), is shown standing near his weird, handmade wagon in front of the studio at 400 Delauney Street, now Rue Magnolia. He constructed the five-story, wooden, frame building in 1895 after his original workshop burned in 1894 It was capped off with a pagoda-like tower. He operated the pottery shop through 1909. (Not Mailed; SC.)

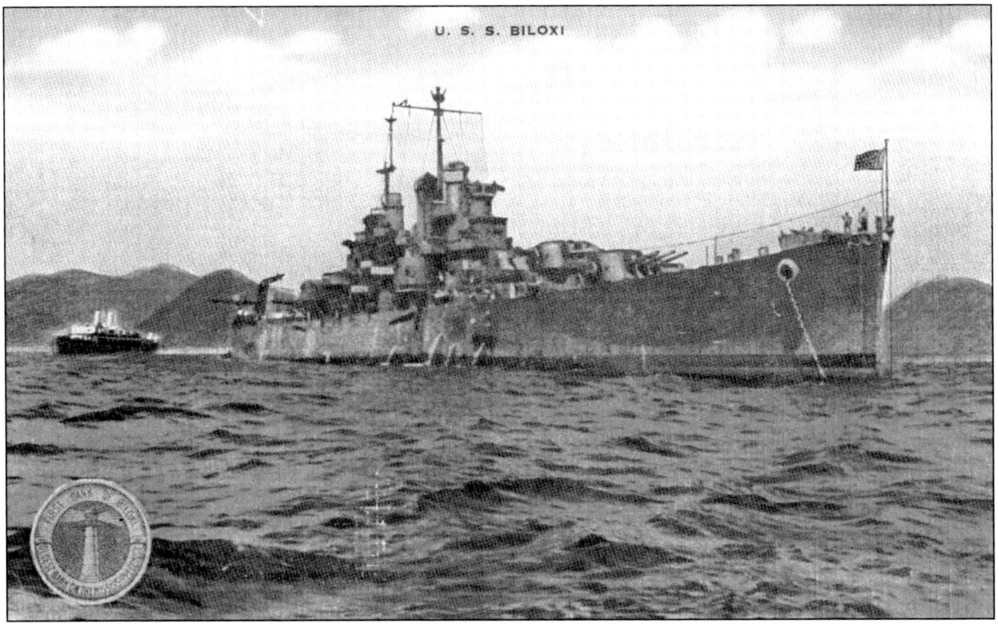

USS *Biloxi*, c. 1945. This official US Navy photograph of this light cruiser was taken during the ship's actions in World War II. Serving in the US Pacific Fleet, the vessel, known as the "Busy Bee," was active in several naval engagements, including the Battle of Leyte Gulf and the invasion of Iwo Jima. The *Biloxi* was hit by a Japanese suicide plane but remained in action. (Not Mailed; BL.)

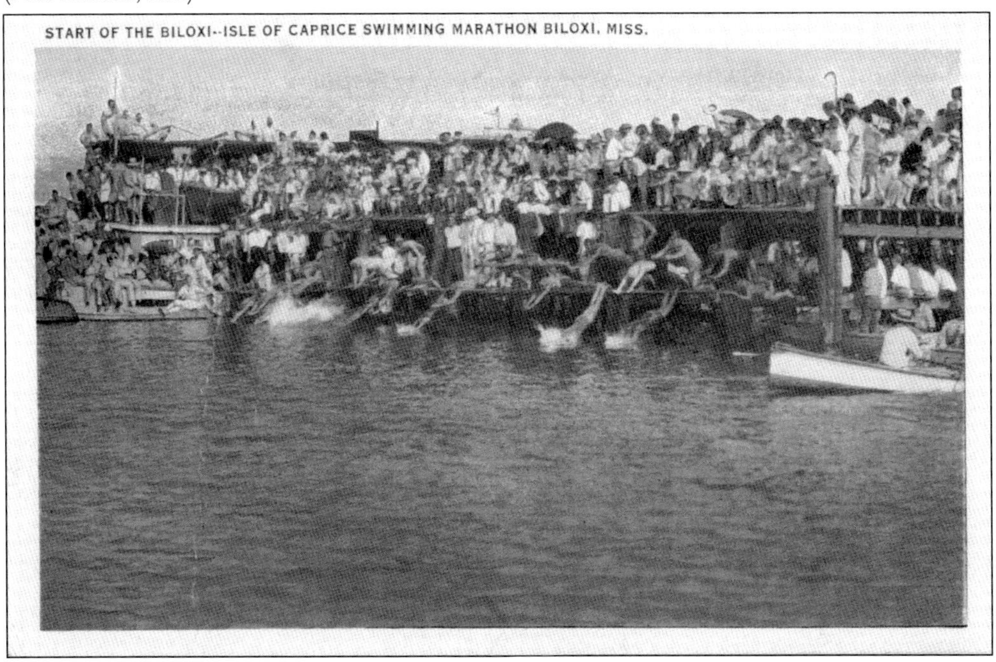

Start of Swimming Marathon, c. 1930. From Biloxi to the Isle of Caprice, the 14-mile, annual summer event was the longest marathon held in the Gulf of Mexico. It drew a large number of swimmers from throughout the South. Bill Jackson, a 24-year-old professional swimmer from Mobile, Alabama, won the race in August 1927. (Postmarked 1937; SC.)

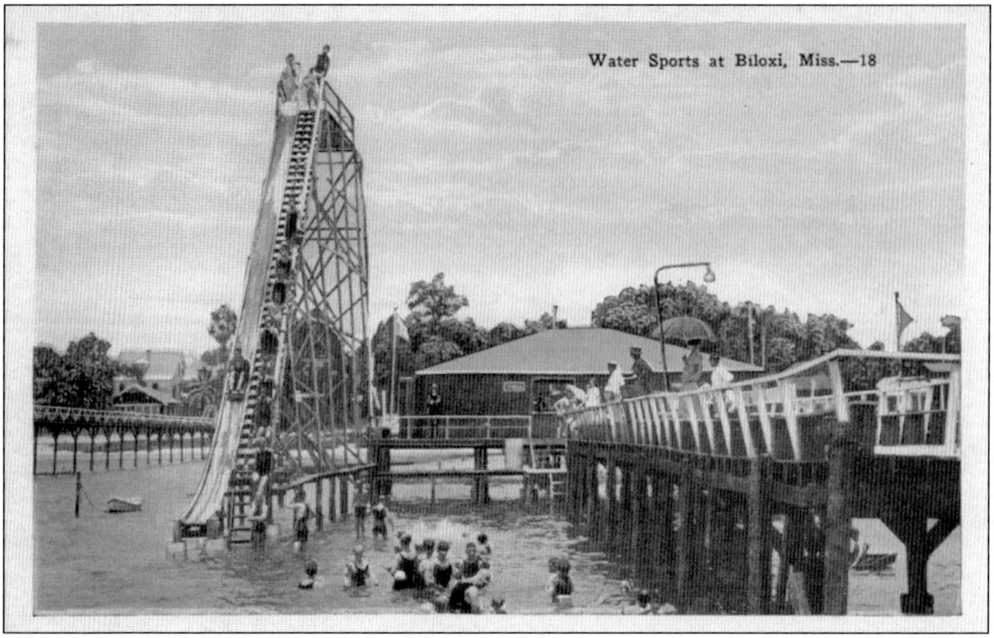

CHUTE-THE-CHUTE AT BATHING PIER, 1920S. Bathers could rent bathing suits, enjoy the long water slide and refreshments, and attend dances in the large pavilion. It was located south of the James V. Hagan home at 418 West Beach Boulevard, on the northeast corner of Reynoir Street. The long, recreational pier was built in the spring of 1921 and closed in the early 1930s. (Not Mailed; SC.)

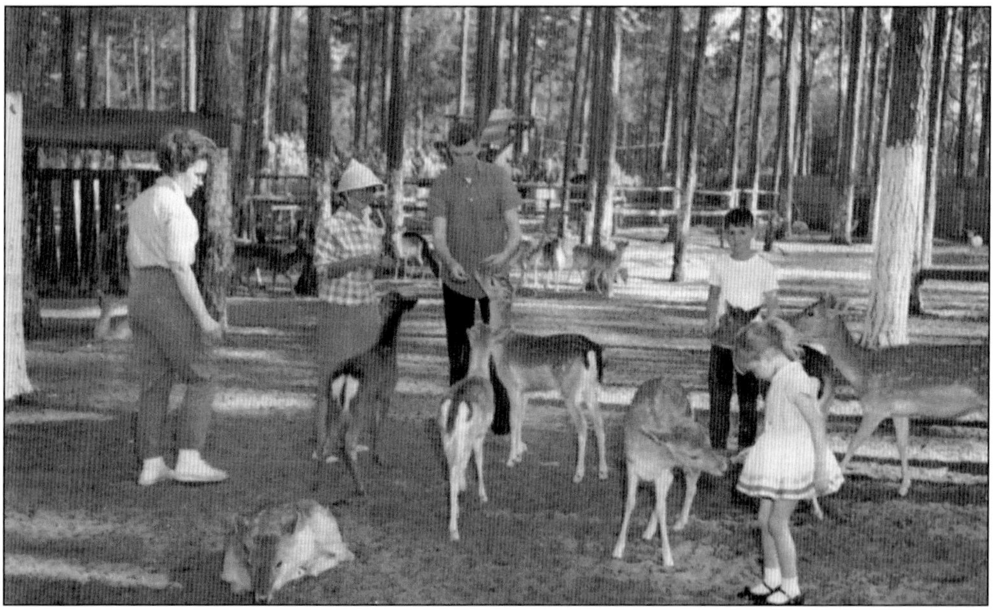

DEER RANCH, C. 1960. This huge attraction was located on DeBuys Road between Biloxi and Gulfport. Locals and visitors could hand feed and pet the tame deer that roamed free on the seven-acre ranch. Also located on the property were the Red Dog Saloon and Theater and an Old Frontier Town, called the Six Gun Junction Ghost Town, where Western shoot-outs were performed hourly. (Not Mailed; SC.)

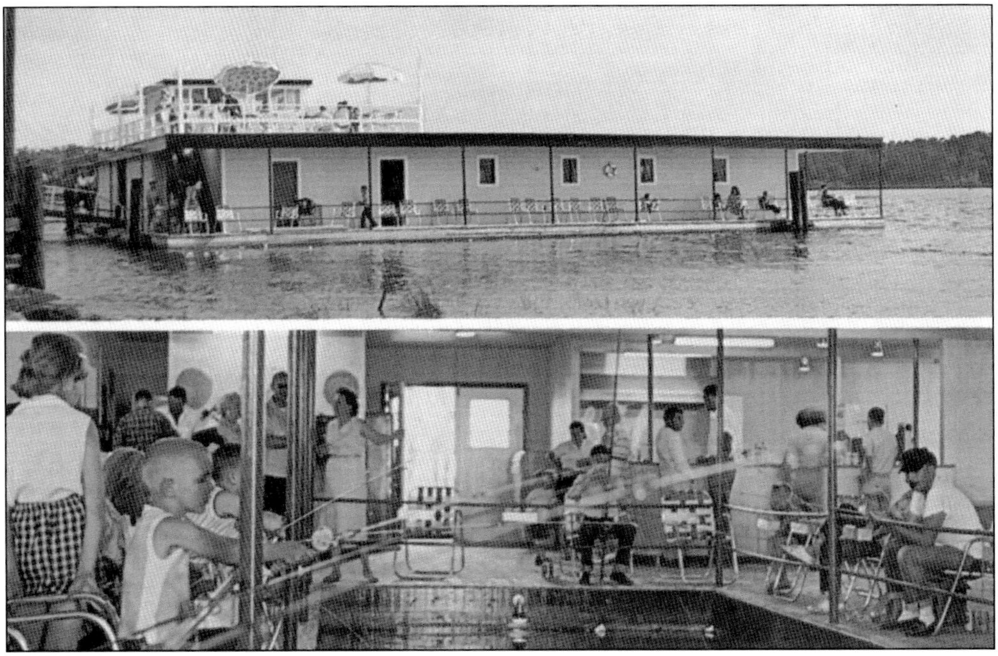

THE FISHING ARENA, C. 1960. Located on the causeway, just northwest of the Popps Ferry Bridge, this recreational spot was the only one of its kind in southern Mississippi. One could fish, drink, and watch television (a Saints game) in air-conditioned comfort. For those who wished to enjoy the outdoors, a sun deck was on the roof; the lower area was surrounded by a covered deck. (Not Mailed; SC.)

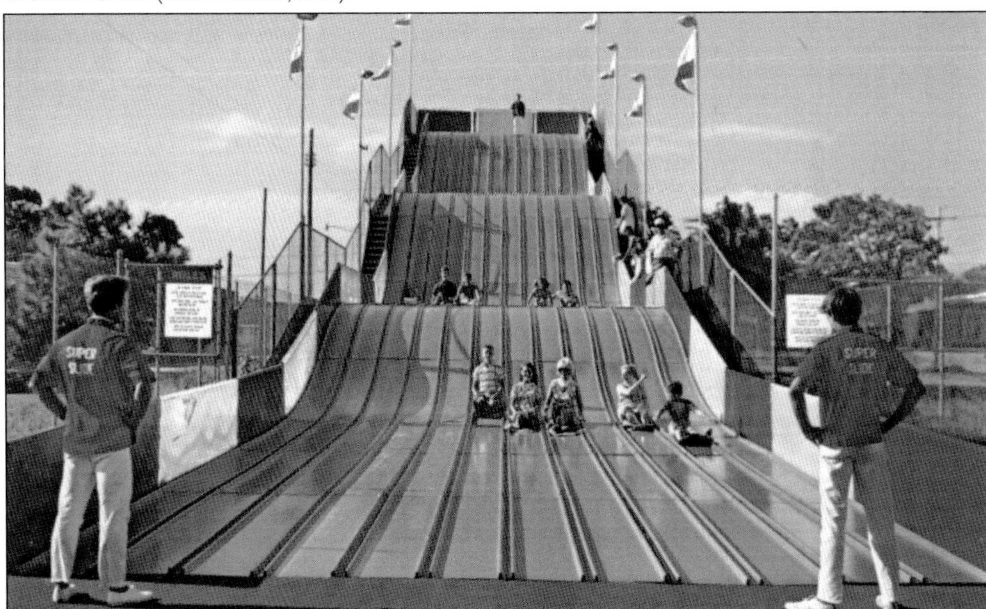

SUPER SLIDE, C. 1960. Adults, teenagers, and children enjoyed this huge summer attraction, located on the northeast corner of Camellia Street and Highway 90 (West Beach Boulevard). It stood 40 feet high and 150 feet long, providing fun, healthy entertainment for the whole family before it was destroyed. (Not Mailed; SC.)

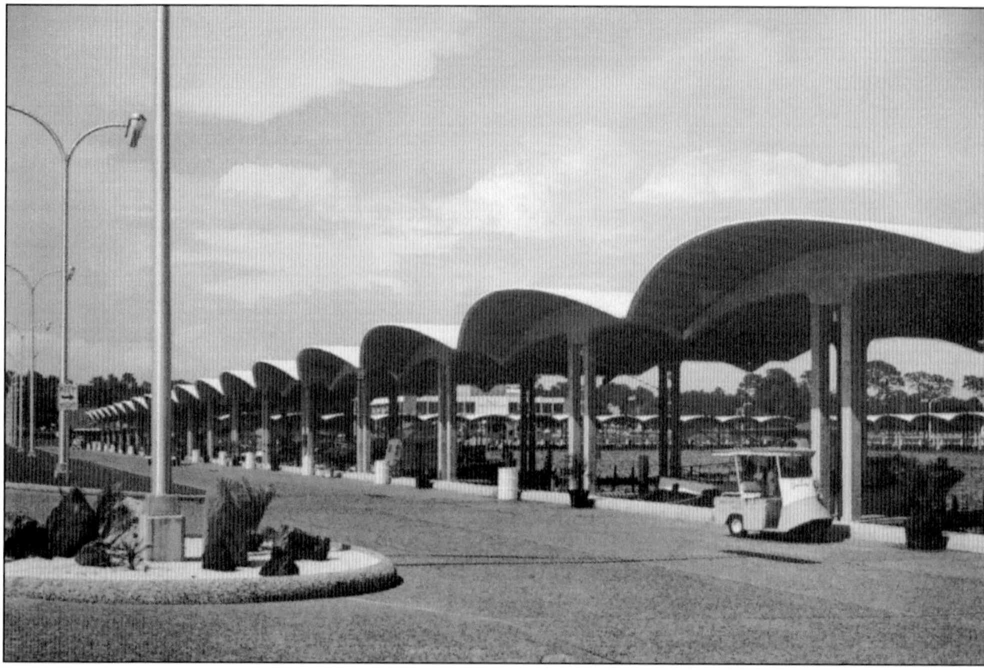

Broadwater Beach Hotel Marina, 1960s. Billed as one of the most beautiful marinas in the country, it offered charter boat services, professional guides, and complete facilities for yachtsmen. The hotel, north of Highway 90, and the scalloped canopies that shaded the boat slips were destroyed in Hurricane Katrina in 2005. (Not Mailed; BL.)

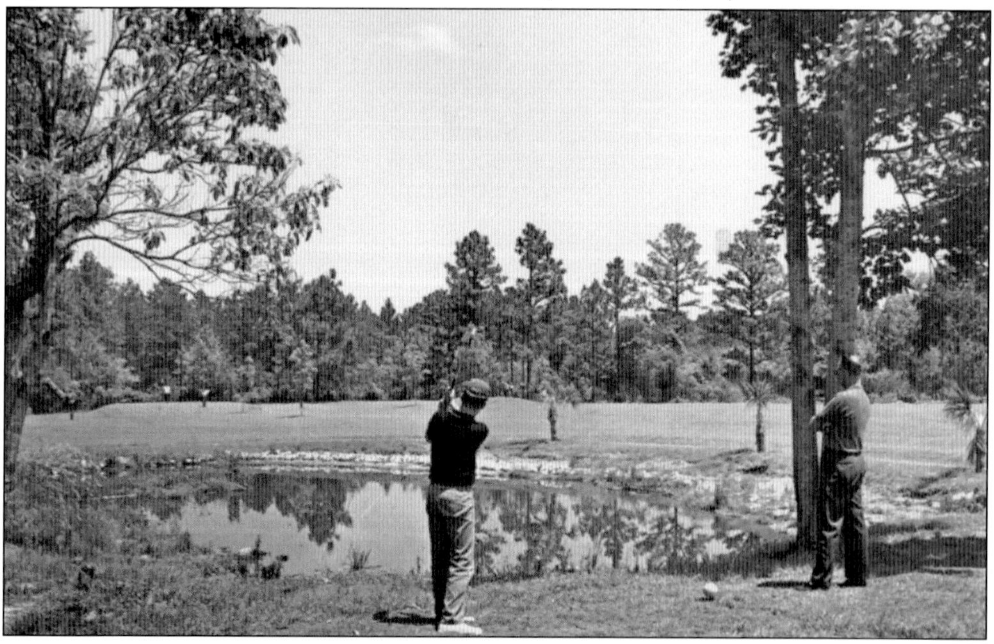

Midway Par 3 Golf Course, 1971. Men enjoy a round of golf near a pond on the 130-yard No. 5 hole. The course was called Midway because it was not located in either Biloxi or Gulfport, but was midway between the two cities. Located on Popps Ferry Road, west of Cedar Lake Road, the area was later annexed into the city of Biloxi. (Postmarked 1971; SC.)

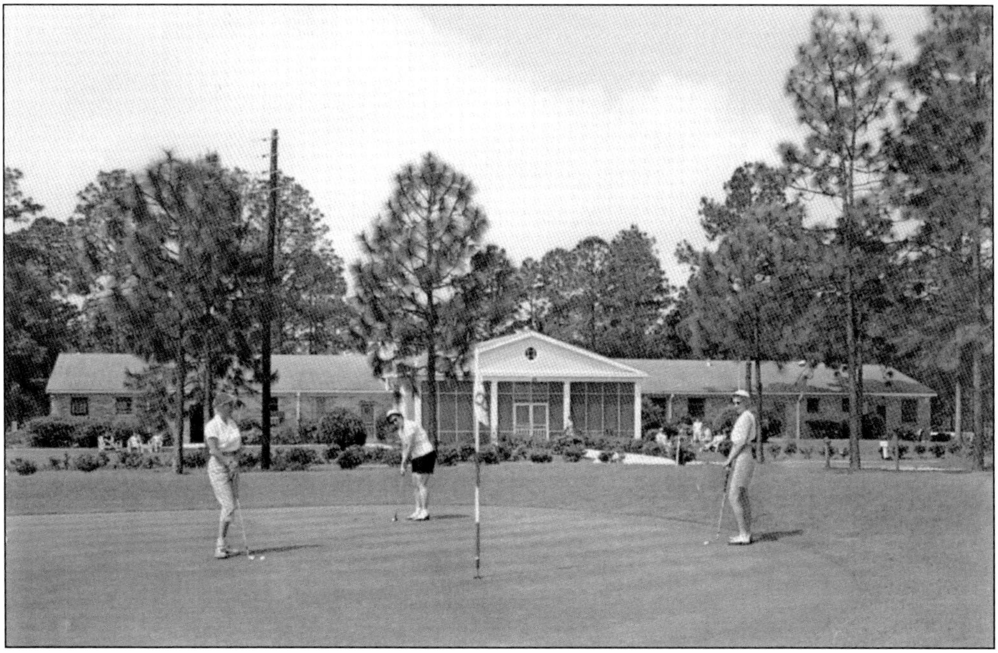

SUNKIST COUNTRY CLUB, C. 1960. Established in 1953 on Rural Route 2, Sunkist was one of the original golf destinations on the Mississippi Gulf Coast. The 18-hole course remains in operation today and is open year-round for the enjoyment of tourists, guests, and members. (Not Mailed; SC.)

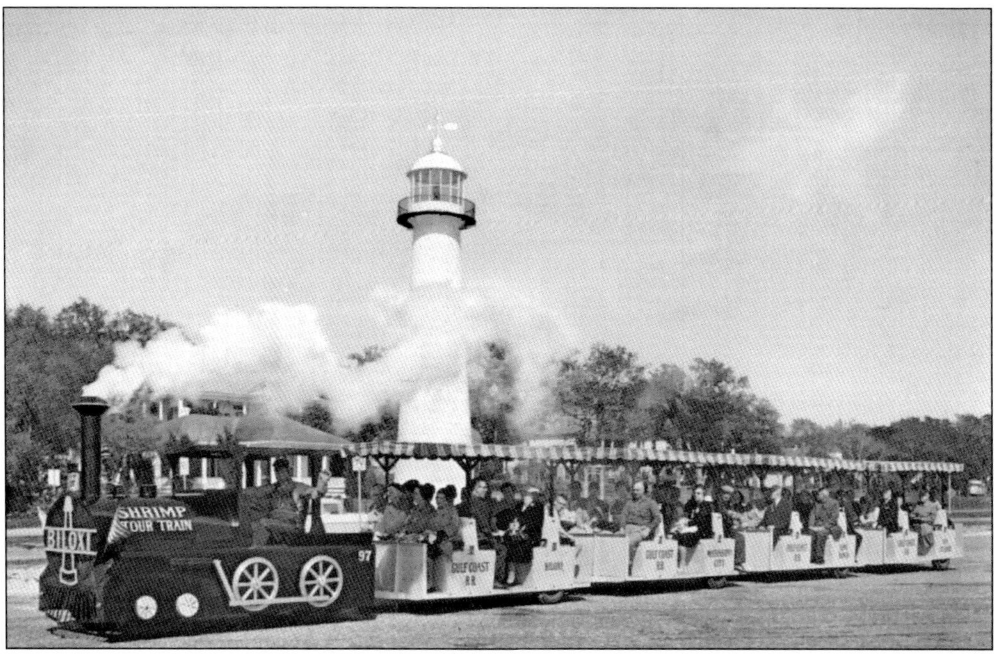

SHRIMP TOUR TRAIN, 1961. Shown at its departure point, the Biloxi Lighthouse, this unique 64-passenger sightseeing train took passengers on a 50-minute, 10-mile ride. More than 46 points of interests were seen during the historic journey, delighting both young and old. It still operates today as Biloxi Tour Train. (Not Mailed; BL.)

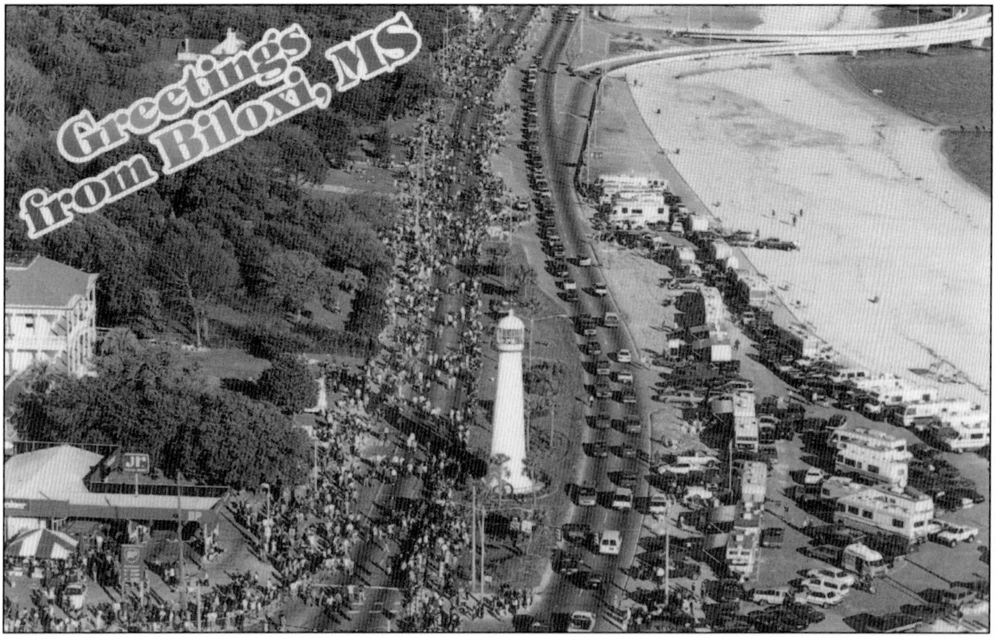

GREETINGS FROM BILOXI, C. 1970. A massive crowd awaits the Mardi Gras parade east of Porter Avenue on Highway 90. The historic Biloxi Lighthouse is in the center. On the left is a BP gas station just below the historic Dantzler House, built in the 1850s (both destroyed during Hurricane Katrina). Campers and vehicles fill the parking lot at right, as traffic flows in the two south lanes of the highway. (Not Mailed; SC.)

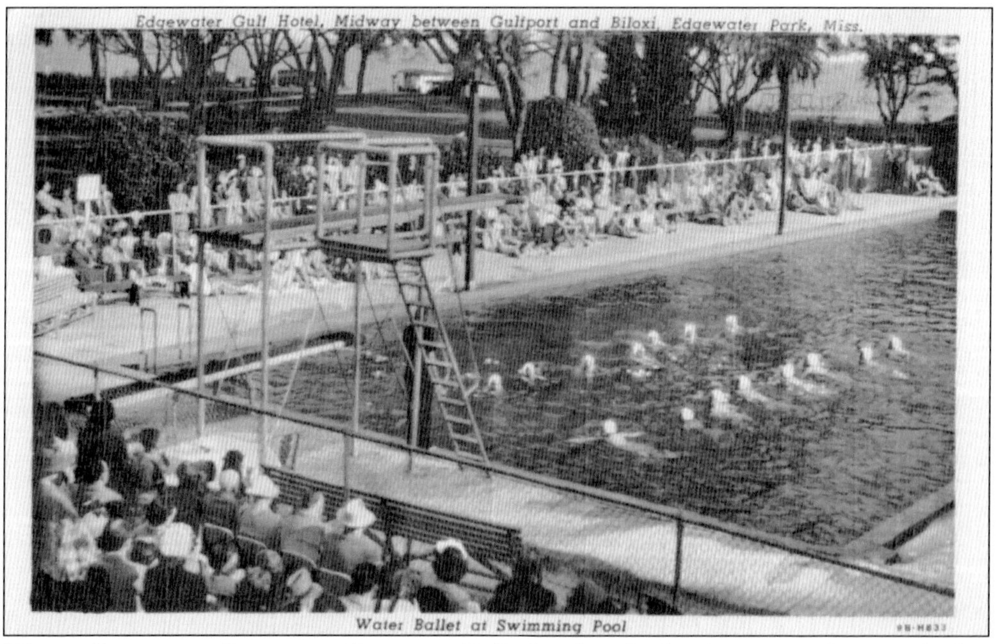

WATER BALLET AT SWIMMING POOL, C. 1950. Synchronized swimmers perform in rhythm for spectators seated around the pool at the Edgewater Gulf Hotel. The hotel was on Highway 90, the Old Spanish Trail, midway between Gulfport and Biloxi. A streetcar can be seen in the background of this image. (Postmarked 1954; SC.)

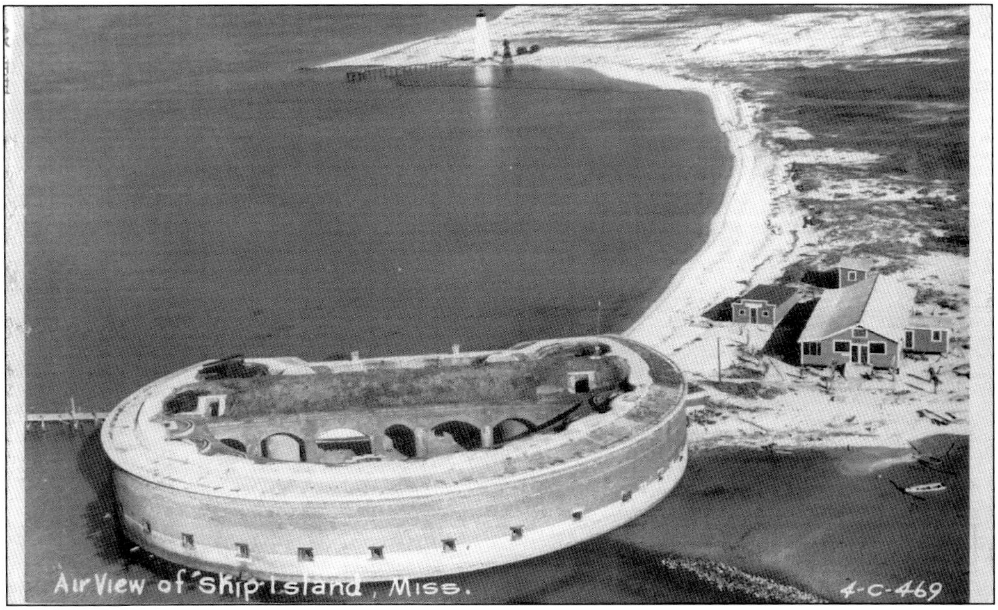

Fort Massachusetts, c. 1940. This fort is located on West Ship Island, a barrier island about 14 miles south of Biloxi. It was built by Union forces during the Civil War and served a home of the West Gulf Blockading Squadron of the US Navy during the war. The historic brick structure has survived hurricanes and is now part of Gulf Island National Seashore. (Not Mailed; SC.)

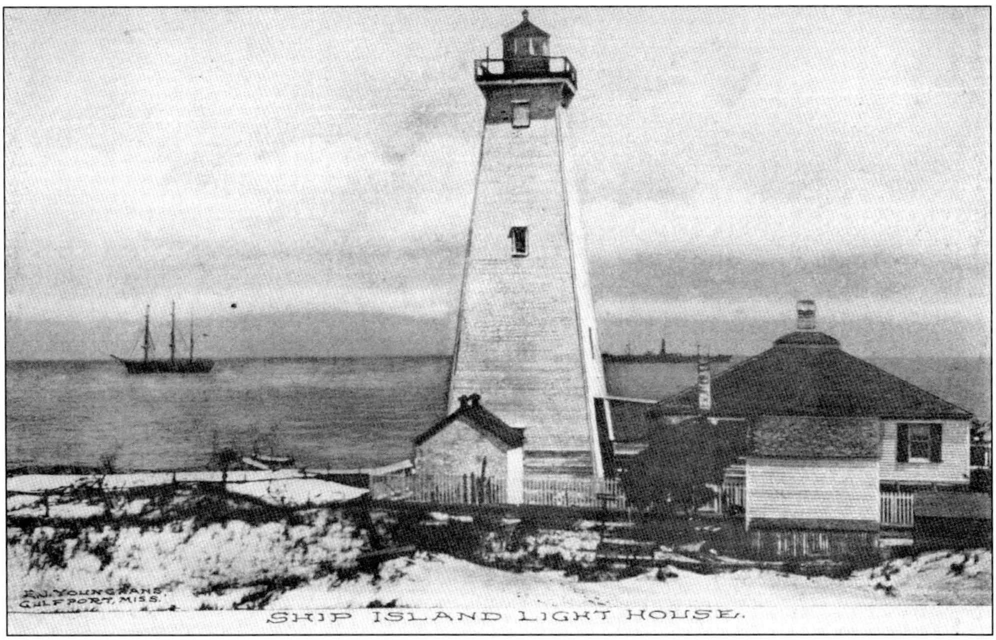

Ship Island Lighthouse, 1911. Built in 1886, this square, open-frame, wooden lighthouse, topped with a lantern room, is shown with a lighthouse keeper's home on the right. It replaced the 1853-built brick lighthouse that had been heavily damaged by waves. This lighthouse was accidentally burned down by campers in 1972. A replica was built in 2000 but was destroyed during Hurricane Katrina in 2005. (Not Mailed; BL.)

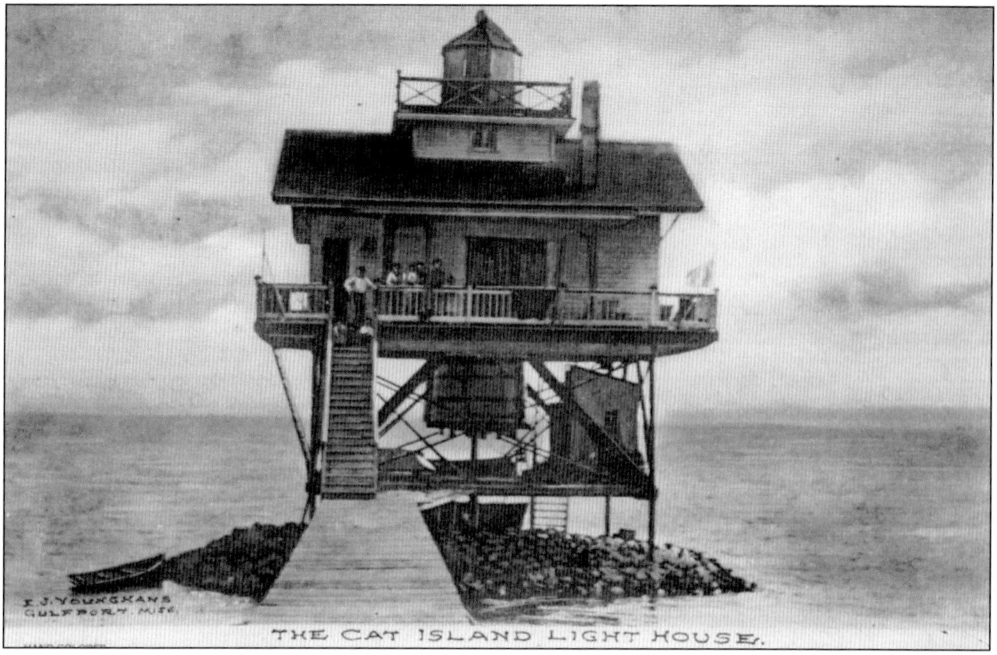

Cat Island Lighthouse, c. 1910. Built in 1871, this version of the Cat Island Lighthouse stood as a beacon off the Mississippi-Louisiana coast. But like previously constructed structures erosion, storms and hurricanes continued to be a problem for this lighthouse. The structure was home to the light and was the keeper's residence. It was deactivated in 1937. It eventually burned in 1961. (Not Mailed; SC.)

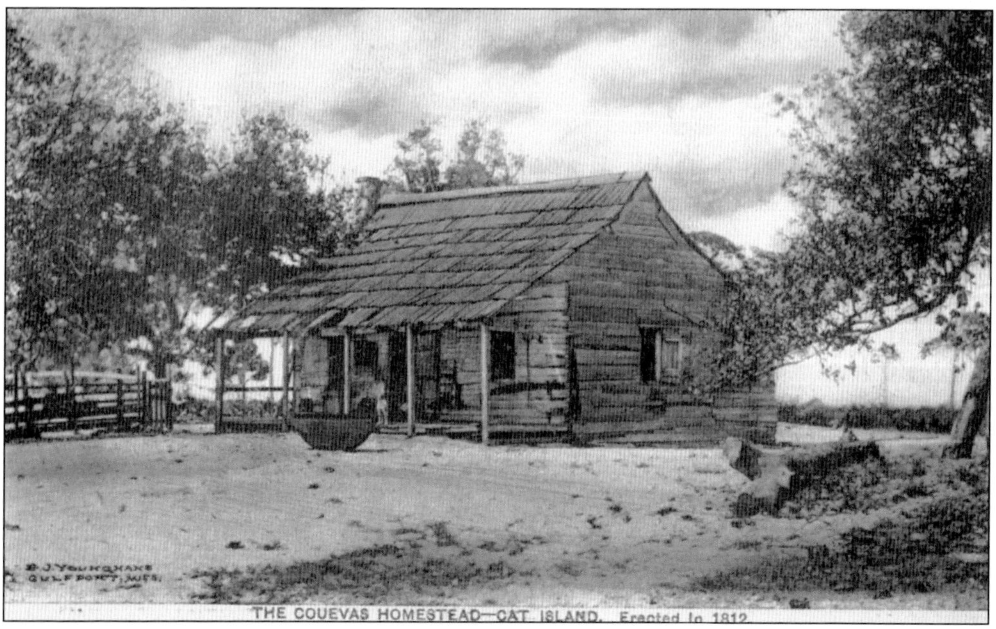

Couevas Homestead, Cat Island, c. 1910. Juan de Couevas's wooden home was erected in 1812 on the barrier island, about 12 miles southwest of Biloxi, on property he received by way of a Spanish land grant. He was a hero in the War of 1812, having served under Andrew Jackson in the Battle of New Orleans. The house no longer remains. (Not Mailed; SC.)

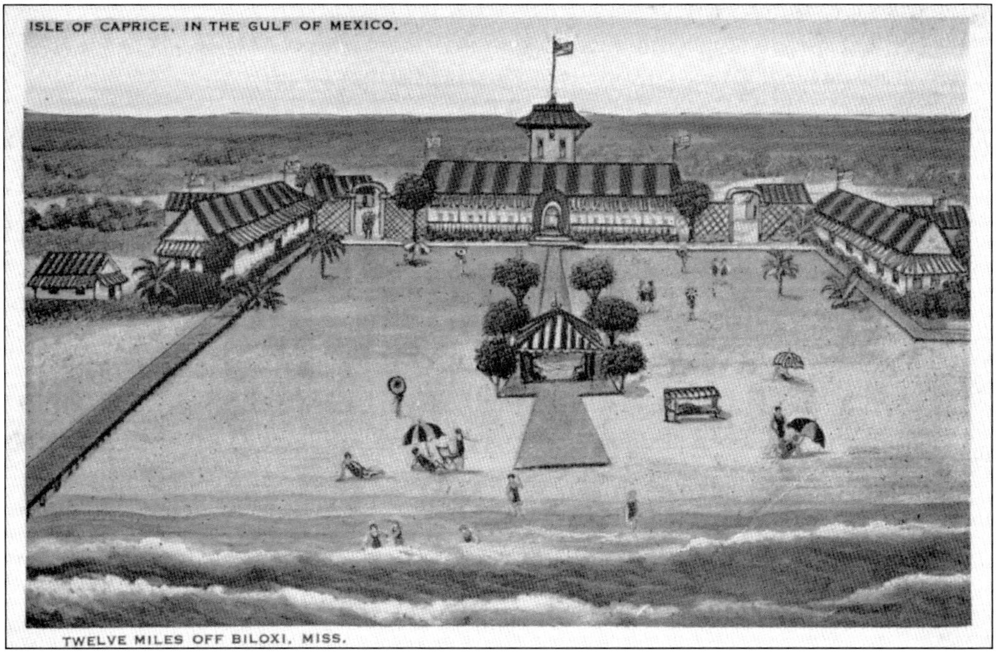

ISLE OF CAPRICE RESORT, C. 1926. May 30, 1926, marked the opening of what became a popular vacationing, gambling, and drinking resort off the coast of Biloxi. Owned and developed by Walter "Skeet" Hunt, its large pavilions housed a restaurant and casino. By 1932, the island was submerged due to storms, currents, and loss of sea oats. (Not Mailed; SC.)

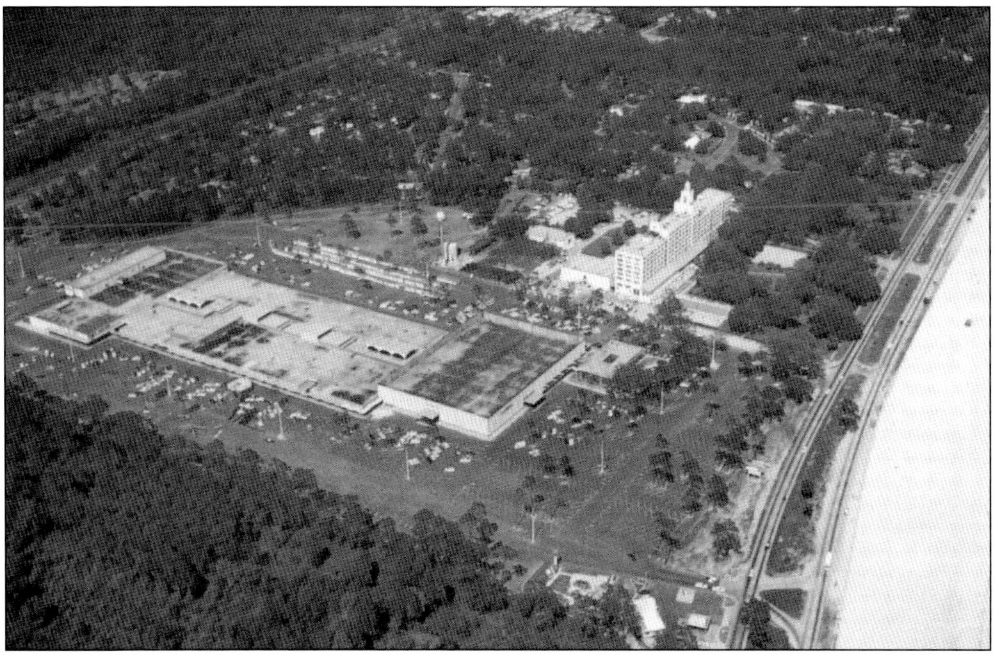

EDGEWATER HOTEL AND EDGEWATER MALL, C. 1968. This aerial view above Highway 90 shows half of the present mall with the stately hotel, which was destroyed in 1971, still standing to the east. Note the hotel swimming pool, the white sand beach, and the seawall south of the highway. (Not Mailed; BL.)

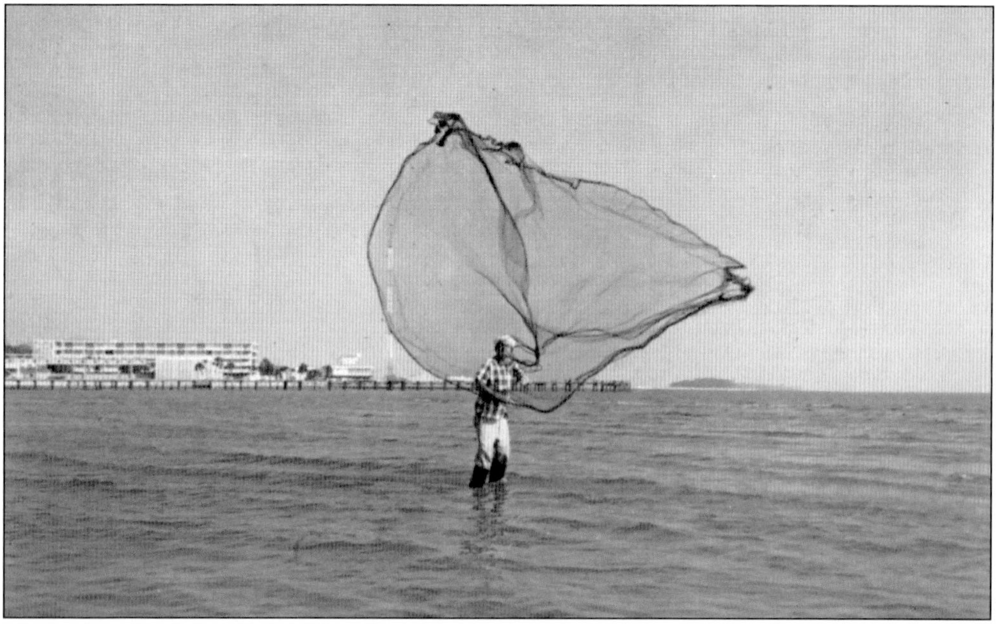

Mullet Net Fisherman, c. 1960. A fisherman is throwing his net while wading in the Mississippi Sound—a common site in Biloxi. Mullet are found in plentiful supply and are often referred to locally as Biloxi Bacon. The Buena Vista Motel can be seen in the background. (Not Mailed; BL.)

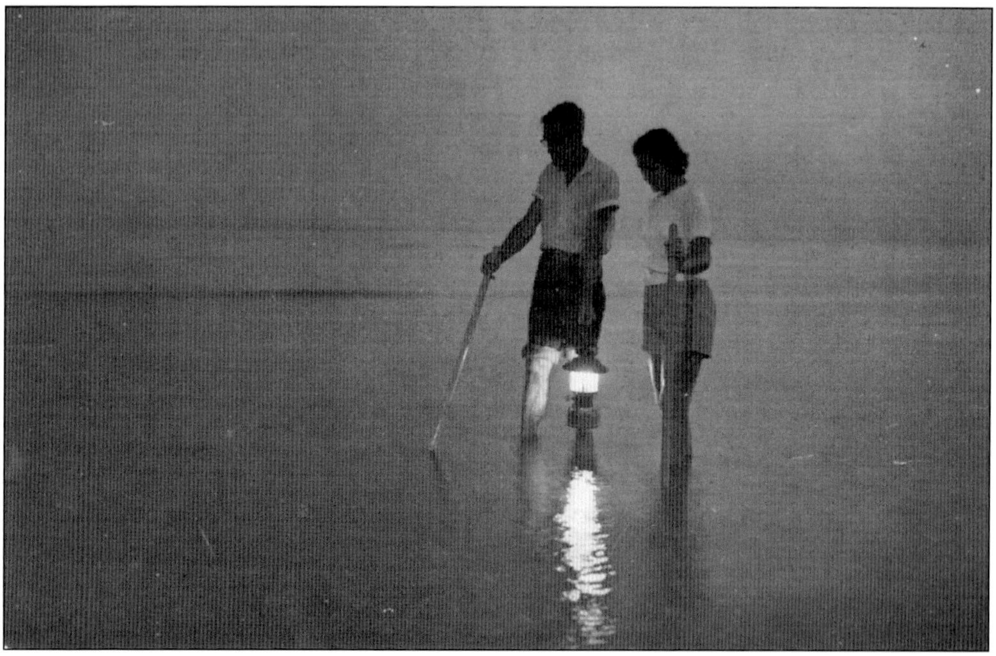

Floundering on the Mississippi Gulf Coast, c. 1960. During the first half of the 20th century, almost every household in Biloxi owned at least one floundering light. The Coleman lantern, or some variation, was used for flounder gigging on the muddy bottoms of the Mississippi Sound or for home lighting after storms or hurricanes. This postcard depicts a couple walking the waterways, looking for their prized catch. (Not Mailed; SC.)

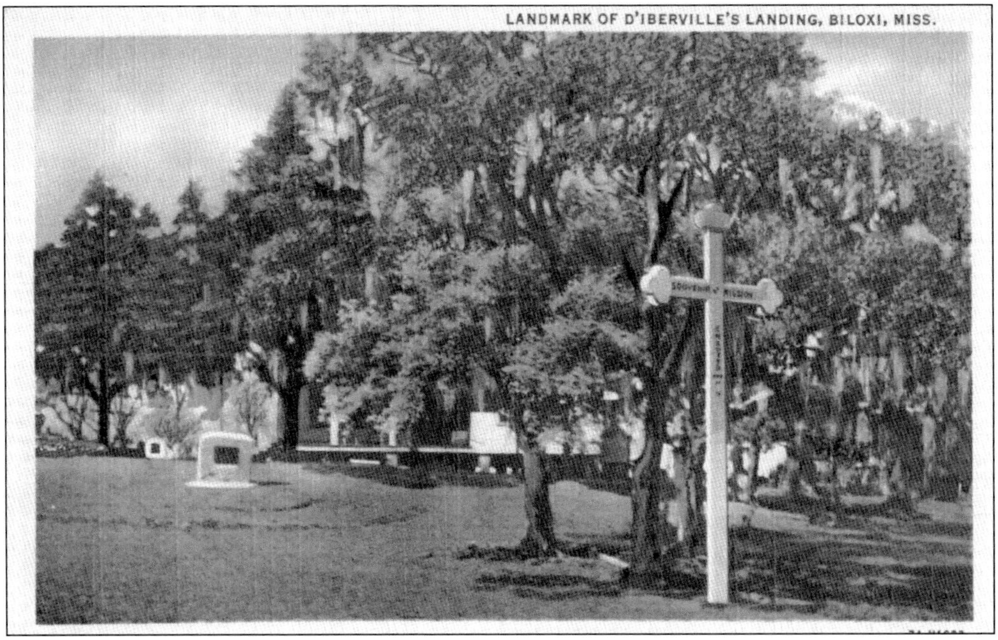

Landmark of d'Iberville's Landing, c. 1940. This cross once stood near a boulder commemorating the supposed landing site by French explorer Pierre Le Moyne d'Iberville in 1699. Spanish settler Emanuel Sanchez was believed to have erected the original cross near a chapel he built for his wife on this property in North Biloxi, now D'Iberville. The land was later purchased by the Catholic Church. (Not Mailed; BL.)

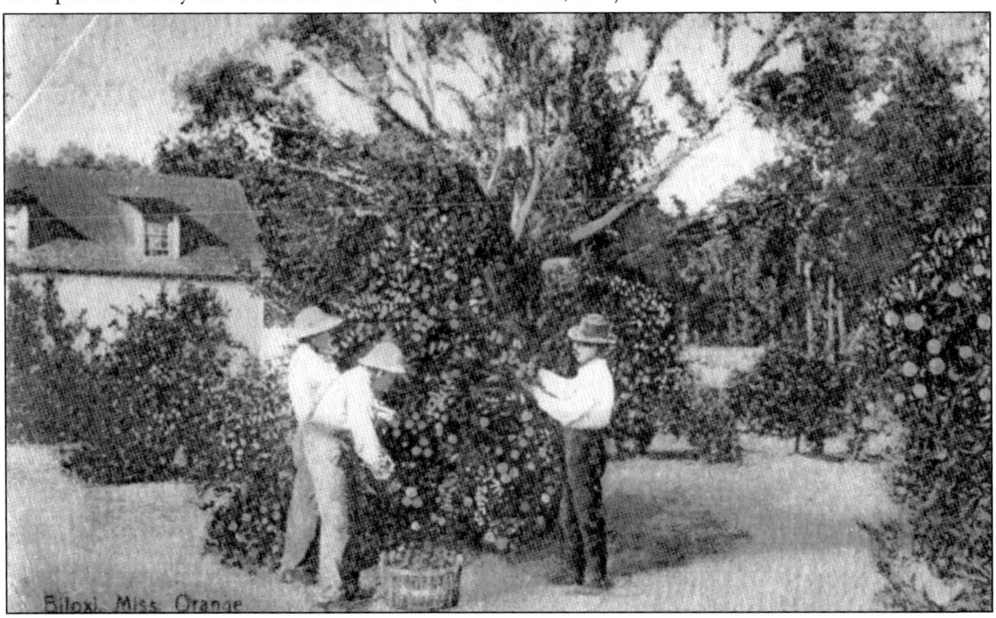

Orange Picking Near Biloxi, 1909. In the days when most locals lived off the land, the climate of the Mississippi Gulf Coast was ideal. Most households had fruit-bearing and citrus trees on the property. Several commercial citrus groves were in operation, growing oranges and satsumas. The occasional snap of very cold weather made commercial citrus growing very difficult. (Postmarked 1909, SC.)

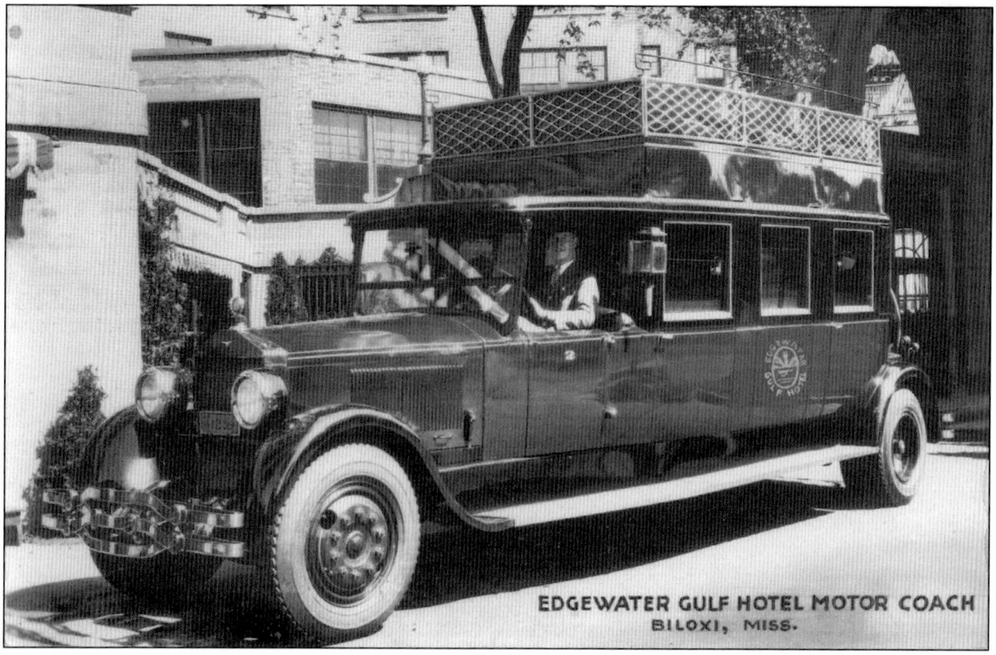

EDGEWATER GULF HOTEL MOTOR COACH, C. 1927. A uniformed driver is seen at the wheel of the resort hotel's private limousine, parked in front of the hotel. Service was provided from all airports directly to Edgewater Park, deep in the glamorous Old South, formerly on Highway 90, in what is now Biloxi. (Postmarked 1929; SC.)

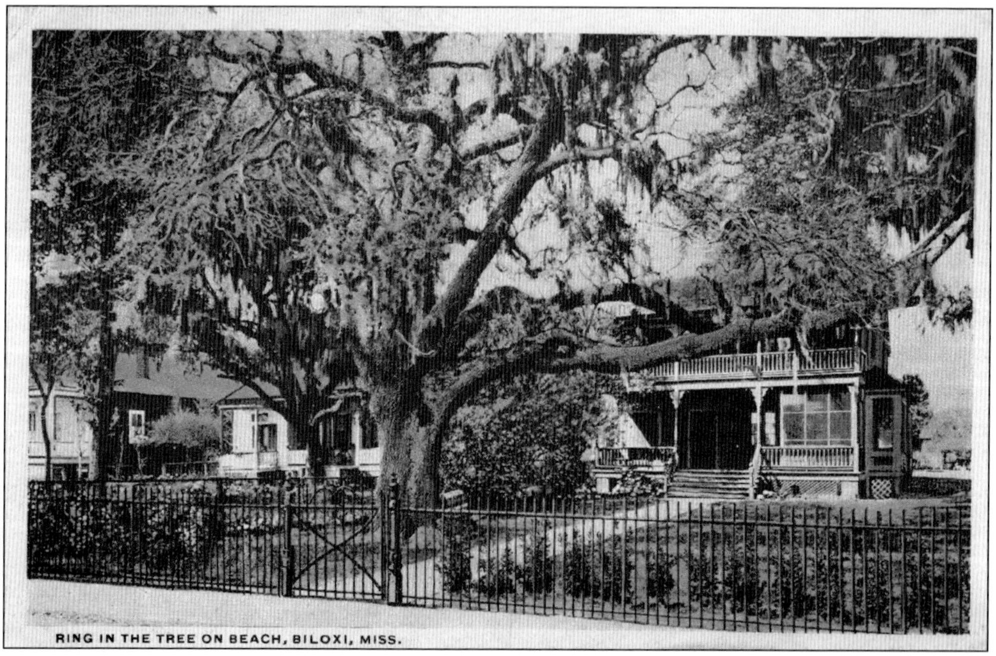

RING IN THE OAK, C. 1915. An old legend states that a Biloxi Indian chief told his daughter, "My daughter shall never wed a brave from a hostile tribe until a ring grows in yonder oak." The next morning, following a violent storm, the ring had formed and the couple was married. It still stands just west of Nixon Street on Highway 90. (Postmarked 1915; SC.)

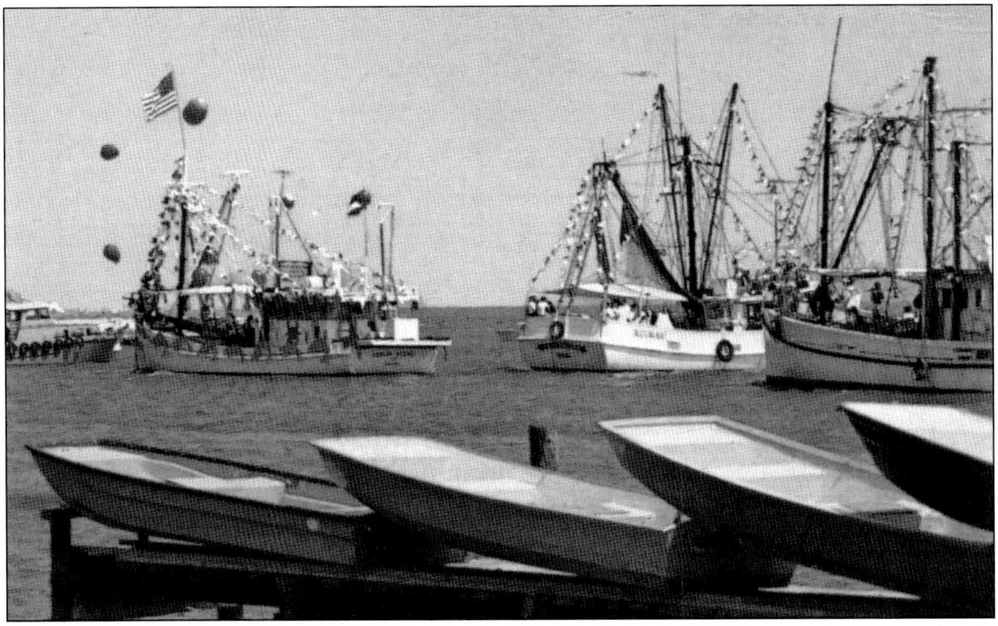

SHRIMP BOATS AT THE BLESSING, C. 1965. The old world custom in which hundreds of gaily decorated boats parade in the largest maritime parade in the south is featured on this postcard. Clerical blessings were offered upon the boats and fishermen for a safe voyage, a bountiful catch, and a speedy return from their fishing trips to the Gulf of Mexico. (Not Mailed; SC.)

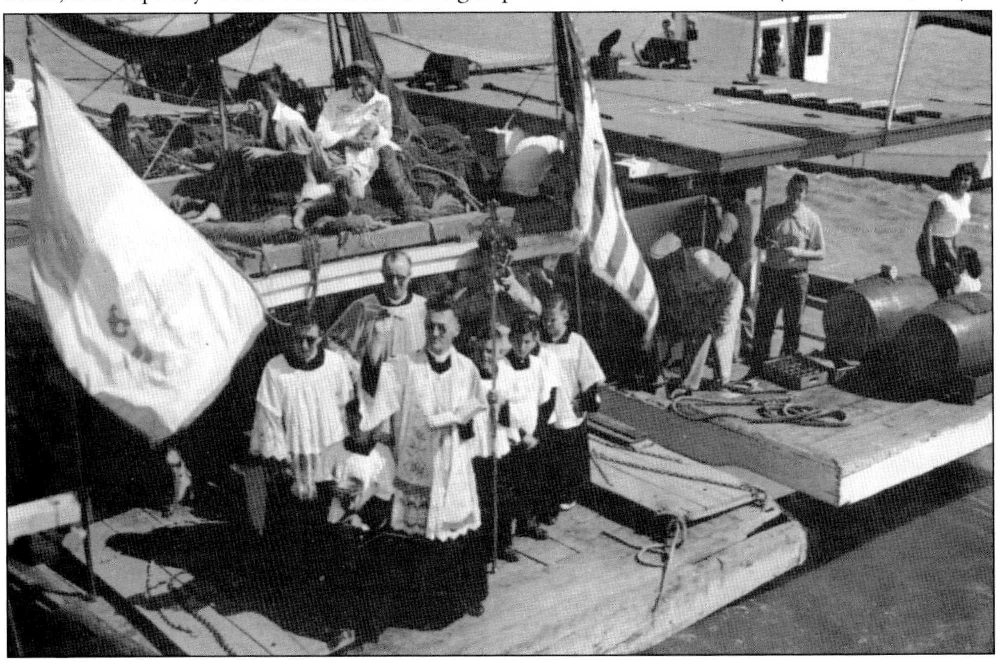

THE OPENING OF SHRIMP SEASON, C. 1952. The Blessing of the Fleet, held annually about the first of June, signaled the opening of shrimp season. Fr. Herbert Mullen, pastor of Saint Michael's Church, is pictured on the stern of the blessing boat along with several altar boys. It was quite an honor for the boat and the altar boys to be chosen to participate in the ceremonies. (Not Mailed; SC.)

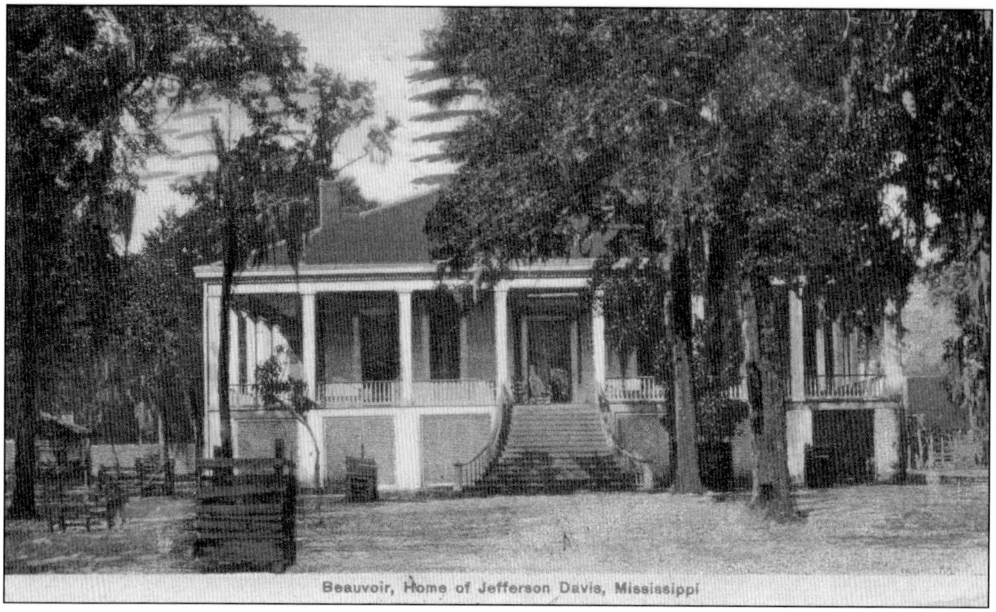

BEAUVOIR, 1901. The word *beauvoir* means "beautiful view." The vast estate that served as home to Confederate president Jefferson Davis certainly lived up to its name. Built in 1852, the mansion was constructed as a typical Gulf Coast plantation home of its day. Today, the museum and manicured grounds are far different from the landscape featuring cattle guards around the small trees shown on this postcard. (Postmarked 1907; SC.)

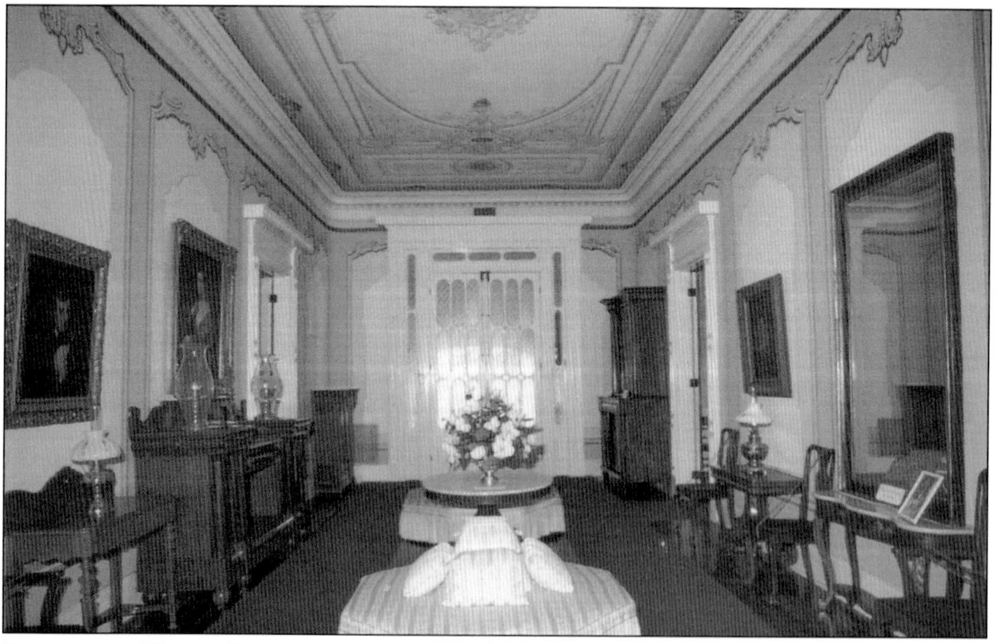

RECEPTION HALL, BEAUVOIR, C. 1960. This view of the entrance hallway of the main house on the Beauvoir estate is restored to the period. The furnishings and magnificently painted walls are featured in the estate restoration. The property houses several outbuildings, the Jefferson Davis Museum, and a Confederate Soldiers Cemetery. This popular attraction is visited by thousands of people annually. (Not Mailed; BL.)

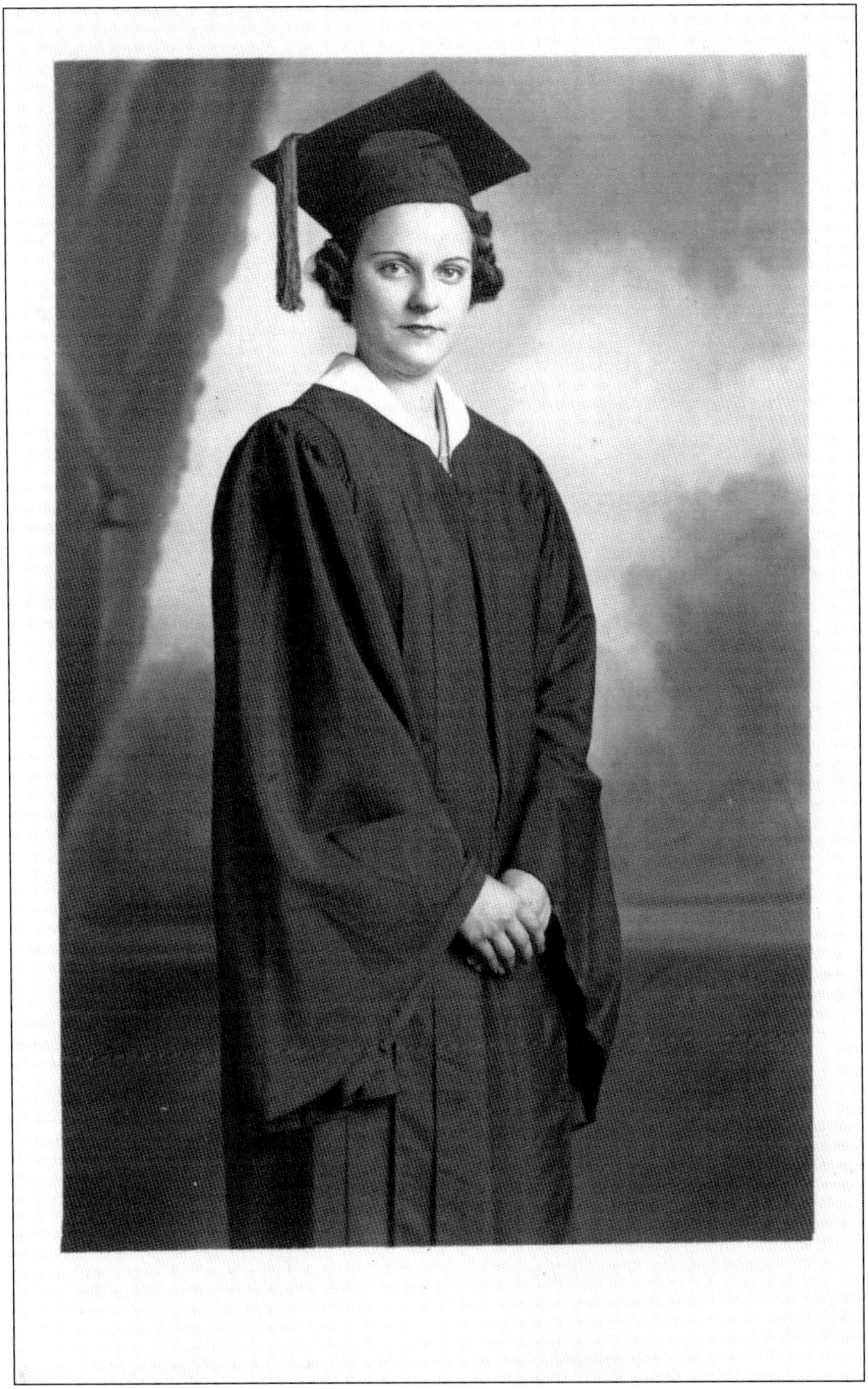

Graduating Senior Biloxi High School, 1940. It was not uncommon in days gone by for individuals or groups to have postcards printed. This postcard of Lily Rose Wentzell, a graduating senior of Biloxi High School in 1940, was an option used for cap- and-gown pictures of the day. Seniors could mail the postcards to friends and relatives as invitations to the graduation. (Not Mailed; SC.)

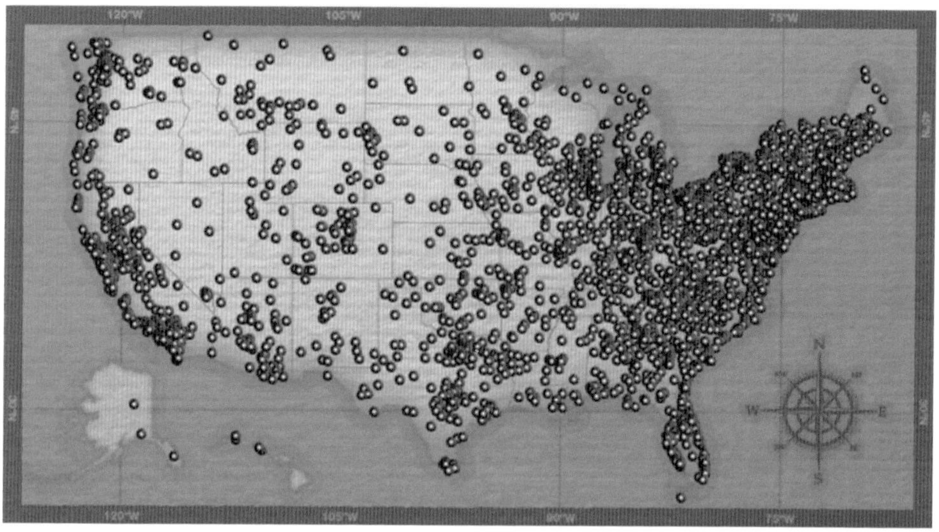